The Fields of War

A young cavalryman's Crimea campaign

———

EDITED BY

PHILIP WARNER

JOHN MURRAY
Fifty Albemarle Street
London

Printed in Great Britain by
Cox & Wyman Ltd.,
London, Fakenham and Reading
0 7195 3356 2

Contents

	Introduction	*1*
1	Warships to Varna	*11*
2	The Brushwood Plain	*18*
3	Cholera	*40*
4	Charge of the Heavy Brigade	*61*
5	The Winter Siege	*81*
6	Building for Survival	*100*
7	Bombardment of Sebastopol	*133*
8	The Attempt on the Malakoff	*164*
9	The Fruits of Victory	*179*
10	Home from the Field	*190*
	Index	*209*

ILLUSTRATION SOURCES

The Publishers thank all the following for their generous help and permission to reproduce copyright material:
1 Mrs Virginia Tregear: 2, 3, 17, 18 Mrs Elizabeth de Clermont: 4, 5, 10, 12 Parker Gallery, London: 6 Black Watch Regimental Museum, Perth: 7 Science Museum, London: 8, 9, 11, 13 National Army Museum, London: 14 Victoria & Albert Museum, London: 15 Scottish United Services Museum, Edinburgh: 16 Mrs Georgina Mayne.

Map of Sebastopol & Balaklava 1855 is reproduced from *Little Hodge* edited by the Marquess of Anglesey, by kind permission of Leo Cooper Ltd. Map of Heavy Cavalry Charge, Balaklava, is reproduced by kind permission of the Editor and first appeared in his book, *The Crimean War: a reappraisal*, published by Arther Barker Ltd.

Illustrations

1   Temple Godman aged thirty-nine in 1871   *f.p.* 24

2   Park Hatch, Surrey (since demolished), the Godmans' country house   25

3   The Earl held by Kilburn   40

4   Godman, Kilburn and The Earl   40

5   English Heavy Cavalry gathering hay in the Crimea   41

6   The harbour at Balaklava   88

7   Ships unloading at Balaklava   88

8   Officers and N.C.O.s of the 5th Dragoon Guards in off-duty dress   89

9   General Scarlett, Commander of the Heavy Brigade   89

10   The Charge of the Heavy Brigade during the Battle of Balaklava   104

11   Major Abraham Bolton of the 5th Dragoon Guards   105

12   Major A. W. D. Burton of the 5th Dragoon Guards   105

13   *The Welcome Arrival* by J. D. Luard   152

14   Interior of the Redan at Sebastopol   152

15   Kadikoi Camp near Balaklava   153

16   Temple Godman in the uniform of a Major-General   168

17   Temple Godman and his four sons at Highden in Sussex   169

18   Active to the last, Temple Godman on the moor   169

MAPS

Sebastopol and Balaklava 1855   16/17

Heavy Cavalry Charge, Balaklava, 25 October 1854   74

EDITOR'S NOTE

Some of Temple Godman's letters have been omitted altogether; cuts (indicated by ellipses) have also been made to a number of others. These deletions have been made not simply because of considerations of length. Many are repetitions; postal, provisioning, and clothing details; or question and comment on Godman family friends in England.

For the sake of the reader, the letters have been divided into chapters and into paragraphs. A certain amount of punctuation has been added and spelling corrected, though it is hoped, without removing Temple Godman's flavour.

Introduction

It is ironic that the Crimean War, which was more fully and accurately reported at the time than any previous war, should have been so misrepresented afterwards. Of a remarkable and interesting campaign, quite modern in some aspects, all that seems to persist in the public mind is the Charge of the Light Brigade and the 'thin red line'. The two incidents together occupied less than thirty minutes; the remainder of the war lasted over two years. There is, of course, interest in Florence Nightingale but she was a long way from the battlefields.

When fighting soldiers eventually read or hear what was supposed to have taken place on campaigns in which they were engaged they tend to smile cynically. Sometimes they consider offering a few corrections, but rarely bother; the task, they often feel, is too large, and scarcely worth the trouble. Fortunately, there are occasions when someone who took an active part has kept records — a diary perhaps — and then a new picture emerges. It may not be the view of the Commanding Officer, or the politicians; it may differ substantially from the official version and may damage a few reputations but it will undoubtedly show what the war was really like. For wars are fought by men, usually tired, cold and hungry, and not by numbers and quaint euphemisms. We tend to forget that 'an attack at Company strength was repulsed with severe casualties' probably means that about sixty people were killed or wounded in an unsuccessful venture. As a piece of military history it is of slight interest but for those concerned, the wounded and the survivors, it is an unforgettable experience.

Among the survivors there will be a variety of memories. To some it will be an appalling and futile disaster, to others a moment of great excitement which gave them a feeling of lasting achievement; to yet others a time which gave them an insight into their own character and potential. Of course, there are almost as many views as the number of men involved.

How far we can perceive the feelings of those concerned in the actual fighting depends on the extent of the personal records. A bare narrative which confines itself to the events of the battlefield tells us little; a detailed account covering a wider range of experience gives us a guide to the writer's mind and the quality of his assessments.

The Temple Godman letters give a valuable insight into the Crimean War for several reasons. One is their completeness. He went out at the start to the Crimea in May 1854 and did not return till two years later, after peace had been declared. Another is their humane perceptiveness. He would write one account for his mother, sparing her the details, and another for his brother whose feelings were presumably less tender. In addition, he is passionately interested in what seem to us relatively unimportant details. This last aspect is perhaps the most valuable for from it we can assess his reactions to other matters. In short, what might seem harsh, inefficient, and unnecessary in the 1970s may have seemed normal, sensible and essential in the 1850s.

Not for a moment did Temple Godman wish to be anywhere else than the Crimea. He missed his home comforts but did not wish to be at home to enjoy them. Many soldiers engaged in hazardous and strenuous activities simply cannot be bothered to make a record of them; they would rather have a sleep or a game of cards, or just forget them. Later, if they change their minds and try to piece the story together their memories have lost some of the details. In hindsight they may feel some self-pity.

There is nothing of that in Temple Godman. He is intelligent and imaginative so he knows quite well the dangers which surround him, and they are many. Some soldiers are too stupid to understand the situation in which they find themselves and therefore appear to be brave; their deficiencies become apparent when the battle demands cool, swift, constructive thought. Cardigan of the Light Brigade was undoubtedly one of these. His orders had been 'to advance rapidly to the front and try to prevent the enemy carrying off the guns'. He was not, however, told to advance in a manner which would guarantee his brigade would be virtually wiped out.

The Charge of the Heavy Brigade, in which Godman took part, was a great success and was just as courageous as the Charge of the Light Brigade. Unfortunately few people have ever heard of it.

It is a curiosity of the British character that we take more pleasure in dwelling on our disasters than our successes. Everybody has heard of Dunkirk, Dieppe and Arnhem but what is known of Mareth, Sittang and Falaise? But even the Charge of the Heavy Brigade was no more than an incident. A disaster there would not have lost the campaign although it would have been a serious setback. When it took place we had already won the Battle of the Alma — and made very poor use of it — and soon afterwards we would win the Battle of Inkerman, which was a very fine performance indeed. And then with all the famous glamorous battles over, the army would settle down for nearly two years and win the war. It would be achieved by solid deeds of courage and endurance, many of them performed by unnamed men. Every opportunity of a quick victory had been frittered away by the ineptitude of the Higher Command. For the long months ahead we had opponents who were renowned for their stoicism and endurance.

THE WAR

How, one might ask, had all this come about, and what had brought the twenty-two-year-old Richard Temple Godman into the thick of it?

The root causes of the war may be summarized fairly briefly. Long before the discovery of oil or the establishment of small nationalist states, the eastern end of the Mediterranean was clearly of enormous importance to any country aspiring to Great Power status. Britain, for example, regarded it as vital to her communications with India; France regarded it as essential to what she hoped would be an expansionist policy; Russia regarded it as highly important as a window on the west. Russia's ambitions were mixed with apprehensions. She knew that the decaying Turkish Empire which still sprawled over a vast area — reaching as far as Egypt — might collapse at any moment and she was desperately anxious to ensure that when it did, she herself would be one of the beneficiaries. Unfortunately her efforts to safeguard existing interests and further others caused her to behave with such heavy-handed ineptitude that she aroused fear and hostility on all sides. Her fears of what the Turks might or might not do with their unwieldy inheritance brought her to war with Turkey four times in the 19th century. The immediate causes which touched off the Crimean War do not concern us here. Suffice to say that after a series of acts which the Russians thought were legitimate defensive moves, and which the Turks, French and British thought were blatant examples of aggression, Turkey, France and Britain declared war on Russia on 28 March 1854.

Whatever the justice of the cause it was an awkward moment for Britain. The army had been run down and neglected since Waterloo in 1815 and, in thirty-seven years, parsimony and neglect can do a lot of damage to any army. Even under the best conditions there can be administrative breakdowns. The miracle of the Crimean War was that in fighting a campaign 3,000 miles away on virtually unknown territory there were not more.

The aim of Britain and France in 1854 was to capture and immobilize Sebastopol, the Russian port and naval base in the Black Sea. The Russian plan was to prevent this occurring and, in due course, to push westwards and capture Constantinople (Istanbul), thereby gaining control of the ingress to the Black Sea. There were minor activities in other areas, such as the Baltic, but the centre of the war was the Crimea, a peninsula jutting into the Black Sea. As the Allies were soon to discover, the Crimea had a climate of extremes, very hot and dusty in the summer and bitterly cold in the winter. Diseases of all sorts flourished in the region, but the most deadly was cholera, a waterborne infection which can kill within hours. Neither the causes nor the cure of cholera were known and it was to exact an appalling toll.

In order to reach Sebastopol the Allies had to establish a base at Varna, in what is now Bulgaria, and cross the Black Sea to a suitable landing point in the Crimea. Initially they were able to land unhindered on the Crimean peninsula north of Sebastopol. On the march south they encountered the Russians on the slopes by the river Alma and won the ensuing battle by the sheer bravery of their exhausted and cholera-stricken troops. Lord Raglan, supposedly in overall command, isolated himself and had no influence on the outcome.

After the victory at the Alma the Allies made a controversial move by marching right round Sebastopol instead of attacking it from the north. This gave them the poor-quality port of Balaklava but they lost so much time that the Russians were able to improve their fortifications considerably. Every week that passed made the position of the Allies worse and the situation of the Russians stronger. The Battle of the Alma had not taken place till 20 September 1854, and it had been followed by an incomplete blockade. The Allies had manoeuvred themselves into a most unsatisfactory position, six miles from the port of Balaklava and at the same time isolated from the interior. Added to this their equipment was old, faulty and unsuitable, as well as being insufficient. Clothing and food were inadequate; there was hardly any fuel. Cholera was the major killer but there were other illnesses too; the nearest hospital was at Scutari, near Constantinople, 300 miles across the Black Sea. Conditions in that 'hospital', some of which was built over a cesspool, defied belief.

The cavalry battles, which comprised the Charge of the Heavy Brigade and the Charge of the Light Brigade, became known as the Battle of Balaklava. This also included the episode known as the 'thin red line' when the 93rd (Argyll and Sutherland Highlanders) stood between a Russian cavalry advance and the port of Balaklava and deflected the four Russian squadrons.

The Charge of the Light Brigade has been too often reported to need much space here. Raglan intended the Light Brigade, a force numbering 673, to advance on the Russians who were trying to draw away some Turkish guns they had captured earlier in the day. From their position in the valley neither Lord Lucan, the Cavalry Division Commander, nor the Earl of Cardigan, commanding the Light Brigade, could see the guns Raglan wished them to recapture. All they could see was a formidable array of Russian guns a mile up the valley. With magnificent courage they reached those guns, sabred some of the gunners but then retired as they had no means of holding their hard-won objective. One hundred and thirteen men were killed and 134 wounded; nearly all the horses were killed.

Heroic though it was, the Charge of the Light Brigade had no effect on the course of the war. The Charge of the Heavy Brigade, in which Temple Godman took part, and which he describes in detail, repulsed an advance by a body of some 3,000 Russians and did it with such vigour that the Russian cavalry morale never recovered from the experience during the rest of the war. The effect on British cavalry morale from then on was that Russian skirmishing was regarded as a nuisance rather than a menace.

The next battle, Inkerman, on 5 November 1854, was much larger. Russian casualties were said to have been over 10,000 and Allied losses approximately 3,500. Inkerman was a confused battle, fought in fog and rain and became known as the 'soldiers' battle' because any form of higher direction was impossible owing to the unexpectedness and obscurity of the Russian advance. Troops were committed piecemeal to the fighting.

After the victory of Inkerman, Sebastopol would probably have fallen easily but no attempt was made to assault it.

The Allied army then settled down for the winter. The weather was appalling; administrative chaos reigned; typical of the supply situation was that 10,000 children's stockings were sent and a huge consignment of left-foot boots. A major disaster occurred on 14 November when a storm sank over twenty ships at anchor. Their stores could easily have been unloaded previously but went to the bottom with the ships. After Inkerman Raglan had ordered the British cavalry up to the Inkerman ridge where it was nearly impossible to supply them; the aim was that they should protect this flank. By 1 December most of the horses were dead or like skeletons and the remnants were withdrawn. Not all officers stuck it out with their men like Temple Godman. Lord George Paget, who had ridden with the Light Brigade, asked permission to go home as the campaign looked like offering little future cavalry work; however, he was shamed into returning. Cardigan lived in luxury on a yacht, and there were others who imitated his bad example.

Public indignation, fed by W. H. Russell's reports to *The Times*, demanded an improvement in the supply situation but this did not occur until the armies had experienced the full miseries of a Crimean winter. In April the siege was again prosecuted with full vigour, and continued again through the following months with steeply mounting casualties. On 18 June 1855 an Allied assault was repulsed with heavy losses. On 15 August the Russians launched an attack at Traktir Bridge, hoping to dislocate the Allied dispositions, but it ended in failure at a cost of some 6,000 Russians; this was the Battle of Tchernaya. On 8 September 1855 another Allied assault resulted in the capture of the Malakoff fort by the French, though the British were repulsed at the Redan. The next day the Russians abandoned Sebastopol. However, they now dug in on the Mackenzie Heights and the war was not yet over. On 16 January Russia agreed that the Austrians should help negotiate a peace treaty and on 30 March 1856 the Treaty of Paris was signed. The last units of the British army did not leave the Crimea until 12 July 1856.

THE REGIMENT

Godman's regiment, the 5th Dragoon Guards, had been formed in 1685. A number of changes had taken place since those early days. Initially it had been called Shrewsbury's Horse after their first Colonel, the twenty-five-year-old Earl of Shrewsbury. Three years later James II replaced Shrewsbury by Richard Hamilton, a Roman Catholic. When William III succeeded James II Hamilton was put in the Tower of London and John Coy, an experienced member of the regiment, given the Colonelcy. At this time each trooper was armed with a straight, two-edged sword, two pistols in saddle holsters and a muzzle-loading carbine.

It was clearly in the Colonel's interest to have his men in good health and well trained but he was not assisted in this by the fact that his officers, who had also purchased their commissions, usually neglected any peacetime training. They believed that their personal gallantry in battle would suffice to win the day and were sometimes killed in circumstances which demonstrated the heights of their courage and depth of their ineptitude. From the start, Shrewsbury's Horse had shown a far more efficient approach to training than many of its contemporaries and this was reflected in its good results. In 1690 another new regiment was formed to fight in Ireland; this was Conyngham's 6th Inniskilling Dragons (or Dragoons). Dragoons were not, strictly speaking, cavalry, but were mounted infantry who used their horses to give them mobility and would dismount to fight. They had the same weapons as the Horse and took their name from their flintlock carbine called a 'dragon-fire spouter'. Until the end of the 17th century they used infantry terms, such as 'company' instead of 'troop'. As time progressed, such regiments with their heavier arms and equipment, and stronger but slower horses, became 'heavy' cavalry, with appropriate functions. In contrast, Hussar regiments (from the

Hungarian *huszar*, meaning lightly horsed freebooter) were principally employed in reconnaissance and light skirmishing.

Over the next hundred years both regiments took part in a number of distinguished engagements, notably under Marlborough's command. In 1788 the title 'Horse' was abolished and all the Irish Horse were renamed 'Dragoons'. Coy's Horse, after a number of other designations, had settled down to being the 2nd Horse. It now became the 5th Dragoon Guards, but for many years was known as the 'Green Horse' from the colour of the uniform facings. The 5th D.G. gained further distinction in the Napoleonic Wars and during the long peace (and neglect of the army) which followed contrived to remain more efficient than many units. Nevertheless at the outbreak of the Crimean War the regiment was under strength and could only muster two squadrons (a total of 300 men) and 250 horses. The regiment was commanded by Lt.-Colonel T. Le Marchant. Going out at the same time were the Inniskilling Dragoons. [In 1922 they would be amalgamated with the 5th D.G. The combined regiment was at first called the 5th/6th Dragoons — a title which successfully infuriated everyone; the 5th D.G. resented the omission of the word 'Guards' and the Inniskillings were equally incensed at losing the word 'Inniskilling'. Five years later, after strong representation the regiment became the 5th Inniskilling Dragoon Guards, which it still is in 1977.]

A proportion of the letters is devoted to Godman's speculations on promotion. Although he was in the thick of the fighting, he seemed likely to gain little advantage from it and in one of the later letters he remarks that if the militia are sent out, he will probably be outranked by men of no military experience whatever.

The purchase system, which was abolished in 1871, was illogical, complicated and unjust. However, it was not unpopular with serving officers who regarded it as a form of gamble and was approved by Parliament as it ensured a good supply of officers at low cost to the country. Although an officer could occasionally gain 'a step' by the death of his immediate senior in battle, the normal promotion procedure was to purchase the next rank vacancy from the person relinquishing it.

Some of these purchases were made at 'regulation' price; others required a higher bid. 'Over-regulation' was, of course, illegal though widespread. Sometimes an officer was promoted for distinguished service but this was an 'army' rank, not a regimental one, and there were interesting situations in which a member of a regiment might hold an 'army' rank above that of the commanding officer of his regiment; it did not affect his regimental position Temple Godman had purchased his initial commission as a cornet for £840; at the end of the war his captaincy was worth at least £3,225. A year after he became a major purchase was abolished and he became a Lt.-Colonel within a year of that.

Explained like this the system probably does not seem ridiculous or corrupt. However, there had been situations when infants or even women had held commissions and where competent officers were invariably passed over; some served twenty or thirty years in the same junior rank. One saving grace was that it helped to create a stable society by drawing officers from the strata with most to lose if there should be a revolution. An officer who had bought his commission and hoped to sell it later would view with considerable distaste any upstart who wished to overturn the existing regime.

THE MAN AND HIS FAMILY

Temple Godman arrived out in Varna in June 1854. He had been born at Park Hatch (now demolished), Surrey, in 1832. He was the second son of Joseph and Caroline Godman, who had twelve other children. He had been educated at Eton, which in the 1840s can scarcely have been comfortable, and was commissioned by purchase into the 5th Dragoon Guards on 17 May 1851. His initial rank was cornet and on 3 March 1854, shortly before sailing for the Crimea, he became a lieutenant. Just over a year later (21 July 1855) he became a captain, but not until fifteen years later, on 22 June 1870, did he become a major. Scarcely more than a year after he was appointed Lt.-Colonel, became a full Colonel in 1876, and retired in 1882 with the honorary rank of Major-General. He died in 1912.

In 1871 Temple Godman married Eliza de Crespigny, who bore him four sons and three daughters. Although at thirty-nine he might have seemed to have left marriage fairly late, some of his sons left it even later; and his grandchildren are therefore still quite young. (One of his daughters married E. S. Shrapnell-Smith, descendant of Henry Shrapnell, who invented the shrapnel shell.)

His younger brother, Frederick, to whom some of the Crimean letters are written, and who went out to the Crimea to see him, became an eminent ornithologist, author of many books; he wrote most of a forty-seven-volume work, *The Biology of Central America*. The children seem to have been very fond of each other in a rumbustious way. In the 1840s when the boys had been sent to bed to be out of the way of a dinner party they decided to dangle young Frederick, with a sheet tied to his leg, upside down outside the dining-room window. Whatever the effect on the guests, it resulted in an immediate and sharp beating for all concerned, even young Frederick.

Temple Godman is clearly quite fearless, both physically and morally. He makes light of danger and is in no way inhibited from expressing justified criticisms of his senior officers. He sees no reason why their ineptitude should be glossed over by such as he — a victim of it. Most of the Generals were too old as well as unsuited for their task; Raglan was sixty-six and unequal to the physical strain. Burgoyne was seventy-two. There have been brilliant elderly commanders but the chances are against it.

Among his final letters Godman tells us that all his possessions have been destroyed in a fire at Scutari. They included a journal he had kept every day. Had it survived it would have been a most valuable document if his letters are anything to go by.

A final point is that Temple Godman succeeded in keeping the same horses throughout the entire war. It would have been a magnificent feat under any conditions but those in the Crimea made it exceptional. It is a convincing testimonial to the blend of sensitivity and practical mindedness that went to make this most unusual and appealing cavalry officer. He richly deserved the laurels that life were to bring him.

PHILIP WARNER

I

Warships to Varna

The Himalaya*   *Tuesday May 30th 1854*

My dear Father — Now I have nothing to do I think it better
to write, and add more as we proceed. We left Queenstown† at
2 p.m. on Sunday (which however did not seem to me much like
Sunday) in a thunderstorm; in spite of the rain all the people
turned out to cheer us as we sailed by. At 4 p.m. we dined, and
before it was over nearly all had left the table and gone to bed.
Nothing could be more unfortunate than our first night, for
towards evening before the horses had time to get used to the
motion, it came on to blow, and increased to a gale, with torrents
of rain, and the sea constantly breaking on us. Ferguson, the Major,
and myself were the only ones not ill. We did not go to bed, and
we, assisted by three or four men who were not ill, were constantly
going round the horses tieing them shorter, and putting those
on their legs who had fallen from the rough sea and wet decks.
They, however, fell faster than we could put them right. Some
got their forefeet over the boxes, and we pushed them back by
main force, for if they had got loose on deck, someone must have
been hurt. They were actually screaming with fright, the canvas
covering over their heads was cracked by the wind, and by flick-
ing them made them much worse. Two horses that fell next
each other gave us much trouble, and at last we had to cut them
out of their boxes, and drag them on deck before they could get
up.

At last morning broke, and I was never more glad. Before this,

* The *Himalaya* a P.&O. screw-propelled steamship — the biggest in the
world at the time of its launching — had been sold to the Admiralty for use as
a troopship and was used extensively during the Crimean War. This remarkable
old ship was eventually sunk by German bombers in World War II when it was
being used as a storeship in Portland Harbour.

† Queenstown is now Cóbh, outport of Cork.

however, they turned her head more round to the wind, which took us out of our course, and they took off half her speed. She then went steadier and the horses did not tumble about so much. Being well tired and wet through I got to bed about 4 a.m. As it did not blow so much, being very sleepy I did not wake till one and so lost breakfast and lunch, for they give us nothing except at particular times.

Monday I was very tired all day, but I have not been at all ill yet. Tuesday evening sighted Cape Finisterre and passed a ship about three miles off, which they made out to be a transport with some of the 11th Hussars; changed signals with her and soon left her behind. She sailed a week before us from Dublin; her name was the *Parola*. Calm weather since Monday evening, horses all well. Got out of the Bay of Biscay Tuesday evening. Wednesday morning had a muster parade and saw several whales about quarter of a mile off, spouting up the water. They do not feed us very well on board. I am getting used to being crowded in our cabin — there is not much room to spare with three in it. All our men were very ill at first, and you can't fancy anything more wretched than they were, strewn all over the floor and deck as thick as peas, so ill they could not move; they have none of them got any hammocks, but sleep where they can. Most of our sea-sick officers came out again Tuesday — and all seem pretty well now. Saw the coast of Portugal most part of the day, and in the evening passed the rock of Lisbon. Thursday still in sight of the coast — passed Gibraltar in the evening about 11 p.m. and had a pretty good view of the Rock, being moonlight. Friday in sight of the Spanish coast all the forenoon, saw the Sierra Nevada mountains covered with snow; they seemed very high, though we were told they were eighty miles off.

I find we only pay 3s 6d for our daily feeding, which is certainly cheap for what we get; Government pays the rest. All the horses well except one or two, and these not seriously indisposed. The screw shakes so I cannot write well. Captain Crispin of the *Fairy* is on board in order to see if the screw would do for H.M. Yacht. He does not like it at all, says he is disappointed with the *Himalaya's* speed, and thinks the screw will in a few years loosen the vessel by the shaking. Our average pace has been 11 knots an hour. This is quite an experiment taking horses on the upper deck, and it can't be a very safe one. They say if the machinery broke they would have to throw some or all of the 190 horses on the upper deck overboard in order to work the sails. The sailors have most of them never been to sea before, they are so hard to get. The weather is beautiful and likely to be so all the way, very warm. We do not expect to know where we land till we get to Constantinople; I suppose we shall go to Varna.* There is an Artillery officer on board, quite a boy, just got his commission. His name is Nicholls; he comes from Chichester and knows the people about there and Midhurst; he is going up to the war.

Saturday — In sight of the African coast all day, passed Algiers but too far off to see the town which is in a bay. Threw overboard our first horse, which however was pronounced to have died of natural causes, and not from the voyage. It is very hot indeed today, not a cloud to be seen, so delightful, the sea as calm as a pond and as blue as paint. Sunday, all well on board, had prayers, very hot weather; I have not much baggage, but I expect to have to leave much of this beind me. We have come all the way about 10¾ miles an hour. Last night passed another transport, but too dark to see what she was — supposed to be the 11th Hussars. We shall be about four days to Constantinople from Malta and I will write again next chance. When we get there we shall know where we are to land. We have just passed Galeta off which the *Avenger* was lost. We keep well outside the islands; can see the coast of Tunis plainly. Monday warmer still; today within a few hours of Malta, where we coal and water and land infantry; stay about twelve hours I believe. Have now done about 2,300 miles in nine days.

Believe me your affectionate Son

The Himalaya   *June 9th 1854*
My dear Mother — We did not leave Malta till about 9 a.m. the 10th. I went on shore again that morning at five o'clock and bought a white wide-awake.† It certainly was intensely hot there. I went on board a French transport which was lying at Valetta, and which had twenty Artillery horses on board, all tied together

---

* A Bulgarian port.
† Soft wide-brimmed felt hat.

by the head and no separation between them. Our horses in such a position would soon have broken one another's legs by kicking, but the French horses show no breeding or spirit. We have had an excellent passage — the second day we saw no land till the evening, when the south coast of Greece came in sight. A very pleasant sail through the archipelago with its numerous islands (which appear very barren, but I believe really are not so) brought us last evening to near Tenedos where we lay to, as no ships are allowed to enter the Dardanelles at night.

This morning broke with a splendid sunrise, before which I was on deck; when we again proceeded passing Tenedos, with Asia on our right, we arrived at the castles of Europe and Asia, which command the entrance of the Dardanelles. We saw the tombs of Ajax, Achilles and Hector on the shore. From this point we passed on either side most picturesque little towns, and numerous forts, with idle-looking Turkish sentries lounging about. All the houses are low and roofed with brick, and though they look well from the sea at a mile's distance I can easily fancy them anything but comfortable residences. The trees are of a very deep green, and the corn, of which there seems plenty, is just turning yellow; the harvest in Malta is over. We passed, since we entered the Dardanelles, the most beautiful little valleys covered with wood and corn, which run into the sides of the hills. The land on either side is high, and seems covered chiefly with short grass; here and there large tracts of corn show that the land must be very fertile. Many parts put me in mind of the Sussex downs, with their undulating surface and short stumpy trees, which in this country I believe are myrtles and olives, but we are not quite near enough to distinguish their species.

I have been perfectly delighted with this day's journey, it is worth coming to see. We have been passing transports all day by dozens, some going up full, and others returning having discharged their cargoes. For every English* we pass two French, but these they are such ships as an Englishman would only expect to see a fisherman in. We overtook today several large English cavalry transports, which sailed long before us, but which are not likely to be in till long after us, as the wind is dead against them. They ran as close as they could to us, but we kept out of

* Godman frequently used 'English' where 'British' would have been accurate.

their way, and pretended not to see their signals to take them in tow. If we get there first we are more likely to get the best quarters. . . .

Your affectionate Son

The Himalaya   *June 12th 1854*
My dear Caroline — I suppose my last letter had about a week's start of this. It was finished in a hurry, and had no sooner left than an order came to say we were to go on to Varna without landing. We had been ordered to disembark on the Asia side of the Bosphorus, and to go into camp, but for some reason which I do not know, were countermanded and accordingly got up steam this morning and proceeded to Varna at 3 a.m. We were eleven days three hours from Cork to Constantinople. We anchored the night before, seven miles below Constantinople (curiously enough in a thunderstorm, as we left Cork); in the morning we steamed up to the city, the approach to which is very disappointing, the country being very low, and not unlike the Thames' banks about Greenwich, only there were not so many houses.

I went on shore where we were to have landed. There was an immense barrack there, where Elliot, and our Brigadier were quartered; anything like the filth it is impossible to imagine. Our Brigadier's rooms as well as the rest swarm with all manner of creeping things, so much so that one would be covered by sitting there only a few minutes. He said his only chance was to keep the room constantly flooded with water. Elliot lived in a store-room full of all sorts of rubbish and dirt. The view of Constantinople, Pera, etc. from the Bosphorus is the most beautiful thing I ever saw, it is impossible to describe it, more like a scene in the *Arabian Nights*, or a fairy scene. The mixture of houses, palaces, mosques with their minarets, with the beautiful green of the trees that grow among them is perfect, but when one lands the effect is spoilt; the streets are so narrow, dark, and winding that one can see nothing. The dress of the people is interesting and curious. From where we were at anchor (opposite Scutari) we could see the camp and barracks; the latter are immense, but filthy dirty and swarm with vermin. I went to see Watson; he lives with two other men in a room, the most wretched-looking place I ever saw, a door on some cross sticks made their table, the only furniture they had, and eaten up with fleas etc.

The 1st Division consists of the Guards and three Highland corps — a splendid division. I believe we belong to this. The Duke of Cambridge* has command of the infantry of this division. The remainder of the troops proceed to Varna tomorrow, so something must be in the wind for they intended us all to remain in Constantinople. I do not know if Watson's company comes on or not: I hear the enemy are close to Varna, but so many reports are current we believe none; however we shall doubtless see them soon. We have lost two horses, and have a few others that will not be fit for work for some time — I expect the rest of the transports will come straight on here. We were fortunate in being at Constantinople during the feast of Ramadan, the minarets were illuminated every night, which had a beautiful effect. I have left as many things as I possibly could at Constantinople with both my trunks, and have bought saddle-bags of Russian leather which hang each side of the horse, and I expect will carry everything, bed and all. I have only taken six flannel shirts, three pairs of boots, some socks, one suit of uniform and one of plain clothes, it will be impossible to carry more. I have also got my tea, quinine, etc. and a few small comforts. The officers at Varna say there is nothing to be got there, and have sent to Constantinople for hams and other eatables. My horses all well, but the Cob has a slight cough, I hope he will soon be all right.

Varna, June 12th. We anchored here last evening at six, so now I can write a little better; there are some French here, also our Light Division; part of the 8th Hussars are here, the rest and 17th Lancers about eighteen miles inland. They give a dreadful account of the place: the town is small and wretched; the officers tell us they are much bothered with centipedes and other insects which crawl all over their beds. There are also lots of snakes and plenty of tortoises all about the land here. We go into camp under a hill between it and the shore, within a stone's throw of the latter. The country is hilly and very pretty, covered with beautiful green trees and fields, not cultivated but fine wild grass, no such thing as a

* Grandson of George III. Commander of the 1st Division. In 1856 he was appointed Commander-in-Chief of the British army and held that post for thirty-nine years.

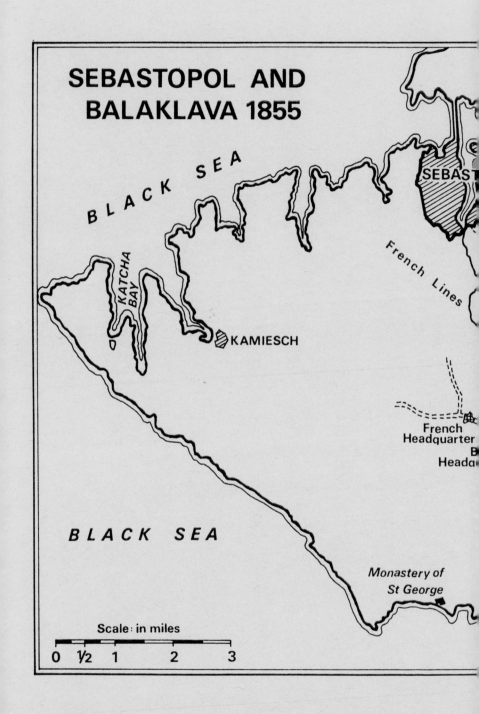

SEBASTOPOL AND BALAKLAVA 1855

BLACK SEA

SEBAST

French Lines

KATCHA BAY

KAMIESCH

French Headquarter

B
Heada

BLACK SEA

Monastery of St George

Scale: in miles

0   ½   1   2   3

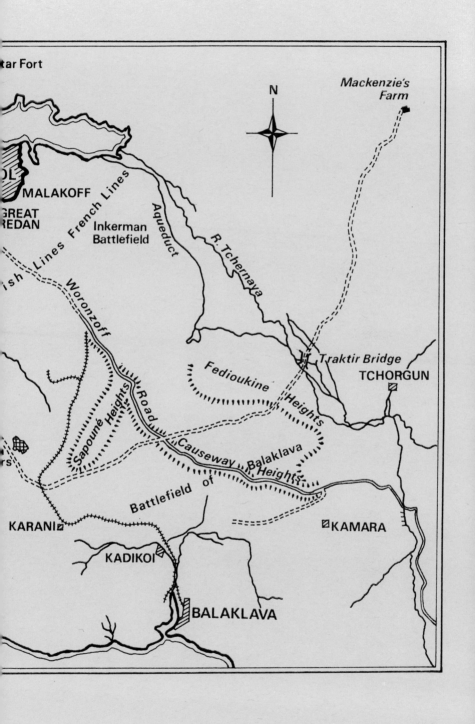

tar Fort

MALAKOFF

GREAT
REDAN

ish Lines French Lines

Inkerman
Battlefield

Aqueduct

R. Tchernaya

Woronzoff

Road

Sapouné Heights

N

Mackenzie's
Farm

Fedioukine

Heights

Traktir Bridge

TCHORGUN

Causeway
Balaklava
Heights

Battlefield of

KARANI

KADIKOI

KAMARA

BALAKLAVA

road. The country appears to be rich, but to be nearly destitute of cultivation. The 8th tell us that troops of wild dogs come and howl round their camp all night, and they are not allowed to shoot them as they are held almost sacred by the people. Some Cossacks are said to have been seen by the patrols from our advanced post eighteen miles from here.

There is such a noise from the horses that I can't write you a better letter and everyone is talking. The post arrangements I hear are so bad you must not calculate on letters, but I will write when I can, and you do the same. This goes by the *Himalaya*, perhaps by Marseilles, perhaps not, at all events you are sure to get it. We have presented an address of congratulation to the captain on our safe arrival. I write by this post to my Father; if we are not marched up the country I may have a chance of writing again by some of the transports, which are expected in tomorrow or next day and return in a few days. I shall hope to hear from some of you soon. Love to all Sisters and Brothers.

Believe me your affectionate Brother

I would give anything to draw. I have a block and will try and take some sketches.

2

The Brushwood Plain

Camp, 2 miles behind Varna   *June 15th 1854*

My dear Father — I wrote to Caroline and intended it to go by the *Himalaya*, but if she is gone it must go by the next conveyance. I have had no time since we disembarked, I have hardly slept for two nights till last night. We disembarked on the 13th and encamped on the shore without accident. The horses were slung over the ship into little boats. The first night the horses kicked everything to pieces and galloped all over the camp; the ropes and piquet poles were so rotten they would not hold the horses, so by the usual false economy of the Board of Ordnance we are sure to suffer in the end. I was up most part of the night and having worked hard all day was consequently very tired. We lost one horse in the night, a horrid brute, which had been kicking all the voyage, and was not worth a pound; he is not yet found. Sir G. Brown* ordered us to move our camp on the next morning, the 14th, which we did, and are now where I am writing from. Last night it rained very hard, and everything I have is damp this morning. We got nothing to eat yesterday till evening, when a Turk brought in some eggs and chicken which we boiled. The horses broke loose last night and eight are missing this morning.

We are in a plain with a lake close to us (in which are quantities of bullfrogs which make an incredible noise). The land is not cultivated, but is all turf covered with low brushwood and trees; it is very pretty, several hills about, and we can see for miles. I am writing sitting on my bed with a book on my knees. There are hundreds of land tortoises all about. Many of our men have had

---

* Commander of the Light Division. He was a veteran of the Peninsula War and greatly respected though strict. He was a passionate opponent of long hair. The Commander of the Heavy Brigade ('our Brigadier'), the Hon. J. Scarlett, had not yet come up from Constantinople. He had formerly been Colonel of the 5th D.G.

nothing to eat since the day before yesterday. The French manage better than we do. All the army is coming here, the Guards have arrived. The Duke of Cambridge came yesterday. They say we are going up the country. I suppose we shall soon.

I landed my horses safely and tied them to a tree the first night. Kilburn* slept with them. The loose horses made the brown break his head collar and get away, but he was soon caught. Kilburn takes much care of them; they are all well but the Cob, which has the strangles, I think it will not signify. I have got my bed up now, and had a good sleep last night till four this morning. The night before I rolled upon the ground, which I found very cold and damp. If we move up the country, which I expect we shall do as soon as the 1st Division is landed, you may not hear from me for some time, but if I can I will write somehow.

The tea you sent is worth anything. I am going to forage in the town and see what I can get. I believe there is nothing to be had but eggs and chicken. As soon as I have done this, I shall cook my breakfast, though I have nothing but some eggs — no bread or biscuit. In a few days we shall get more settled, and get our rations more regularly. Our Brigadier is at present kept at Constantinople. Varna is a horrid town, the houses of wood, scarcely any shops, and more dirty than any Irish village I ever saw, a few cafés, in which you see sullen-looking Turks cross-legged in clouds of smoke. It is very hot here in the middle of the day, and will be warmer when summer comes on.

We hear Austria has joined us. They say the Russians are falling back. I have no more to tell you now. Love to all.

Believe me your affectionate Son

Camp, Varna　　　　　　　　　　　　　　　　　　*June 18th 1854*
My dear Father — The *Himalaya* having taken her departure, my last letter to you was sent by the French post on the 15th which goes out every five days. On that evening we had just finished our dinner when an orderly brought a package for the paymaster, which turned out to be letters and papers; I had one among the number, dated June 3rd. Letters are very acceptable out here, and the disappointment of those who did not receive any was very great.

* Godman's regimental servant.

Our camp is outside all the rest, so we don't get as many good things (i.e. eggs, milk, etc.) as those nearer the town, however we are now more comfortable, and I hope shall be more so. We get our rations regularly, tho' sometimes not till midday, being two miles from the town. We have not yet got a commissary or interpreter attached to us, but are to have one directly which will make us more comfortable. We get $1\frac{1}{2}$ lb. bread and 1 lb. of meat a day, the former is nearly black with plenty of dirt in it, not made with yeast. It is good and wholesome food but turns rather sour the second day, not exactly what we should eat at home if we could help it. The meat is hard and sometimes more like carrion than human food, but since we reported it to Sir G. Brown, we have had pretty good mutton and bullock. All the officers put their meat together, and a woman cooks all in a large tin; we make up a bag of money among us, with which some chicken, rice, pepper, etc. is bought, and all boiled together makes a good wholesome stew. We all dine together at 4.30, each bringing his tin mug, plate and knife, and helping himself out of the general stew pan. Hitherto we have always had enough to eat except the first day or two. The doctor manages the mess and the officers get what he orders them when riding into town. We go to the shops and buy from the Turks, and you see officers riding home with two chicken or geese under their arms, which are immediately killed and put into the pot — with the exception of a few little things we buy, we live exactly like the men. It is a good plan to keep up a mess if possible, as it retains a good feeling among the officers, which is everything at this time. After dinner we smoke our long pipes and then go to bed when it is dark, for a light in one's tent causes all the insects to come in. Our tents are full of ants, which cover every eatable, besides these there are lots of large green and blue lizards, beetles, centipedes and other insects to share our houses with us. The frogs at night are very thick, and if there is rain all our clothes get damp.

I am quite well and happy, I have a great deal to do, but not in the writing line as formerly. Our men have been rather discontented, and the Duke of Cambridge spoke to them about it on parade yesterday. It is unfortunate having a fresh major now, who, I fear, is not popular with the men. If our Brigadier could come up from Constantinople, we should, I am sure, do better. Ours is the only corps that has complained. The men generally, for the future, will be able when not marching to get a pint of London porter daily, for 1½d. There is a canteen man established with a tent; he keeps beer, soap, candles and eatables, though very dear. It is intensely hot, thermometer 92° in the shade; how we can march in this weather I can't tell. Stocks* are abolished. The Light Division is some miles in advance. The Duke of Cambridge's Division is here, and the Division under Sir de Lacy Evans† disembarks tomorrow.

There appears a difficulty in getting from here to Silistria,‡ as they say there are thirty miles without water. This place is hard pressed; the Turks are holding out most bravely, but they say can't stand more than a few days more. The enemy are in great force, supposed to be 70,000 this side of the Danube. I hope they will not take Silistria before we arrive, or it will cost many lives before we can drive them out. I expect we shall meet the enemy near Silistria, where, or near which, no doubt there will be a hard fight, as the Russians intend to make a stand. The French are coming up fast, the English also; as soon as they come, they will, I expect, concentrate farther north, having marched up by divisions, and then the three Allied armies will fall on the Russians and drive them across the Danube. This is the talk here, but no one knows for certain what is to be done. The Admiral, Lord Raglan§ and the Duke, etc., met here Friday and had a consultation. I expect some plan is determined on. Lord Raglan is gone back to Constantinople. The Duke and Staff are encamped on a little hill close to us, in several *large* tents. Of course this is more comfortable than the town — this is what he calls roughing it.

My tea and chocolate are most useful, especially the latter. We breakfast as we can, not together, and get eggs to eat with our bread if we can; no such thing as butter here. The horses get barley and chopped straw, which they eat pretty well, but mine are not so fat as when we left England. They cut green forage

---

* A stiff leather band worn as a uniform collar — smart but uncomfortable, and widely detested.

† Sir George de Lacy Evans commanded the 2nd Division.

‡ A town on the Danube which the Russians were besieging.

§ The Admiral was Lord Dundas, later referred to as 'D—d Ass'. Raglan, the Commander-in-Chief, was sixty-six. As Lord Fitzroy Somerset he had served on the Duke of Wellington's Staff and lost an arm at Waterloo. He was brave and diplomatic but lacked any previous experience of commanding troops in the field.

every morning — no one seems to own the land; very fine grass grows. There is only one cornfield near here, and that the Turks mount guard over with soldiers every night. The Turks we have seen are really good-looking soldiers, much better than I expected to see; they must be brave fellows. We are obliged to be armed to ride two or three miles into the country. All the horses we lost were brought back by Turks, from some miles off, except one, a great brute which we don't want to see again, the rest stand quiet now.

The French are very civil and seem to agree well with the English — what a change *since this day thirty-nine years!* (Both days on a Sunday.) Who could have thought we should be encamped together in friendship? And who knows what may be the end of this alliance? We had a visit yesterday from General Yusuff;* he was much pleased with our Cavalry. He is a very distinguished officer. The dress of the Zouaves is extremely picturesque; they must be very rough and ready troops. The great dodge here is to ask a Frenchman to get you what you want; they are delighted to do it, and walk into a shop, put down what they think a fair price, and take what they want and walk out, getting it for about half what we can. Everything they have seems well arranged; we shall no doubt soon do quite as well.

Our papers have come to June 3rd. Tell Mr Rennell I intend to write to him but can't get time at present, and you are of course entitled to my first spare time. We are more settled now, our kits are smaller: we left lots of things at Constantinople, and leave more with the Consul here. The officers have all bought ponies for about £5 each, to carry tent and everything; mine goes on my third horse.

If you buy a map of the seat of war, you can follow me, as I will tell you in my letters; we are now on the north side of the lake behind Varna, on rising ground behind it. If at any time you do not hear from me, you might find out about the regiment from Duckworth's people, or Joseph might hear from the Halfords. Messrs Grace & Co., Constantinople, have been employed by the regiment to take care of baggage we leave, to take charge of parcels from England, forward letters etc. to us, so you know where my portmanteaus are left, and you can send letters that way if you like. I

* A French divisional commander.

believe the English post will soon be arranged on a better footing; till then I shall use the French as a safer way.

June 20th. As I knew we should leave this soon, I would not send my letter till we marched, which we do tomorrow morning at 4 a.m. to Deverend or Devenish — it is not marked in my map; it is about eighteen miles from here to the north-west and I believe a beautiful spot. I expect it is on our road to Silistria, which place it may be the intention to relieve, if not too late. We heard firing the other night, which they said was at Silistria; this must be at least sixty miles off. The 13th Light Dragoons march with us; I expect we shall have a good deal of outpost duty, patrols, etc. Some of our men are left behind with fever from the sun and damp at night. I am quite well yet. I shall take to quinine if we get to a bad place. I had a little this afternoon. I think this cannot be very healthy; it is where the Russians lost so many men before Varna in '28. The heat is intense; and thirst excessive — our only chance is when we get inland it may be cooler. At the place we are going to there is nothing to be got, so I hope the commissariat will take care of us; here we can at least buy eggs and chicken, and the ration bread is wholesome. We are to take so little baggage that even the doctor is hardly allowed to take anything besides his instruments, so when we get ill, I don't know what we shall do. I have curtailed my kit again to three flannel shirts, two pairs of drawers, etc. in proportion, with a few comforts of different kinds.

We had a marching order today, my Cob carries the baggage quietly, tent and all goes on his back. I wish our Brigadier would come up. When you hear of a regiment marching you little know all the labour and trouble attached to it. Our men have to carry axes, buckets, piquet poles and rope on their horses, which are already too much encumbered. I am sure if we met an enemy on the road, we could do nothing. We are made to do this in order to curtail the baggage of the army; it will never answer. Lord Cardigan has remonstrated strongly, but with no effect. I have no time to call my own, being called upon for one thing and another every minute.

This is a pretty country, but a very barbarous one. There are plenty of deer and boar in the woods they tell us. When you go out, you see large and small tortoises crawling about, so unlike any other country, and plenty of small animals between a rat and stoat; I don't know what they are. The few books I had were obliged to be left behind. How we should all enjoy England again after this country. The infantry certainly have a great pull over us: when they march on to their ground, their work is over as soon as tents are pitched, which takes about ten minutes; our work can never be said to be finished. Some of the ponies here are very good, both handsome and good action. Every officer must get one for his baggage. On Sunday they were selling (really good ones) from 25s to £10. I have been so bothered while writing this that it will account for the writing. I will write again when I can; I have no table and am obliged to write on the ground. Best love to all at home.

Believe me your affectionate Son

Camp, Devna   *Sunday June 25th 1854*

My dear Caroline — One of our officers is going into Varna in an hour, so I send this by him, as I may not have a chance again for some time; there is no post from this. We marched here on Wednesday about eighteen miles, and a nice day we had of it: up at 1.30, tents struck at 2.30, everything soaked with the dew, which is so thick here it is like rain; I have more fear of this than anything else, after the intense heat of the day. Newspapers and some letters came today, the former to June 8th. I suppose I shall get another letter the end of the month. We had an excessively hot and fatiguing march here, though we started at 6.30. The country most of the way is lovely; the south side of the lake is exactly like a most beautiful English park, only without a house. There is no road, only a track through a vast plain covered with a prickly bush which at present is one mass of pretty yellow flowers.

After immense trouble we started; the pack ponies as fast as loaded would persist in kicking their loads off again, but at length we arrived baggage and all, though part of this did not come till late at night. To add to our discomfort, the meat we had had served out for two days was so bad before night it had to be thrown away, and the men were minus meat for that and the next day. There is nothing to be had here except a few chicken, which we have nearly cleared off the country. We live on our rations and generally get a pint of beer, but not the men — our meat is killed and eaten immediately. Yesterday we had biscuits as we could not

1 Temple Godman aged 39 in 1871

2 Park Hatch, Surrey, the Godmans' country house, now demolished

get bread. We are now encamped in a broad valley, enclosed by hills — very picturesque country, but extremely wild; it is the high road to Silistria and Shumla.

The Light Division of cavalry, consisting of 17th Lancers, 8th Hussars and one squadron of 13th Dragoons, all under Lord Cardigan, are close to us, the Light Division of infantry eight miles in rear; about eight miles in advance is a small body of French infantry, cavalry and artillery, a small force which came here across country from Varna. Last night their outposts were attacked by some Cossacks, but they very soon retired again, so you see we are not very far from them now. Some Englishmen just come from Shumla say the Russians are in full retreat from Silistria. This, if true, must be from the Austrians threatening them in flank. They say we are all to go up the country directly, but where to I don't know. One squadron of the 17th and one of the 8th go tomorrow. There was a patrol from the 8th which went within a few miles of the enemy last week. They report the road difficult, as it passes a forest thirty miles long and there is but little water, but the same road was passed by the Russians on their way to Varna in '28, and they were encamped on this very spot, so I suppose we can go the same way. We can't impress on our men the necessity of looking out very sharp at night; though so close to the enemy, they seem to look on it the same as if we were at Ballincollig,* and I fear will not be undeceived till some are shot on their posts; we only hope others will not suffer for their carelessness. I *hear* Lord Raglan is at Varna. Our Brigadier is not yet come up — I wish he were — I fear he will be detained at Constantinople till the rest of the brigade arrives.

We are all well and have only a few slight casualties in men and horses, the former only slight fevers. They say we are to give up our tents and travel without any covering; this, I should think, would not answer in this climate. I have left all my horse clothing. My stud looks well at present, the Cob rather rubbed by the baggage, which I had to hang over a plain saddle. I would give anything for an English pack saddle; those of the country don't fit my Cob. The horses take to the barley very well now. It is wonderful what messes and dirt we are glad to get, such food as we should not look at at home, but notwithstanding we are all well

* One of the Regiment's previous troop stations in Ireland.

and happy. We mess now by troops; we found altogether made too many. Our ration costs 1½d a day, which is stopped from our pay; this with 6d for rice or beans, when we can get them, feeds us; not very expensive is it? Please send me from time to time a few wafers* like the enclosed; mine are all smashed and lost; you can put a few in your letters. Lord Cardigan and his two squadrons just off, *without tents*, and hardly any baggage. This is so unlike the Peninsular; no villages where we can put up men and horses.

Devna is a wretched place — any village you saw in Connemara is much better — hardly anyone to be seen, not even chicken. The only amusement we have is shooting hawks and crows; the former are very plentiful and very large. There are lots of animals here which I take to be marmots, something like a stoat. The other amusement is dog hunting, all go out in the most fantastic dresses, and whip a half-wild dog out of the bush and then have a grand hunt, to the great astonishment of the solemn old Turks, who stand by, looking fearfully disgusted at our wickedness, for they hold the dog almost sacred. They come down by packs at night and howl a concert round our tents. Every Turk about here is armed to the teeth, and they do not look on the Christians very kindly. I should not like to trust much to them.

There is more cultivation here, all barley, which grows in patches. We have plenty of water; a small river runs through the valley and turns several mills. We are well in front of the army now, and I hope shall be pushed on and see some service; you no doubt get better news in London than I can give you, though nearer the spot. I seal my letter with the wafer I mean. I expect this is a very difficult country to march an army through, on account of the commissariat. There seems plenty of cattle at present. Our faces are all blistered and burned by the sun, you would hardly know us. Mosquitoes have made their appearance. Massie, who was with Captain Livius† in Germany, is here on Lord Cardigan's Staff. Best love to all at home. I shall be sure and write when I get a chance, if it is ever so short, and shall always be glad to hear. Don't forget the wafers.

Believe me your affectionate Brother

* A disc of paper used for sealing letters before envelopes were used.

† Livius was the tutor I was to go to at Bonn on the Rhine but he seemed such a shady sort they would not leave me there. (Footnote by Temple Godman.)

Camp, Devna   *Sunday July 2nd 1854*

My dear Joseph — I suppose you are now enjoying yourself in London society, your summer campaign being over. Here I am still and likely to remain for the present, though, for aught I know, by the time this reaches you, I may be at or on my way to Silistria, and within a short time of an engagement with the Russians, if the news we hear today is correct. A captain and eight men of the 8th Hussars have just returned from Silistria, where they went on patrol last week. They saw the enemy's outposts across the river at some distance. Silistria is terribly knocked about and the fortifications nearly destroyed — the Turks must have fought like devils, and they say there that the enemy has only retired and entrenched themselves till a reinforcement 140,000 men (which is said to be on the march) joins them. Among these they say are the Imperial Guard, but tho' this is news direct from Silistria, I do not place much dependence on it. At the same time it is very likely, because the Russians have left the siege and *retired*, though not *retreated*, as they are entrenched; what their object can be I cannot understand, unless to attempt Silistria again; after being reinforced.

Anyhow I expect a forward movement soon, and we are likely to occupy the line of the Danube. Omar Pasha* is gone back to Shumla. Some think we shall have a dash at Sebastopol, others at Odessa. This I suppose would not be difficult to capture and would make fine winter quarters for the army. I don't see how we are to get through the summer without fighting, though some think we shall. For my part I hope not: a very little of this goes a long way; it is very well now in fine weather, but would be very bad in wet weather. As soon as our army can be concentrated, it will never be in better order and spirits to advance, and though there must be hard fighting if we meet, no one seems to doubt the result.

The heat is intense though there is generally a breeze; in our tents the thermometer goes up to 115°. Last night we had a storm which seems not infrequent here; fortunately I foresaw it and slackened my tent ropes, for the rain makes the canvas stretch so that it would split or break the pole. In the middle of the night several tents blew down, to the great discomfort of the occupants, and turning out of bed in the rain to slacken your tent is not pleasant, though necessary. My wants are few here, and comforts

* Commander-in-Chief of the Turkish army.

fewer, only three shirts and two suits of uniform, with a brown holland coat and trousers. My indiarubber bed has gone smash in one compartment, though I can't find the hole, yet if I lie on it an hour, all the air goes out. I am glad I brought a bed to raise one off the ground — by spreading the indiarubber on the sacking of the bed, it keeps the damp off from below, and two blankets and my cloak keep me warm, for sheets are long since discarded. My cloak is often quite wet in the morning from the dew.

We see our dinners walk into camp in the morning, in the shape of some fine old cows, which are killed, cut up, and put into the pot; the soup is pretty good when mixed with rice, but the meat is about as hard as one's shoe. Sometimes we ride out and get a lamb and a goose, which makes a good dinner, but these are scarce now. The Light Division is come up. Lambs were to be had at first for 1s 6d but not now; other things as cheap. We have a small river we bathe in every morning. We are obliged to go out with loaded pistols as these people (who are Greek Christians, though they seem to me to have no religion or civilization at all) have shot at some officers and men. They are all well armed, and look on a man's life as nothing. There are the most curious birds, lots of storks, black and white; they let you go within a yard or two of them, also quantities of eagles and immense falcons. . . .

I suppose there is not much to do now at P.H.* but rabbit shooting in the evening. How pretty it must be now! I should like to see it but I expect it will be some time before I do. . . . I rode up a hill yesterday near our camp, from which I could see the lower range of the Balkans for several miles, and also had a good view of the surrounding country, which appears much the same as this — an immense plain, prettily wooded, and covered with brushwood. The town, Devna, is a wretched place, just like the pictures one sees of a Hottentot village. All the houses one sees are built of mud and hurdles, and thatched with a small enclosure round each. You may go from one end to the other and hardly meet a single person.

Part of the Royal Dragoons have arrived, the rest will soon be here. Lord Cardigan is gone up the country on a patrol to watch the enemy; he has been gone a week. I have written home so lately I shall not write again today, till I get a letter which I suppose I

* Park Hatch.

shall receive in a day or two. I don't know what I did with the key of Chubb's lock which I sent home, if it was not to be found. Is the haymaking over at home yet? The barley here is nearly ripe.

My horses are well; the brown looks a little light, the rest are improving. The brown was lame the other day, I think from the heat of the ground on which they stand. The French dismounted their cavalry to bring them here, where they will find great difficulty in remounting; indeed there are only ponies to be had here, so I don't know how they will get mounted.

Believe me your affectionate Brother

Camp, Devna   *Saturday July 8th 1854*

My dear Father — Your letter from London of June 17th reached this on July 6th; though directed to Hanson, I don't think it ever goes through his hands nor do I think it the best way as these gentlemen seem very independent sort of people. Other officers get theirs *through the post* via Marseilles, by putting on three postage stamps, I believe up to $\frac{1}{4}$ oz. I have never paid any letters received yet; I don't know if you prepay them. I can send letters the same way so I am going to try this, and you might try the same mode. It is a great pleasure to get letters out here, and to know all going on at home, and if you continue to write every fortnight, I know when to look for them.

As there is no saying how long we may be here, I thought it a pity to be so near Shumla without seeing it and accordingly obtained leave, and started on the 6th at three in the morning. The party consisted of Inglis, NcNeile and myself, with my and McNeile's servant, an interpreter and a spare pony. I rode my chestnut horse and also took the Cob. We went slowly along and arrived in about eight hours; the distance must be quite forty miles if not more. On our arrival a man appointed on purpose gave us a stable and lodging, the latter was tolerably clean, nothing but a room without any furniture; the shed for the horses also did very well. We slept on the floor in our cloaks (as we did not bring any other baggage) and, what with fleas and mice which ran over our faces, did not pass a very refreshing night, but it might have been worse. There is no hotel, only the most dirty description of café; there we got some sort of food, such as it was. We returned the next day, leaving at 6 p.m. and arriving in camp at two in the morning; I rode the Cob home and he carried me well. There was a drill this morning at five, so I have not had much rest the last three nights, and pretty hard work; however I am very glad I have been. There is nothing but a rough track, no road; we were fortunate in having a fine moon for our return, or should have lost the way. The country is pretty: we pass through an immense plain, the last of the Lower Balkans on the left gradually running down into it; these hills are beautifully wooded — in the distance an immense way off we could see the magnificent chain of the Balkans. The plain is covered with brushwood, and the turf extends nearly the whole way, very little cultivation, and this nearly all barley. Where this does grow the luxuriant crops plainly tell the fertility of the land — what a country this would be in better hands!

Shumla is situated in a recess of a mountain (part of the Balkans) and is amazingly strongly fortified; it holds at present about 20,000 men. I suppose the garrison in a siege could not be less than 50,000. In front of the city is the plain, which stretches away north and seems to be endless. The town, like all in Turkey, is very dirty, the houses low and built of mud and hurdles, with tile roofs. The bazaar is good and curious, though nothing but Turkish manufacture is to be had here. The people are dressed in the most picturesque manner; all sorts of races in their different costumes form a most curious spectacle, Turks, Greeks, Armenians, Circassians, etc., and every man carries an immense bundle of arms in his girdle, which they would not scruple to use on the slightest occasion. We rode all round the fortifications and visited a large hospital, where we saw a number of wounded Turks and Russians from Silistria, some of them dreadfully maimed. They seemed pretty well cared for, though I believe their surgeons are very bad.

We have to get up early every day, and all parades must be over at 8 a.m. Omar Pasha came here and reviewed the troops the other day; he was much pleased, and said he never before then had seen cavalry. The artillery unlimbering pleased him much; he says the Russians would have no chance with us. He appears a very intelligent man. I was at Shumla the day he inspected the 5th which was unfortunate.

They do not seem to be moving more troops up here, and there is a report we are all to go to Odessa or Sebastopol by water. Of course everything is a secret, still, since the enemy has retreated so far, I think it likely we shall be landed somewhere else, instead of marching so far. We must get some good town for winter quarters; it would be impossible to stay here. The Turks can hold the line of the Danube in case of another advance of the enemy, which is not likely with the Austrians on their flank. If we go to Odessa we could take them in rear, and that would make a good place to winter in. Bucharest, I am told, is a very fine city. I only hope now we are here the English people will not allow the Emperor to make fools of us by some paltry treaty, or that we are to come out here for nothing after all. From our latest papers (23rd ult.) it seems certain the Austrians and Russians are with us now.

What a horrid thing was the loss of the *Europa*;* I cannot fancy any state a man can be placed in so dreadful as a fire at sea, especially in a transport. I often thought of this in the *Himalaya* where there was so much hay and fire about. The Queen's head on your letters is useless; it always comes crossed through with a pen.† We expect our Brigadier daily. I hope to get a table made here, for it is very inconvenient writing on the ground. I wrote to Joseph at his club a short time ago; did he get it? What are the names of the men who came from his regiment to the 5th? Our Major,‡ or Lt.-Colonel as he is by brevet, *is* related to the Tredcrofts, but how I don't know; one who is in the Artillery was with us at Ballincollig, and I believe he called him cousin.

This sort of life suits me very well, for I am fond of change and excitement, and I do not mind roughing it as long as I have my health. The only thing I regret is the loss of books; these I cannot possibly get, and feel the want of them much, but I keep a kind of journal which takes up some time. The Czar when turned out ought to get some corn besides grass, I think; horses without this

* This ship, carrying part of the Inniskilling Dragoons, caught fire 200 miles out of Plymouth. The Commanding Officer and seventeen others lost their lives.

† The explanation of this and other remarks which follow about the postal service is that letters posted to addressees in the Crimea would have a value to collectors. Few of them, of course, would be preserved. To have this value they needed the official cancellation stamp which was a crown or a double 'o', or the number 48. However, some were cancelled with the stroke of a pen, and this made them useless to the collector. Officers' letters required a 3d stamp; other ranks' letters travelled free.

‡ Apparently Major C. W. M. Balders.

get too low in condition. I like what I saw of Nicholls very much; he is now at Varna. Tell me what letters of mine you get, and when you write say what you and people in general in England think of the war and state of affairs. Our papers are irregular, though the letters seem to come right — everything is kept so quiet, we know nothing of what is in contemplation. This goes today and I must close it, or shall be too late for the post. Love to all.

Your affectionate Son

Camp, Devna   *July 12th 1854*
My dear Fred — They have at last made arrangements for the letters here, and the post goes out every five days. I got your letter on the 6th but suppose by the time you get this you will have left England for your summer tour in Switzerland, or wherever you are going. The weather is intensely hot — the thermometer averages from 110° to 115° in our tents, and in the sun it goes up to the top, so I don't know how much higher it would go, if it could. We generally have a breeze in the day, and but for this I don't know what we should do, at least the men, for they are many of them done up. They never gave us any canvas trousers before we started, as they did the other regiments; and the men can scarcely bear their leather overalls. Fever is becoming more prevalent, a sort of low fever, and many men with cholera, diarrhoea, etc. One is obliged to be careful now, and they say it gets hotter every day till September, when fevers become more common.

I began to take light wine and water, but this made me very ill. I then took to beer, which I intend to give up, as they say it is very unwholesome, and take to very weak brandy and water, and water when I can't get brandy. We get little now besides our rations, since General Brown's Division came. The eggs we buy are nearly all bad, and the ham we bought is consumed, so that for breakfast I am reduced to ration bread and biscuit and a raw onion; it agrees very well with me. I have discovered some bees near here and I go and buy some comb now and then. I have plenty of chocolate left for the present, which is a great comfort, and we can buy very good coffee about here. Sometimes I and Kilburn go out with forage nets and a sickle, and cut grass some four or five miles off, as all the green food near here is consumed. Sometimes the people take it into their heads to shoot at you, so it is not safe to go unarmed. There is a very heavy dew every night, and this morning my clothes were just as if they had been out in the rain.

We have been obliged to flog two men since we came; of course in the field the punishment must be summary. On the whole they behave well, though they have much to try them, having little to eat and much hard work. Sir G. Brown is inclined to be very severe if he gets a chance. I do wish they would send us on; we shall lose many horses before long. Lord Cardigan came back yesterday with his two squadrons having been to Silistria, where he saw some Cossacks, who soon made themselves scarce across the Danube. They are terribly knocked up, both men and horses. Our brigade is nearly all up, only one more ship to come. We expect our Brigadier today.

What a horrid thing about the Inniskillings. The other day I was riding home to camp from Varna, when we were quartered there, having been to market, when an engineer officer overtook me and we fell into conversation; he told me he had been ordered off to Silistria that day and was then going to wish his brother (in some other regiment) good-bye. He told me he never expected to return as he was the only engineer officer, if even he was able to reach Silistria, which the Russians were then all round. He was an officer of some service and seemed a nice fellow. Yesterday I heard he had been killed with three other English officers, crossing the Danube with the Turks — such is the uncertainty of existence.

Omar Pasha inspected the troops the other day and was very much pleased. A ration of rum was afterwards served out to all the men. The various reports we hear seem very absurd, every day there is some new shave. We hear the Turks have crossed the Danube with a loss of 300 or 600 men, and the Russians a heavier loss; also that the Austrians are at Widden. Some say we are to leave this and go to Sebastopol or Odessa, and leave the Danube to Austria and the Turks.

It has just come on to rain; when it does, it comes through our tents, and when the sun shines, it strikes through also. You never saw such rain as comes down here in thunderstorms, which are very frequent. The Duke of Cambridge's Division was absolutely washed out of its camp the other day. There is a very good place for bathing here, a large tank fourteen feet deep with beautiful water; only so many officers bathe in it. There were some pony races here yesterday, but dog hunting in the evening is the usual amusement; they run famously. The change of temperature is such that since the storm, the thermometer has gone down to 25° and will probably be as high as before in the course of an hour. A storm at home soon passes off and is forgotten, not so here where it puts out the fires and spoils the men's dinners, which were not overgood before, and leaves the soldier with a damp blanket to sleep in.

Lord Lucan* inspected us the other day and took the command of the regiment himself, an unusual thing. However, in about ten minutes he managed to club it most effectually; pretty well this for our Cavalry Commander, who sets up to be an exceedingly smart, sharp hand — however we are all liable to mistakes. We have constant reports here that we are going home immediately; we hear this again today. I must say that, glad as I shall be to see England and home again, I should be sorry to come home without first seeing some Russians. I was sorry to hear so poor an account of yourself; you must take care. I think I did well to bring out Daly's chestnut and the Cob; these are rather picking up condition and the chestnut does not look so small here as I used to think him. They were not one bit the worse for their forty miles to Shumla and back the next day. The young bay horse would never have stood this feed and knocking about. Write and tell me what you are doing, and if going abroad, direct to me, 'British Army in Turkey, *Marseilles*'.

We sent a picture the other day to *Punch*† of a Dragoon in Turkey, in marching order with all the things he is supposed to carry, drawn by Campbell, did you see it? It seems an age since we left Cork; the time passes so slowly. When we bathed we found this morning a sergeant of the 8th Hussars, drowned last night. The post goes out today 13th at midday. I have no more to tell you at present, but hope I soon shall. Write before long.

Believe me your affectionate Brother

Camp, Devna   *July 17th 1854*

My dear Father — It appears to me that letters travel quicker from me to you, than from you to me; I don't exactly understand

---

* Lord Lucan was considered to be incompetent but brave.
† Not apparently published.

why this is, perhaps it is only fancy. Our mails leave this the 3rd of every month and every fifth day after, consequently this goes tomorrow. The mails in are uncertain, but generally come the day after ours leave; there was one in today and brought me your dispatch of July 1st and for a quarter of an hour while reading it I was almost back again in England. Your letter came with two Queen's heads, one of which was crossed through with a pen and the other unstamped, evidently useless; the *letter*, too, was unstamped so I cannot think how this came. I also received a letter from our depot at Newbridge with three heads on — one sheet of common notepaper. This seems a cheap and sure mode of transit. I don't know if you pay your letters, but I never have to do so; perhaps Hanson keeps an account against me for them, though I do not think this likely.

Everyone here talks of peace and going home; I suppose this arises from their expressing their wishes and trying to imagine they will come true. From your letters and our latest papers (July 1st) peace does not seem to be the cry in London, especially as I hear six more infantry and two cavalry regiments are to come out directly. I was much pleased with Lord Lyndhurst's speech the other day on the Eastern question; he spoke out the feelings and opinions of the British nation. I was also glad to see Lord Clarendon state in so straightforward a manner the intentions of the ministry. Lord Aberdeen seems to want energy and decision to carry on the affairs of the country at so critical a moment, however he has a difficult and very responsible game to play. I hear often what is going on through our Major, whose brother is in Parliament and seems much mixed up with the leading men of the day and who appears a clever man from some of his letters which I have seen. Do you think this ministry can stand much longer? If a new one were to come in, more active operations would no doubt be the consequence, as this would be a popular move in England. Men and officers are getting tired of this inactivity; everyone seems to imagine that he came out for a summer's hard fighting and then go home; many wish themselves back. For my part I don't mind as long as I have my health, which I am happy to say I have had hitherto.

We get more biscuit than bread here; this is wholesome, but as it is ship biscuit and preserved in tar sacks because of rain, it tastes more of tar than English flour, but this I do not mind. We have changed our ground a quarter of a mile, which is necessary in this climate now and then, and we are now not so near the river. Sow fever and dysentery had laid up many of our men, but they got over it in a day or two. We have lost one man, but that was from some cause which would have happened in England and he was a man who had drank a good deal. Nearly all our officers have been laid up from the same cause; Halford has been very ill, but is, I hope, better this evening. This place would be unhealthy in the autumn. I take as much care of myself as possible and am very glad I have lived so quietly hitherto; those who have not will not stand much chance out here. Last night there came down such a rain as I never saw before, as if it were poured out of buckets, and our tents which keep out neither sun nor wet, had as usual a small shower inside like a mizzling rain. I keep a waterproof rug at the foot of my bed, which I draw over when it rains, and am therefore comparatively dry. I am very glad I brought a bed, though only eight or nine inches from the ground; it is a good thing to preserve health and, being of wood, is not very heavy. If you hear of anyone coming out, tell them not to come without one.

Our Brigadier is come, which we are glad of. One half our brigade is here; they leave the rest at Varna, so as to keep Lord Lucan there, for he and Lord Cardigan would be sure to fight if together, so we suffer for their folly. Lord Lucan inspected us the other day and taking the command of the regiment clubbed it completely; he is a regular muff. General Thackwell* would, I expect, have been better. There seem to be a good many muffs among the chiefs. General Brown, though rough and disagreeable, seems a fine soldier, one of the old sort, cares for no one; he has a magnificent division, works them hard, but they are in fine order. Stocks are discontinued for the present, a great comfort. We see none of the delicacies you read of in the papers of preserved potatoes and numerous other things. The officers buy potatoes from the canteens, but the men never get any.

I rode into Varna last week; the town has improved in as much as the French have established cafés, etc. Sir de Lacy Evans's Division is situated on a hill near us, in the most lovely spot you could possibly imagine. . . .

* General Sir Joseph Thackwell — a Peninsular and Indian veteran.

These paper reporters send home very *highly coloured* reports of all they see and hear. Our present system of piqueting horses does not answer; it is, I believe, to be altered. I have got a small table and camp stool made by the artillery wheeler, which makes me much more comfortable. I saw in *The Times* that Campbell's* ship is ready for sea and that he, being so popular, had no difficulty in getting men. I am sorry to find the cholera has broken out again in the West Indies. Sidebottom, from whom you have got a cook, keeps a very magnificent table for all the swells about his part of the country; he himself is one of the greatest snobs I ever set eyes on. I was sorry to hear Mr Napper is about to leave Ifold; is there any part of the property you think of buying? I am getting rather tired of Devna and should like to go off to Odessa. We heard yesterday from a man who saw them that the Russians are still in force before Silistria; I suppose this is merely their rear-guard.
. . .

Believe me your affectionate Son

Camp, Devna   *July 27th 1854*
My dear Joseph — I wrote to Caroline this morning, and as I don't know where you are, I write to your club, as most likely you will be in London to parties. I did not tell them in my letter we have the cholera† in our camp for fear of frightening them at home, but such is the case, and this is the reason of our moving. The Light Division of infantry got it first. They were encamped about a mile from us and higher up on a hill; they took it one morning and before night sixteen men were dead — no case lasted more than three hours. The next morning they struck their camp early and marched away about five miles to fresh ground. I expect this valley is unhealthy, and the men *would* drink the river water, which is very bad, and also the country wine; all warning is useless. They, I believe, lost thirty-five men and two women but since they moved, they have been more healthy. The Light Cavalry have had some fatal cases. We have lost three men: the first of heart complaint, the second of typhus fever after a few hours' illness, the third in a

---

* Presumably, Sir Colin Campbell.
† In fact, there was also plenty of cholera in London in 1854, including an outbreak at the Tower of London.

few hours of Asiatic cholera, and a man now dying of cholera, who I expect to have to bury *myself* this evening, as the clergyman of the division is gone on. I can tell you this work is anything but lively, when you see a man go to hospital and die in a few hours, then put in his grave with nothing but his blanket rolled round him, and not knowing who may be the next. The place too is beyond everything dull and we have no books for we can't carry them — and no chance of doing anything yet; any work would employ the men's minds, and we should do better.

Nearly all our officers have been ill with fever and ague. Montgomery is gone to Constantinople to get well. I fear this country will never do for him and many others. The heat is so great, and food so bad we have no chance of picking up strength after illness, and there are only a few bottles in the hospital, as they will allow us to carry hardly any medicine. One of our men fell off his horse into the river the other day and was drawn under the mill which smashed his leg and would have killed him, only some of our men held the wheel from going round; he is now doing well. Our horses are getting very thin. I do wish they would send us to Sebastopol or Anapa, where we might have a chance of seeing the Russians.

Write and tell me where you are going abroad, or if at all. Call at your club now and then as I shall sometimes write to you there. I hope those two men have joined the 5th from your regiment. I saw the picture of your inspection in the *Illustrated*.* When the papers come they are immediately read through by all and then this temporary pleasure is over. They don't come at all regularly.

I expect several of our fellows will sell in the winter. If we are quartered at Scutari we shall no doubt get six weeks' or two months' leave, which I shall spend in travelling, as it would only be useless to come to England for a fortnight and then to return to this barbarous country. If we have a hard fight before winter, I *may* then come home and see you, if only for a week or two, and should then take a cut across Europe; but the time is yet some way off and I have a good deal to go through between this and then.

We have flogged two men since we came here, one is since dead of cholera. Poor fellow he was a very smart soldier, but his career was anything but a bright one, as about half was spent at punishment or in prison. I am in for anything but a pleasant afternoon,

* *Illustrated London News.*

having first to flog a man, who has been given over to us to operate upon (the extreme penalty of fifty lashes), his regiment having marched. As the Adjutant has to stand within arm's length to count the strokes, I have the full benefit. It is a very disgusting sight; a few strokes properly administered makes a man's back the colour of a half-ripe plum, blue and red, and towards fifty every stroke draws blood. I have to see that the farriers lay it in as hard as they can. After this I expect to have a very different occupation, that of reading the service over this poor cholera patient (if he dies) who the doctor tells us is dying; he is Swinfen's servant. Such is life, however I suppose I shall see worse things than these.

Rather an amusing scene occurred here the other day. Two Turks, having stolen two troop horses, tried to sell them to the infantry. They were of course discovered and immediately delivered over to the Provost, who there and then tied them up and administered fifty lashes (no joke from such practised hands). The Turks would not undress, so had it done for them, when they began to yell and scream frightfully, tho' the men could not half flog at first for laughing, but afterwards they did *pitch* it in, to the great delight of the Bulgarians, who stood by crying 'Bono Johnny' — they always call the English 'Johnny'.

Tell me about the new kennels; what prospects of game, shooting etc? Have you had any rabbit stopping? How is Fred, and where is he? I shall write to him soon.

This is a bad place to be ill; tents keep out neither rain nor sun, and one can hear the sick in the hospitals groaning and crying out with pain. I dare say it will all be in the paper about the cholera here. I hope it will not frighten them at home; it is sure to be in as there is a *Times* reporter* with the Division. My horses are doing very well.

Believe me your affectionate Brother

* *The Times* reporter was W. H. Russell whose frank dispatches helped to remedy the supply situation but were also considered to be giving information and comfort to the enemy.

3

Cholera

Camp, Kotlubei   *August 7th 1854*

My dear Mother — We struck our camp and marched here
July 28th; it is about five miles on the Shumla road, and as it is
high ground and open, it is more healthy than the valley of
Devna. . . . I will now tell you a little of the news of the place. We
are encamped here alone on an immense plain, and near a poor
little village. Much the same as all about here. The 1st Dragoons
are five miles from us, and the rest of our brigade still remains at
Varna. The Light Cavalry under Cardigan are about twenty miles
in advance at Tannibazaar; the Division under Sir G. Brown are
also about five miles from us. A melancholy thing happened there
the other day. Captain Levinge, who commands a troop of Horse
Artillery, not feeling well got up in the night and by mistake took
a bottle of laudanum, thinking it some other medicine; he died
the next morning. I believe he was a very good officer.

The movement of the army is not meant for an advance, but
merely a change of ground. We shifted again today about a mile
in order to get a fresh spot, which is necessary here every ten days
or so. I don't imagine we shall remain here long as the water is
getting low, and we are obliged to draw every drop out of wells
and one fountain half a mile from our camp. We received our
papers today up to July 22nd. I see John Bull is very anxious for
an attack on Sebastopol, nor is he more so than everyone in the
British army out here; I am rather inclined to think that the authorities are consulting about it now — at least several things look
like it.

I believe I told you Sir G. Brown had gone in a steamer to the
Crimea with one or two Engineering officers; this was true, and
he has now returned. Now he must have gone to look for a landing
place. He went so close to Sebastopol that he very nearly got shot,

3 The Earl held by Kilburn, painted by John Ferneley at Newbridge Barracks, Ireland, 1852. The Earl served through the Crimea and was shot in 1869 after being for 19 years Godman's charger. Kilburn died in 1889 aged 61

4 Godman, Kilburn and The Earl photographed by Roger Fenton in the Crimea before September 1855

5 English Heavy Cavalry gathering hay in the Crimea, from a contemporary issue of the *Illustrated London News*

for as they were at breakfast on deck (I hear) several balls came into the ship, and one through the funnel, but they sent a shell right into the middle of the town, and then went off. They say that on every point of the coast Cossacks were posted, one of whom on their approach galloped off into the interior. Sir G. Brown is not come back, but is at Constantinople where Lord Raglan is, also Marshal St Arnaud* who also went. He is said to have climbed up the mast on seeing the town, declared he could take it in a very short time. I believe the best point for landing is about eight miles from the town. I expect they will send cavalry also if they go, and every man they have would not be too many. If they risk an engagement (before they arrive at the town, which it is almost certain they would do) without cavalry it may go hard with them.

You must not believe all you see about us in the papers, viz, that we formed part of the patrol to Silistria — it is not true — also that our men were quite done up marching to Devna. It was certainly very hot and the horses were tired with a twenty-mile march, but I have often seen men as tired in Ireland, so that was not unusual. As to their riding without boots I can only say that I, who inspected the men and rode with them, did not see it, so this can't be true either. There is a reporter to *The Times* with Sir G. Brown's Division who puts in all he hears, and I expect more than he sees.

No one seems to imagine that any move north is at all likely this year, though we have constant reports about going to Sebastopol which may be true in the end. It would be a very good finish to the campaign before going into winter quarters, and will be a harder nut to crack if left till next year.

This is the hottest month in Turkey, the thermometer seldom below 90° in the shade, and often much higher; I don't feel it so much as I did and don't mind it now; it seems to agree with me for I am very well indeed. The sun on our head is unhealthy. I always wear (when not absolutely on duty) a white wide-awake, with a turban folded thickly round and a tail on my shoulders. You have no idea what the sun will strike through here. I see a long account in *The Times* of Omar Pasha's review; it was

* Marshal St Arnaud was the French Commander-in-Chief but he was a very sick man with not long to live.

one of our men's helmets that he tried on, and thought very comfortable.

We are getting on better here now in the feeding way, there being no other regiments near, and a sutler* has set up a canteen today, so we shall do very well for some days to come; we get more accustomed to our ration beef and cook it better than we did. The canteen man brought some pale ale 2s a bottle, a great treat, and a little does one good in a hot climate. I was glad to hear a pack saddle would be sent, and have written to Watson, who I believe to be at Scutari to go to Hanson and make him forward it when it comes, so I hope to be able to give you some account of it before long. The commissariat gives us coffee, but as it has to be roasted on a spade, or whatever we can get, it is never very good, and sometimes hardly drinkable. We also get rice and rum, which is very wholesome I believe. As to potatoes we have only had one case since we came to Turkey, and only two days' porter. The ovens being at Devna we get as many days' biscuit as bread.

Poor McKinnon is gone to Varna to pass a medical board, and go home if he can; if he does not pass, he will throw up his commission. Anyhow, I fear he will lose money, but he is sure he will die out here, and, I think, has frightened himself about being here in this climate. He promised to call at Lowndes Square or Connaught Place when he gets to London. I find saddle-bags are not good things, as one has to turn out everything to find what one wants. Next year I shall take my portmanteaus. I don't want anything from England at present; I have enough tea, etc. left. Chocolate is to be had at Varna, not the sort I brought in tins. . . .

There is a very unusual complaint here: everyone has too much money. We get our pay every day, and as mine is 13s 6d a day, it mounts up, and I have got £49 which I should like to transfer to Cox & Co., if I could, having no good way of carrying it about. I brought out about £50 and after all I have spent, have now what I tell you. We know what it is to have a pocket full of gold in Bulgaria, and in spite of this to have a bad dinner. Our men do not know what to do with their pay; some send it home, but those who have no families think nothing of giving 2s for a bottle of porter

* Camp follower or private trader.

when they can get it. Their rations and living altogether does not cost more than 1½d or 2d a day. I think they put a great deal of nonsense in *The Times* about the dress of the troops; they are not so bad as they are said to be; I mean not so much encumbered or strapped up. Tell Mr Rennell I shall send him a line now. If we go to Sebastopol I will let you know. I hope we may, but perhaps you will hear as soon as I can tell you.

Your affectionate Son

Camp, Kotlubei   *August 12th 1854*

My dear Father — You see we are still here, nor do I think there is any chance of moving at present, though we still hear reports about an expedition to Sebastopol, which however I think is more than doubtful, because the French do not wish to join us, at all events this year. I expect we shall loiter about the place till it is time to go into winter quarters. I am sorry to say the cholera has been bad here, but it has not been so bad in the country as at Varna. We, like other regiments have come in for our share, but I am in great hopes it is passing over, and they say that toward the 15th we may look for cooler weather.

I remembered Joseph's birthday yesterday; it was that day three years I returned to Ireland, after Exhibition leave. It is very dull here, nothing to enliven us but newspapers, which do not come more than once in seven or eight days. I expect a post in next Tuesday, and I hope there may be a letter for me. I had been thinking of a trip to the Danube, and also Silistria, which I should much like to see, but as there is just a chance of our being ordered off to somewhere, it is of no use to ask for leave. Our Brigadier is still with us; he sticks to his old regiment, and I dare say will follow us wherever we go. There has been a tremendous fire at Varna; the town was fired in four places at once, and it is supposed it was done by Russian spies. Much of the commissariat magazines were destroyed. McKinnon has passed a medical board and has leave to proceed to England, so I suppose he will start by the next conveyance and will probably very soon be in London, when perhaps the Mellings may see him. . . .

There are quantities of beautiful blue birds here, I think they are orioles; also lots of hoopoes with a topknot. We have both in our case at home. I have heard no more about the pack saddle, yet suppose it is on its way to Constantinople before this.

Your affectionate Son

2nd Cavalry Division, Camp near Varna   *August 18th 1854*

My dear Father — We have had a dreadful time of it the last week or ten days, having suffered more severely than any regiment out here, considering our numbers. I did not tell you much about it before, but I hope now the worst is over and that we shall be more healthy here than at Kotlubei. In about one month we have been more than decimated, having lost thirty-four men out of 295, and our surgeon, poor old Pitcairn, who died the night before last. We left on our ground at Kotlubei nine men who could not be moved, with Duckworth, who has also had cholera, and who I fear will never recover as he now has typhus fever. Our vet. surgeon was also left ill, but I hope more frightened than hurt. Our Colonel is also ill on board a transport here, so you may fancy what a state the regiment is in. Our horses are half starved, not having had above 10 lb. of barley the last four days and coming off a long march today, fancy Lord Lucan *telling us* they looked thin.

I am very glad to get to Varna again: we are encamped on high ground overlooking the sea, which seems quite like seeing home again. Thank God I have been very well through all this sickness, which is very bad in a tent. Fancy a sick man on the plains of Bulgaria as we were, with very little medicine and no comforts or, one may say necessaries, such as arrowroot for the sick. One of the doctors told me that if they had had these things, some lives at least might have been saved. Even medicines were wanting, and we have now just come off a three days' march without so much as even a pill with us. The only thing we had to give our convalescents was common sailors' biscuit; no wonder they could not get better. We have had nothing but biscuit and pork for three or four days; the latter I don't care to eat in this hot climate, not having much appetite, indeed I seldom touch any meat now and live mostly on rice, of which we get 2 oz. a day. I find this agrees well with me. Our men are quite done up, but I hope will soon recruit here.

There are still reports confidently asserted that Sebastopol is to be attacked this year — and Monday next is said to be the day for the embarkation of the infantry, which are now falling back on Varna. The Cavalry are to follow the infantry. One of Lord Lucan's aides-de-camp told me today, we should be there this day fortnight; for my part, I *don't believe* we shall go there this year. These A.D.C.s are always great men in their own opinion. The Guards marched today, and no one who *knew* the *London guardsman* could have supposed him the same man; he is so weak and wasted. What a misfortune that so beautiful and luxuriant a country should be so unhealthy; but I believe it is more from mismanagement than the nature of the climate. The bay is full of shipping, and quantities of gabions* on the seashore, as well as fascines, used in siege operations, and more are being made; no doubt Sebastopol was intended if this sickness does not put us off it. The French expedition to Gusleudgi lost 4,000 men of cholera. I do hope we may go to Sebastopol. Our men have quite got their spirits up since we came here; this cholera is a fearful disease, and I think the doctors can treat it *about as well* as they can the plague. I have seen men within the last few days doing work quite well or talking, when suddenly down they dropped like a ninepin, and in the course of five hours dead and buried.

I must now finish as I am going to bed. I am very well and should like this kind of life if we only kept tolerably healthy. I am in hopes we may, now we have changed. I have lots to do and get plenty of scolding for anything that goes wrong, though I am at work always, and hardly ever let alone for a minute. You may fancy the state of the regiment, and how many disadvantages we have when compared with others. No colonel — no major — no paymaster — no surgeon — no vet. surgeon — one captain *hors de combat*, and an adjutant† of four years' only service and experience. I shall write next mail if here.

Your affectionate Son

Camp, Adrianople Road, near Varna   *August 24th 1854*

My dear Caroline — There was a mail in on Sunday last, and among the letters was a bundle tied up for poor Pitcairn, who I

---

* Gabions were wickerwork barrels filled with earth to make trench parapets. Fascines were bundles of brushwood used for filling ditches.

† Godman himself.

told you in my last was dead. This bundle I did not untie till Wednesday, yesterday, when I found yours of July 28th which I had supposed to have miscarried. I am writing this in a hurry and am in great trouble; my poor friend Captain Duckworth, who has had cholera, died this morning, poor fellow — he was the best friend I had in the regiment. Thank God I have had good health so far, and the cholera seems to have spent its force. We have lost in all thirty-six men, one captain and our surgeon. We had no more cases since we came here.

It is said we are all going to Sebastopol, and I suppose we shall start next week if we go. The artillery are embarked and all the transports are here, also numerous steam-tugs. They say we are to land about thirteen miles from the town. Our regiment is in such a state, I should not wonder if we did not go. We have no colonel, our major is ill at Constantinople, our senior captain dead, two lieutenants and a cornet on the sick list, our paymaster gone home, our surgeon dead, and quartermaster been ill for six weeks and the vet. surgeon hardly expected to live. Having lost so many men, it is very likely we shall be cut out of this expedition. We have suffered more from disease than we should probably have done in two general actions. I have bathed every day since I came here; it agrees with me. The weather is much cooler now, and I suppose the commencement of winter is at hand: they will have to be quick at Sebastopol.

I send you a little remembrance from the Black Sea in the shape of a few shells I picked up while bathing. I am glad you enjoyed yourself at Goodwood races; I should much have liked to be there. I shall be glad of a few more wafers next time you write. The saddle, I suppose, is on its way. The things my Mother is going to send with it will be most acceptable. We get on better now cooking, but 1 lb. beef or a chicken does not make much of a dinner; however, it agrees with me. Being near Varna we can get some comforts, occasionally a ham, or a tongue off some of the transports; jam is a great luxury — we get this too sometimes. The biscuit does not go down well without something, and we can get no milk here. I bought 2 lb. of indifferent salt butter the other day for 6s. I shall like some jam sent out when we go into winter quarters. . . .

Believe me your affectionate Brother

Camp, Adrianople Road, near Varna   *August 27th 1854*

My dear Father — It takes some time to fill this paper so I begin before post day, which is not till the 29th. I have so much to do that I have not much time for writing, especially on weekdays. All officers have to be at stables at 5 a.m. and there my day begins, from that time till ten at night I have hardly a moment to myself. Since we came to the camp I have not been out of the lines except to ride two miles to the sea and bathe, which I generally do daily, and once to Varna to attend Fisher's funeral; you will see by Fred's letter that he is dead. I write to Fred by this mail to P.H. Varna Bay is quite changed from when we arrived; it is now full of shipping of all kinds, from the huge man-of-war to the little French transport or small steam-tug. Three or four boats a day come in and go out to Constantinople.

It is now no longer a secret that Sebastopol is to be the point of attack. Marshal St Arnaud issued a proclamation to the army yesterday that in three weeks the French eagles should be flying over this town. The ships are all told off in their proper divisions, and immense steam-tugs ply about the bay — all is activity and preparation. The shore is strewn with gun-carts, ammunition, gabions, etc., which are being shipped as fast as possible. In the meantime the infantry are concentrating around Varna; and the Light Cavalry are expected tomorrow. The soldiers whose spirits have been at a low ebb, as well they might from all this sickness, are now on the rise; and everyone looks forward to the fall of Sebastopol. I know nothing of the strength of the garrison, but I suppose that has been well ascertained. I hear there are about 20,000 Cossacks. Sir J. Burgoyne,* the great engineer, arrived here last night, having been packed off from London at six hours' notice. Lord Raglan talking to Brigadier Scarlett yesterday told him he would embark with the 2nd Division; but whether he meant Scarlett or the 5th D.G. he could not say. I fancy that the Artillery and the infantry are to go first and secure a landing, the Cavalry following. I hope we shall take our tents; some people doubt it. It would not be pleasant in the trench these cold nights without. I suppose the place will be carried by assault, for I believe they have two or three years' provisions in the town. I hear when we get to a

* A veteran of the Napoleonic Wars; he was seventy-two.

certain point the fleet will sail into the harbour and smash all before them; but they cannot do much till some fort is taken. Caroline's map will probably be useful now. They must either fight to the last or be taken prisoners, as no doubt the retreat will be cut off. Some people say the place is mined for six miles round, but one hears all kinds of reports. No doubt if we had gone two months ago it would have been much easier, as they have been fortifying it all the summer, and our men were then stronger and less impaired by climate. It is wonderful how they have improved since we came here from up the country. The Guards especially were so weak some of them could scarcely march, even without arms and packs. As to baggage, I suppose they have more than half the rest of the army. But perhaps it would not have done to have gone some time back as our presence was required to raise the siege of Silistria. If we can take it, what a blow it would be to the Russian ambition in the south. The only difficulty I see is, who is to keep it? We cannot, and the French must not, and the Turks are not fit to have even what they have got. I cannot see how this will put an end to the war, even should they take Kronstadt also, which appears not very likely. The only chance is to keep them shut up as they are now and work them well here and in the Baltic; in time we shall no doubt bring them round, or the better sense of the people will prevail against their tyrant ruler.

This being done and peace established the second act will commence, the question being how will the French be got out of Turkey. I cannot help thinking little of their principle as a nation, and I fear they will give England some trouble yet. They are very civil and the best feeling exists between the two armies, whenever the two nations meet at a drinking shop, they invariably get drunk together, and frequently after one of these meetings, you see the immense Highlander arm in arm with the little Chasseur, or the Zouave. Some of the French troops, especially the African corps, are the most soldierlike-looking men it is possible to imagine, and they have always fought well, the Zouaves especially are a splendid body, but terrible ruffians. They seem to keep them apart from the English as much as possible, and I think this is as well. Every now and then there is a fight in the streets, and the poor Frenchmen are sure to come out second best from the effects of Johnny's fists; in spite of these little fracas no ill feeling exists. Sometimes you see two soldiers making signs, and one showing the other his regiment which is rather amusing, as of course neither understands a single word and they talk for an hour in this way.

I saw Watson two days ago, he is quite well, has been on board ship between Varna and Scutari about three weeks, he is now landed. I suppose he will go also to Sebastopol. I am glad to hear so favourable an account of the crops at Merston, and hope those at Park Hatch will also turn out well. I should very much have liked to have been with you in the jolly little cottage at Merston, and have not forgotten old Charlie's beer. I have drunk beer out here, but fancy it does not agree with me in this climate, so shall not continue it; we also get a pint of porter as ration, at least we have had the last few days. This does not agree either, though very good, and it does the men good; we get a glass of rum nearly every day, sometimes I take it, sometimes I don't, but on a cold evening I think it wholesome.

I spoke to Hanson's son, who is his agent at Varna; he says my parcel will be forwarded to him from Constantinople, so I hope to get it soon, he had not heard of it yet. He is making a large fortune, I believe by robbing officers, and selling everything at a most exhorbitant price. Since I came here I have had some honey and butter, etc., the latter was salt and not exactly what we should call good at home, but here it does very well. I don't expect much marching now this year, but you can send the saddle when you get a chance; as to comforts, you say you sent me some powder for sauce, this is very useful. We get about two tablespoonsful of brown sugar a day and 2 oz. of rice, it is quite enough. Milk is not to be had here, but when near a village we get goat and sheep's milk, if there are *not too many soldiers* about, then it does not go far. Prepared chocolate would be useful now, the other is not very good without milk; coffee is better, and we can buy many things in Varna. I have a tin and a half of tea left. When we get into winter quarters I will get you to send me out some things. The preserved soup, makes very good soup, and is most useful when on the march, for then the commissariat is generally behind, and perhaps we get nothing but what can be found in villages, of which the inhabitants persist in saying 'Yook, Yook' ('No, no') to everything you ask for, until you search the house yourself and find eggs and bread. One cannot get fresh meat on the march, for if you carry it, it is sure to get bad before getting in, and pork and biscuit don't do every day in this climate, a little is very well. I made myself ill the other day eating pork, as I was very hungry, and could get nothing else, I could not touch anything for a week after. The other evening on the march, I had to forage for my horses, for they had not had a mouthful for twenty-four hours, and a hot march, so I got my sack, and after much trouble I found a stack of barley sheaves, of which I brought as much as I could carry on horseback, and my horses I am sure would have thanked me if they could.

Monday 28th. I took some quinine yesterday, not being quite well, it seemed to do me much good, so I took some more today, I expect it is very wholesome when much fatigued or pulled down by the heat. What is Joseph going to do with himself now? I suppose he will not be able to go abroad again while the war lasts on account of his regiment being likely to be called out, for certainly the whole of the regulars must soon be out of England. If I were him I would take to farming. I am sure I should like this, and when I get tired of the service and knocking about the world, and get older, I should much like to live on a farm. It must be very interesting if one understood it, if not profitable, but I have a good deal to go through before I ever set foot again in England. Tell Joseph I shall expect to hear about the shooting, etc.

It was in general orders last night that we are to be attached to the 4th D.G. having been so cut up by disease and lost our senior officers. I dare say I shall see more of young Fisher now, it will only be pro. tem. till we get another major or colonel, for I don't expect ever to see Le Marchant* again, nor do I wish it, he is not at all liked, and no one would have much confidence in a man who left us as he did, just when the cholera was raging (being ill himself) when everyone was required to be present. I think at such a moment it was every man's duty to remain, however ill, unless his

† T. Le Marchant, son of the distinguished Cavalry Commander killed at Salamanca, had been put in command of the 5th Dragoon Guards when Scarlett had been given command of the Heavy Brigade. Le Marchant seems to have been very unpopular and was described as neither a soldier nor a gentleman. He gave up the command and went home on half-pay. Cholera at Varna left the regiment much under strength and Raglan, who appears to have disliked the 5th, put them under the command of the 4th D.G. (Lt.-Colonel Hodge). Hodge was popular and understanding but soon handed over command temporarily to Captain Burton, the senior captain. Burton handed over to McMahon in December 1854 after commanding the regiment in the most important battles.

doctors insisted on his going. The men were left there, and why should not the officers stay with them, but in my opinion it is a regular case of *Aegrotat animo maius quam corpori.*

I find my glasses* very useful, there is a general order for all officers to wear them when marching etc., also a compass. This order came out while we were at Devna, and we were supposed to provide ourselves with them, though where to get them no one knew, of course they are not to be had there. . . . The Guards and Highlanders embark tomorrow; the Duke of Cambridge is away at Constantinople not having been well, but he is expected back tonight. Doubtless we shall all be off in a few days and shall probably be there by the time you get this. I hope Campbell's ship will come to the Black Sea.

I am glad I did not bring out the Czar, he would never have stood this work. The brown is rather thin, and these cold nights don't improve him. The Cob is as fat as a pig. If we are to take but one horse I shall take the brown if in good order, I could not get a better mount. I don't care about an indiarubber bed, I sleep on mine now not blown out. A kind of quilt on the bed ticking is as comfortable as anything, I am quite used to blankets and never wish for sheets. I sleep well, and as soon as I am awake I have to get up. My tub too is broken, the air gets out; I must buy one at some sale, it is rather too large. You ask if I can get calomel; I can, but don't like to take it living in a tent and in these days of dysentery, but I don't require it yet.

The Guards and Highlanders broke up their camp, and marched this morning 29th to embark. The sea air has quite set them up again. I am going to give up the adjutancy now there is a death vacancy, some man can be made from another regiment. I find the work out here too harassing, I am never left alone for a minute. Balders advised me to give it up as soon as an opportunity offered. When I took it, I expected to serve under him, but have had a very disagreeable Commanding Officer, and now I don't know who we may get; he may for what I know be a worse. Scarlett told me he was quite satisfied with me, and if he could stay in the regiment he would like me to remain, he said I had done very well. I am sure I have had no easy time of it. I have now a good opportunity of giving it up, and have attained my object which was to gain a good

* Field-glasses.

insight into the interior economy of a regiment, in case I may ever be a Field Officer. I have now done the duty for two years and don't care to go on, for the little extra pay is no object to me. It must all be settled at the Horse Guards, it may be four months or so before I am gazetted.

Your affectionate Son

Camp, Adrianople Road, near Varna   *August 27th 1854*
My dear Fred — On the 25th I got your letter of August 5th enclosing one for Standage — poor fellow he never received the news of his father's death, as he himself was taken from this world the day before. He had cholera at Kotlubei and was brought to Varna General Hospital, where he died. I will write to Brown at Godalming, and through him his friends will know. We have lost many of our best men, in all thirty-nine, or about one in seven. We have only lost two here, one of these was a relapse, the other died just as he arrived, being very ill. Did you hear that Pitcairn died at Kotlubei?

Duckworth died here on the 24th in a ship, being the best place we could get for him, both of cholera, only apoplexy ended the first, and extreme weakness caused the death of poor Duckworth. As you know he was the best friend I had in the regiment, and now he is gone I shall miss him much; he was my captain. We attended him and did our best for him, the cholera is a dreadful disease to see, and very painful, but he bore it well and never complained. He would not let us write to his friends for two posts; the 3rd will bring them a letter from Scarlett, as I know a little of his brother Herbert I shall write him all particulars. We shall sell all his things except what his friends are likely to want. Fisher died in the General Hospital here, and we buried him the day before yesterday; it is a melancholy business, we have lost one out of six officers. McNeile, Burnand and Ferguson are ill, but not dangerously; they must go away for a time to recruit health. I have spent a wretched summer and have seen many sad scenes. This day thirteen weeks ago we sailed out of Cork harbour, as fine a regiment as ever went on service, now how are we thinned. However things are looking much brighter now, cholera greatly on the decrease. . . .

The other night I heard a man near my tent very ill and groaning. I knew it must be cholera, so I got up, for I thought it was the sentry, but it was not, the night was so dark I could not see who it was, but the groaning went on, and I went to sleep. In the morning a dead Turk was found about ten yards behind my tent; poor wretch he had died like a dog without help, but these people instead of looking on death with fear, think it the best thing that can happen.

I was very sorry for Standage for I had taken an interest in him because he came from near us; he was a very good soldier. I thought of you at Goodwood race-time; I should like to have been there also, to ride over those beautiful downs, go where you may I believe there is nothing like Sussex. This country is hilly, wooded and beautiful, but barren, savage, poor and miserable. It makes one think twice as much of the numerous comfortable happy homes in England, which one sees on all sides. I always wear a flannel belt, as well as a native shawl, which I roll round my stomach; they say this is a good thing and the natives all use them. The army, too, have mostly taken to them. I expect this letter will find you at P.H. where the partridges are, or will be, falling under the murderous fire of your double barrel, just as the Russians will be I suppose within a short time at Sebastopol.

For military intelligence see the letter to my Father by this mail. The infantry here all wear a moustache, as yet it has not obtained a luxuriant growth, they look half-ashamed of the martial appendage, to which they are not yet accustomed — it will certainly make them look more soldierlike. There is a general order that *no one* need shave *at all* in Turkey, it is a great protection in heat and cold. The Guards wander about quite unlike the rest of the infantry, not knowing how to amuse themselves — it is rather fine to see these London swells in difficulties. What a sell this must be for Thompson, who I believe changed into the 5th on purpose to wear a moustache. The weather is cooler now, though occasionally we have hot days as usual; as I am writing, it is 105° in my tent. I am more used to it now, and do not mind it, if the sun does not strike on my head. I shall think of you on September 1st. I hope you will have good sport, Fisher of the 4th D.G. is here, but I have not seen him to speak to yet. The last time we met was shooting on the hill at Park Hatch. I have not read all about the

46th court-martial,* but I think both the two officers deserve to
be cashiered and the regiment seems to come out very badly. ....

Your most affectionate Brother

Camp, Adrianople Road, near Varna   *September 8th 1854*
  My dear Father — I wrote to you so lately that I have not much
to tell you now, but as I may not be able to write again for some
time, it is as well to let you know. . . . We have had no more cholera,
but the general complaint is remittent fever, which though I don't
think is very dangerous, yet when a man gets it here, it soon knocks
him up, and there is no chance of regaining strength in a tent and
on poor food. We have only three subalterns now left for duty,
three are gone to Scutari; one on board ship, and one here unwell.
I think none seriously ill though. McNeile, I think, must go home
directly if he wishes to get well; he is very delicate and ought never
to have come out. His family wish him to leave the service, and I
think he will, for it would be madness for him to attempt to stay
on. All those I liked most are gone now. Burnand is at Scutari and
I think he must go home too.
  I am happy to say I am very well; before I left Kotlubei I got
exceedingly weak from the heat and ill feeding, together with the
effect of seeing so much sickness round us and the dullness of the
place. Since I came here I have bathed nearly every day which I
think has done me good, and now I feel as strong and well as ever
I did, and there is something to think of now to interest me. We
are very short of officers and our Camp Officer is not a first-rate
one, which is a pity as we are so soon probably to be in action. Our
second captain, who exchanged with Johnson, knows about as
much as you do of his profession.
  The troops finished embarking Monday, and Tuesday and
Wednesday they went to the rendezvous in Baldjik Bay, from which

  * While the 46th Regiment was stationed at Windsor, Lt. J. E. Perry was
court-martialled for attacking a fellow officer, Lt. R. Greer, with a pair of
candlesticks. It seems that Greer, a notorious bully, had dragged Perry out of
bed and generally humiliated him. Perry was found guilty but the C.-in-C. did
not confirm the sentences and Perry was court-martialled again on a fresh set of
charges. A fund was opened to help Perry but he was once more found guilty,
a verdict heavily condemned in *The Times*. The Press described the affair as an
open scandal but the publicity seems to have reduced the amount of senseless
bullying in the Services.

I saw them sail on Thursday — an immense line of ships as far as the eye could reach, guarded by the fleet, and an immense cloud of smoke which extended for many miles showed what a number of steamers were among them. Lord Raglan told Scarlett that as soon as they had landed they would send back ships for us. The Greys are coming up from Scutari and it is expected we shall remain all the winter in the Crimea. I think we shall embark about the end of next week; we are looking forward to the luxuries of the *Himalaya* or some other fine steamer, the good dinners, comfortable beds with sheets, and not obliged to turn out in the cold at five in the morning. The nights are now *very cold*, the days not so, I believe the rain will soon set in. I expect we shall have rather a rough time till settled for the winter, and then there will be plenty of work, for the cavalry especially.

I was sorry to read of the almost total destruction of Cubitt's manufactory, how fortunate our house is done, it would have upset everything.* There is some boar shooting near here, and if I have time I shall go and get a shot; an officer told me he went the other day and waited near a fountain, and he shot a fine pig. This was Wheatcroft of the Inniskillings, who you remember I went to see at Dundalk when I joined, he is now near getting his troop. I see Wyld has published a map of the Crimea; *if possible* I should *much like* to have one sent by post, or the first opportunity. Caroline sent me one of Sebastopol before I came away. . . .

The Bashibazouks, who were disbanded here because they could not train them, are committing robberies and murders frequently. I saw an Araba† driver two days ago in the road, with his head broken and his throat cut, evidently robbed of the pay he had just received from Government — they were all paid the other day — no one seems to think anything of a murder here. I suppose you have heard several times of the taking of Sebastopol, but I fancy it will be some months before you hear in truth it has fallen. We may have a go in at it this year, but unless it is a certainty that we can take it within a given time, we shall no doubt leave it alone till the spring.

I rather wish I was in the Light Cavalry, as they are always sent

---

* Thomas Cubitt & Son was the firm responsible for building much of Belgravia.

† A heavy screened wagon.

on in front, and if I can get a troop I might exchange to advantage — for by that time all I cared most about in the regiment will be gone, in fact most of those who were in the regiment when I joined. Any captain in the regiment who was really a good officer would be certain to get a Lt.-Colonelcy in a very short time. I wish I was higher up. I expect Scarlett will soon be a Major-General and I suppose we shall now have a good Field Officer put in Le Marchant's place. I hope he will never rejoin, for I think no one will speak to him after all he has done. Finding himself quite incapable of commanding a regiment, he went to Lord Raglan and reported the regiment to him as unfit for service, thereby trying to escape himself at our expense, but everyone has found him out.

They say the landing in the Crimea will *not* be opposed. I hope not for I should not like to be out of the first brush with the Russians after all we have gone through. They make us pay income tax, which I think is rather too bad as we pay in another way, however the war must be supported, it takes over £1 off my monthly pay. Watson told me that Edward Kirkpatrick was likely to make his appearance in the East; I advise him not — he will find the greatest difficulty in getting on, no houses to live in, etc., besides the risk of climate, and after all the country would not repay him for his trouble in coming here.

All the things you sent will be very useful, I must write to Grace who is our agent, and as I know the name of the vessel, no doubt the box will reach me in time. I should like to have had it to take with me for the first few days' landing. All my winter clothes are at Constantinople and I don't know how I am to get them. I am going to try and buy some arrowroot to take with me, as I hear there is plenty at Varna; it is a capital thing because so easily made and very wholesome. Brandy we get here, but not very good. Halford also has a box coming out from Fortnum & Mason. The ginger is useful and would have been most acceptable a short time ago. I am always very glad to get any letters — you don't know how we all look out for the mail. I should like the Hampshire paper when there is anything particular in it, and any other paper with important news, as ours often miscarry. In my next I hope to tell you how the Russians are looking. The Cob is most useful to me out here; he is as fat as possible and just now taking a roll in the sand before my tent. My love to all, I don't know when this goes, but if anything else occurs I will add a line before I close it.

Your affectionate Son

Since I wrote last we are ordered to take all our horses and baggage, but shall not land with them at first.

September 9th. We have had a miserable twenty-four hours' rain, which makes clothes and all damp. I expect winter is setting in and we ought to get under cover. It is very cold today. I find from the doctor, arrowroot is not nourishing, this is a great sell, it is so easy to make and to carry. . . .

Screw-steamship Jason, *off Sebastopol*   *September 30th 1854*

My dear Father — We marched from our late encampment on Friday the 22nd and embarked the same morning in Varna Bay on board this ship, and some on the *Simla.* We got all the 5th on board except the baggage, and a few horses, which I found myself left at night with on the shore, and no preparations for them; I had about fifty men. We expected to have got all on board in one day, however we made the best of it. We put up a tent or two, made some fires, and fortunately I found a commissariat close by, with some meat and biscuits so that we did get something, which was more than I expected. We cooked our meat in pans and on sticks, and it is wonderful how well it went down. After I had posted my sentries over horses and baggage, I was glad to roll in my cloak and go to sleep, for I could not get at my baggage. I slept well having been up since 3 a.m. and at work all day without much food. I can't write very well the ship shakes so.

We sailed at 4 p.m. the 26th, having by the help of the French sailors embarked all the brigade. We towed a ship with the Royal Dragoons on board. We had not been long out when it blew a gale and we parted from the ship we towed, the two enormous cables having snapped like string. We fully experienced the truth of Byron's lines:

> There is no sea the Traveller ere pukes in
> Whose waves are more deceptive than the Euxine

I am not sure my quotation is quite correct.* Our orders or rather our captain's orders were to go as far north as Serpent Island; but we kept too far south and the gale carried us away. The next morning we saw all the transports separated, and then lost sight of them. Nor have we seen them again till this morning. The *Simla* and *Trent* are close by us. We quite lost our way, and were forced to lay to — at last the sun came out for a moment, and an observation being taken we found ourselves far south of the Crimea, instead of at Eupatoria. We are lucky not to have fallen in with any Russians, as some are known to be about. One steamer went right down to the Bosphorus the other day, a very bold thing. We have had a tremendous tossing, but are fortunately all right, with the exception of the loss of eight horses.

At nine this morning we steamed through our fleet in a bay outside Sebastopol; it was a magnificent sight: there is the town, and a fleet blockading on each side the harbour; it appears very strong indeed. We could not have had a more lovely day for the view, the coast is fine, and part high, the town is backed up at some distance by mountains, or high hills, which gradually slope down to the sea. We can see camps on shore, but whether ours or not I can't say — I expect they are ours. We saw a pretty little engagement as we steamed past the town. A French steamer was standing into the harbour mouth just (I suppose) to try the range, when she was fired on from the forts, and we saw the shot strike round her; whether she was hit I can't say. Then an English steamer (*Retribution*) stood in too, and they blazed away for about ten minutes. We saw this about one and a half miles off. We see cavalry on shore, supposed to be Cossacks.

I shall write as often as I can to you, but I suppose I shall be pretty busy for some time to come — and sleep with one eye open. We heard before we left Varna of an engagement† — which of course you know of by now, or soon will. I don't think from what I heard the cavalry were in for much — I am in great hopes we are in plenty of time yet. It was a severe trial to one's temper to hear of all that was going on and be obliged to wait for the brigade

* Godman went a bit astray:
       There's not a sea the passenger e'er pukes in,
       Turns up more dangerous breakers than the Euxine.
† The Battle of the Alma.

being embarked. We land in a bay, I believe called Balaklava, a few miles east of Cape Chersonese; the ground rises there, and then there is a good level plain between this and the town. We left four or five French line-of-battle ships at Varna, taking troops on board; this shows our naval superiority — we have not as yet been obliged to put a single soldier on board our ships of war. As to my pack saddle it had better stand over till winter, I don't think there can be much marching in the Crimea; if there is we must march very light. What a pity we did not come here three months ago. I have not yet heard of my box, and don't expect to get it for some time, because there can be no regular channel of communication established on shore. I saw by the papers that Cubitt's fireproof floors do not answer. Is this true or not? You say you keep my letters; I am glad of this, they may be useful as reference when I get home. I hear there are three bags waiting for us, so no doubt there is one for me from you.

Evening, September 30th. Since I wrote the last a large bag of letters has arrived, with yours of the 3rd and 11th inst. The mail went out today, I could not send this. Letters here are most acceptable, but now we have much other excitement. This battle seems to have been a severe one, and the true British spirit was found as bold as ever. I hear the way the Highlanders and others carried the entrenched positions was most gallant. The former, they say, never fired till the enemy fell back, but rushed in regardless of the heavy fire and literally drove them out with the bayonet only. The French were quite astonished, as were also the Russians too I expect, for they calculated the position would hold out six weeks against 80,000 men. I really believe nothing can stand the British. The loss, of course, you saw, was very severe, but not to be wondered at. Our Brigade Major, who is an old 5th man, heard of the loss of his brother, Conolly 23rd Regiment, on our arrival here. I am glad I have no relations in the army out here. Lady Katherine Balders I am sorry to say has lost her brother, and a nephew wounded.

The cholera prevails here, but chiefly among the newly arrived and unacclimatized regiments. The Greys have lost an officer, and the 21st Regiment, which landed from England a few days since, has buried 200 men, but then I suppose their strength is about 1,000. They have not been in action — the disease has greatly abated the last few days. The Russians I hear have it badly in the town. Our men are in very good health, but we have sent home several. Everyone is in the best spirits and no one doubts but that the place will be taken. They say if they had had Cavalry at that engagement the other day, an immense number would have been made prisoners, or at all events prevented from entering Sebastopol. They certainly should have waited for the cavalry, for a few days could have made no difference as far as the weather goes.

October 3rd. We landed the day before yesterday and had to bivouac on the shore. I found an empty cart in which I took up my abode for the night, not a very comfortable lodging. The Cavalry are encamped about four or five miles from the town, and we are harassed night and day with piquets and patrols. We cannot have much to do with the siege, unless in case of a sortie, or in clearing the streets when they get in. An army of some 30,000 or 40,000 men is expected up to the relief of the town, in which case there must be a good stand-up fight. Our inlaying piquet has just turned out in a great hurry after two squadrons of Cossacks, but the latter know better than to stand a charge of even a dozen of our men. They come near and shoot at us. There are about 1,000 sailors dragging up guns out of the fleet, which are to be put in position for the siege. The grand attack will not commence before Friday. Our infantry are close to the walls, just out of shot. Shot and shell constantly come bowling in, just up to their outposts.They say it won't be an easy job, this side of the town is not so strong, but the west side is very strong. We came across plenty of forage, and miles of splendid vineyards — the grapes are famous, and the French carry them away in faggots. We are just ordered to be ready to turn out, some Cossacks or someone are coming, so I must finish as the post may be gone on my return. In great haste.

Your affectionate Son

4

Charge of the Heavy Brigade

Camp, Balaklava, near Sebastopol   *October 6th 1854*
My dear Father — My last letter ended rather abruptly, as we
got the order to turn out the brigade but though we remained
saddled all day we were not called upon to go out. It was merely
that our patrol had been driven in by a large body of Cossacks.
These gentlemen keep us well employed, though often 200 or 300
together they never dare attack even a piquet of thirty men of ours.
I am longing to have a go in at them, and hope to get a chance
before many more days. There is such a scarcity of officers in the
brigade that we are on duty nearly every day.

Tomorrow I am on inlaying piquet, but I must tell you what this
means or you won't understand. An outlaying piquet is a body of
men, say perhaps thirty or forty (or stronger or weaker as the case
may be) who go about five miles out in front or rear of the army
to give an alarm of any approach of the enemy, and if driven in,
to keep them (the enemy) in check as long as possible, to give the
main body time to get under arms. From this body detached men
are again placed forward to give notice of anyone coming from the
enemy, these are 'videttes'. The piquet is commanded by a captain
or lieutenant. You may imagine it is a responsible and often harassing post; you are generally out for twenty-four hours, and of course
must not ever be off the alert, especially near so untiring an enemy
as the Cossacks. An 'inlaying piquet' is a body which remains in
the lines, ready, under arms, to turn out at a moment's notice in
support of the outlaying piquet. A 'patrol' is a body which is sent
to reconnoitre the country. We have daily skirmishes with the
Cossacks; they nearly surrounded our patrol yesterday and drove
them in before they saw them, but tho' supported by a considerable
body of cavalry they did not even fire at us, though we were only
about a dozen strong. Today our patrol was fired on, some shot

and shell. We are protecting this town and port, or rather village, from the army in our rear, said to consist of some 15,000 or 20,000 men, these are the fellows we skirmish with daily.

I rode about three miles up to look at Sebastopol the other day; from the hill above, you can see at about a mile off right into the town and harbour. There lay the fine ships of war, and there are the inhabitants walking up and down, and the enemy working hard in their trenches outside, for they are very busy fortifying themselves, and are doing much this way day and night. You can see the great black guns on the forts and looking through the embrasures, and if you show yourself too much, a puff of smoke curls from the walls, and a shell hisses over your head — they have all the ranges very well, and drop them very close. Yesterday Burton was looking on, when a shell fell within twenty yards and killed a sergeant and wounded two men of the 63rd.

I regret extremely we were not at Alma; if we had been we must have taken all their guns, and lots of prisoners, or cut them to pieces. Though the Light Cavalry were there, they will get a medal for doing nothing. The day before Alma an officer told me a shell went right into one of their horses and then burst. The Cavalry may say what they like hereafter about that affair, but they were hardly under fire — I would have given anything to have been there. I saw a horse in camp today which had a bullet through his ear, which first passed through the body of the adjutant of the 23rd. They suffered most severely, but behaved most gallantly. Our brigade major lost his brother, I knew him; he was struck by a round shot in the chest. Another in the same regiment I knew, lost his foot. Watson saw the action from the fleet, he being in the siege train was not engaged. I saw him today — he looks very well indeed and is in excellent spirits, during the fight he will be in a battery north-west of the garrison, his saddle never arrived.

Halford writes again today to Grace to send his and my parcels, and I hope to get them soon; we are not very well off for food. I can't bear to hear of our servants being so fastidious; it really is too bad. Here are plenty of the sons of the highest men in England living on biscuit and salt pork and, so far from complaining, are glad to get it. When we landed we had a lump of pork to carry, about three times the size of one's fist — not the better for being carried about — and some ship biscuit, this was all we had for three days. Yesterday we got some very skinny mutton, and tomorrow pork again, no bread here. Our mess when cooked, for we put three or four fellows' rations together, puts me in mind of what keeper makes in buckets for the dogs, however it agrees very well with me.

There is not much sickness since we came here; we have had one cholera case, and there have been one or two fatal ones in the brigade, where men went off in a few hours, without any premonitory symptoms. However the disease seems nearly expended. Several officers are ill, but ours all well. One of the Inniskillings died on board ship today, but he had been ill some time. McNeile and Burnand are both away sick, and not likely to rejoin. I heard from McKinnon; I hope he will go and stay with you — he is a very good fellow and a perfect gentleman, whose only fault is that of being poor. I expect he is too busy at present about an exchange, but no doubt would come sometime hence. You will see by the papers that Le Marchant is dead, but I heard from him today dated September 22nd. The Russians had two new white forts outside the town, and last night they painted them both brown as they were too good a mark.

You see we are what they call, disregimentized, and attached to the 4th D.G. All this is most absurd. After we had suffered so much we were certainly attached in orders and then encamped beside the 4th D.G., but Colonel Hodge behaved very well, and I don't think he came once into our lines, or interfered with us in any way. We have no more to do with them, or they with us than you have. I am sorry to say their colonel is left behind very bad with dysentery. Everyone agrees that our horses *look better* than any regiment, of course the Greys excepted, who look first-rate, but then they have lost no men, or hardly any, have done no work, and had the best of forage.

The people about here are very civil, always take their hats off to us, their countenance is not at all like the Turk, but more flat, and the women have rather the look of the Chinese, tho' some are very good-looking. This appears a very fine country, full of vineyards, and pretty well cultivated, the houses quite superior to the Turks', tho' sacked by the soldiers. Our dinners are cooked by wood brought from the houses, doors, tables, floors and even a piano has been seen on the fire, it is a pity, but the French are great destroyers. You may often see a good fire of a mahogany bed, or chest of drawers; they think nothing of pulling down a house for fuel. There was a large wine house and press near here, and the men got the barrels to sleep in, for we have very few tents now, and most men sleep out — the dews are very heavy at night and we occasionally have a smart shower, but on the whole the weather is fine and healthy. I am in a tent with three others and we are obliged to sleep on the ground, as there is no room for beds, but beyond it being rather hard and cold it does not matter, as I have a waterproof rug, and we always go to bed tired, and get up early, and if cold sleep in our clothes. . . .

Your affectionate Son

Camp, Balaklava　　　　　　　　　　　*Evening, October 12th 1854*

My dear Mother — The post goes out tomorrow morning so I must write a line to say how we are getting on. Here we are still *before*, not *in* Sebastopol. Every day we hear the siege will commence 'tomorrow' or rather that the batteries will open, but I think it will be two or three more days yet. There will be an awful row when they do commence. The French have their batteries ready, but they have not so many guns to place, nor so far to take them as we have. Our lines are getting very near the town, within 1,400 yards; they work hard day and night.

I saw Watson for five minutes this evening, he is quite well, his company were under a heavy fire in the trenches last night, and they had to retreat very quickly. Two days ago the enemy kept up an incessant fire on our works from about 7 p.m. till eight the next morning; we could see the flash of every gun in the night sky and could hear every shot and shell hissing in its flight. The result of all this fire was *one* rifleman killed, and two or three more wounded, no other harm done. They say there is a gun slung in the rigging of one of the enemy's ships, to give it a good elevation. They also say one of our batteries is to sink this ship in two hours, when they open. It is expected after a short time the place will capitulate, or if not they will take it by assault, but I believe they will not risk the troops at this till the place is well pounded.

This is a beautiful country and fertile, but not much cultivated. The weather fine, but cold at night. We had one piercing cold day and sat shivering round our fires, one side scorched the other very cold. Our men have only a few tents and can't all sleep in them. It is bad work sleeping out, and the dew of early morning wets us through, as we are all in the saddle daily before daybreak, in case of an attack, it is hard work. My servant has got a famous house, a large cupboard he got out of a house, this he gets into, shuts the doors, and goes to sleep. I am very well. It is curious, out of five officers who messed together when we commenced the campaign, I am the only one who has been able to do duty the whole time, two being dead and the other two very seriously ill for some time, though now recovered; indeed there are not more than two others who have kept off the sick-list. I don't mean to boast of this, knowing the chances of these things, but merely to be thankful for it.

It is said that 40,000 men are on their march south of Perekop to raise the siege; these, if joined to the 20,000 now in our rear, will be a formidable force. They also say Lord Raglan expects an engagement with them in two or three days. I believe these men were seen by some ship coming down the isthmus of Perekop; but no doubt the papers will have all the information. People must not be impatient about the siege, no one knows but those engaged, what infinite work and trouble must be undergone before the fall of such a place can be effected. We have had daily skirmishes lately, yesterday our patrol had to retire before a force of 300 cavalry or more — we were but forty strong. They did not hit one of our men, but we knocked over two of their horses, and one was an officer's, about forty or fifty shots were fired. Today our piquets were attacked by Cossacks, but soon driven back by our skirmishers, several shots exchanged, but no one hit. I went out to see the fun, these Cossacks will never show a front, and are not in themselves formidable, but they give us much trouble by their constant attacks. They were foraging in a plain today about a mile from us, but when we tried to cut them off, they dropped the hay and ran like a pack of hounds to the hills, they got more shots at them in the evening.

I and two or three other officers rode into a village to look about, two miles beyond our outposts, it was a beautiful spot among the mountains. When we got there we found through an interpreter who was with us that twenty Cossacks were in the village, so not wishing to be taken we turned round and rode back, thinking discretion the better part of valour.

My box is not yet come, I wish it were. We got from the ship here some hams 2s a lb. and some cheese, chocolate, paste, etc. so we are doing well just now. Things very dear, and the ships are stripped by crowds of hungry officers, as soon as they come into harbour. We also got a small pig. I hope my Father's cob does better now, tho' it was bought out of a cart, one often picks up a good horse in this way, indeed one of our best troopers Bolton bought out of a Dublin hack car. I am still adjutant, I would rather not be just now, as I should be more engaged in outpost duty, but if all reports are true we shall have enough work soon. I could not bear to go home without a good decided action. I am sure if we get them in the open they will remember it.

This place where we are is rather weak, and not many troops, but several strong batteries have been thrown up round it the last few days, we have 1,000 Marines here, and if attacked they must send a division of infantry from the trenches to help us. The French have thrown up very strong batteries to prevent the army attacking our force, which is engaged in the siege. I have got your letter of September 18th and will write to Joseph soon. I don't want more clothes at present, and could not carry them; three shirts have seen me through the summer, and I have one of those woollen jersies which is quite enough. I hope the map will soon come. McNeile and Burnand still ill at Scutari. I did not bring my filter on shore. I wish I had as the water is muddy, but I am used to this and don't mind it. The health of the army tolerably good, considering exposure and work, which is hard enough now. Best love to all.

Your affectionate Son

Camp, Balaklava   *October 17th 1854*

My dear Caroline — We are now in the middle of the siege. Our batteries, which till now have not fired a shot, were finished last night and opened this morning; the roar of the cannon is without an interval, and tremendous to hear, occasionally an explosion comes. We are getting on well, the round tower was silenced in an hour or so, and I believe we have sunk the *Twelve Apostles*, their largest ship. One of the Lancaster* guns has burst, I believe without harm, they are doing great execution. Meantime the sun shines as usual and everything looks the same, as if here were no such work of destruction going on, and probably every hour is sending numbers of the Czar's unfortunate troops into the next world. I have not heard our loss today, we had a very heavy fire yesterday and day before, but not many were killed. The French made a mistake in one of their batteries, which the enemy enfiladed, and they lost about fifty men.

I went close up yesterday, one is obliged to be careful about this, as if they see you a shell is sure to be sent after you. I could see them pitching shot and shell into the trenches among our men, and very well they fired too. You must know, that our army only encloses the town from the south coast, to where the main creek runs up past the town, so the rest and other side, which is by far the strongest, is open to the enemy; they say every inch is mined. The French hold the extreme left on the sea, also their 2nd Division defends the rear of the army; this they have done admirably, by throwing up works. From our extreme right, Sir de Lacy Evans's Division, I could see the enemy as plain as possible, on some hills about one and a half miles off, said to be about 35,000 under Constantine. They are also in our rear, and I don't think their numbers are well ascertained. More are expected up every day, and I can't help thinking, and so do most others, that there must be an engagement very soon.

We have been saddled all day in expectation of a turn-out, and Lord Raglan expects an attack daily, so that the sooner they come the better, and let us have it over. We were confined to the camp all day and threatened with arrest for leaving it, but I could not stand hearing and not seeing the work, so rode up this afternoon; it was a splendid sight, and from where I was I could see the shot and shell tearing up the ground, and coming in among our batteries. We have not got it all our own way as some expected, and I think today the besiegers and besieged are about equal; we have silenced one fort and knocked the others about. The fleet pour in constant broadsides. The enemy blew up the French magazine at 10 a.m. They had not made it well; they say they lost fifteen guns

* A range of 4,000 yards and great accuracy was claimed for these much-prized weapons.

and 500 were blown up, but I expect this is over the mark. We shall be engaged tonight repairing our works. It will be two days before the French are ready again. The Russian fire is admirable. We have turned out two or three times since I last wrote, but only ending in a skirmish, though once the whole army was said to be advancing, and pistols were capped and got ready etc., but they did not like to face us, or had some reason for not doing so, as about they went.

My first box has reached Grace at Constantinople and he has let me know, so I wrote today for it and shall no doubt soon get it. We have been doing well lately, having bought hams, cheese and chocolate off the ships. These are very exciting times certainly, and I like the life very well, I always was fond of change. The mail goes out tomorrow morning. Remember me to Mademoiselle when you write; I get on with French pretty well, but would give anything to be able to speak it well. I find we have not yet sunk their ships. I hope the next mail will send you news of the fall of the place, but unless we get on much faster, and are let alone in the war, I don't expect it. Love to all.

Your affectionate Brother

Camp, Balaklava   *October 19th 1854*

My dear Father — Your letter from Bognor of October 2nd reached me this morning. I don't know why I did not get it two days ago when we received the papers of the same date. I read the letter while a tremendous cannonade was going on, and it seemed such a mockery to think that on the 2nd inst. the news of the fall of Sebastopol was posted over London and announced in *The Times*; how such a report could appear authentic seems strange. Yesterday I believe we did not make much progress, and the Russians mend in the night all the harm we do their batteries. Indeed we do not seem to get on very fast, but the fact is when we landed we made too little of the great work before us, and everyone said we should be inside the place in about twenty-four hours. Confidence is all very well, but I think no one ought to boast too much before operations are commenced. Perhaps the Engineers are satisfied with our progress, and though one is on the spot and looking on, it is not easy to ascertain the true state of affairs. I expect it will have to be carried by assault, in which case we shall most likely lose many men by mines. This morning as usual we were out before daybreak, in a thick fog, nearly wet through, only an occasional gun could be heard, but the fog no sooner cleared than a tremendous roar commenced, which has been going on ever since.

Yesterday we had just come in from our usual parade, and I had dispatched my letter and was sitting at breakfast, when the Videttes began to circle (i.e. the alarm on the approach of an enemy) in a minute the trumpets sounded to saddle and turn out, which we soon did, and then I and all thought we were in for a regular engagement, as the enemy were coming on in force. Having arrived under the ridge where our outposts are, we halted, and the Russians were seen coming over a little line of hills on the opposite side of the valley in skirmishing order. There was a very large body of infantry, and we *suppose* guns, though they took care we should not see them; on their extreme left, for they extended about one and a half or two miles, was a body of regular cavalry, as near as we could tell about double our number; in front of all came a cloud of Cossacks. The 'Bono Johnny', alias Turks, dropped some round shot among them as they advanced from three batteries, and also some of our artillery opened, the former made excellent practice, but owing to their being so extended I don't think much harm was done. However, it made them *leave that*, and they retired a short distance, but they there seemed to encamp, or rather bivouac, and the cavalry dismounted and watered and made fires, which I thought the height of impertinence under our noses, but *just out of shot*. We could see all they did which made it more provoking, they remained there all day, keeping a sharp look-out on us.

Sir Colin Campbell, the Highlanders' Brigadier commands the infantry about Balaklava; he is said to be a good officer. He sent up for some infantry and two regiments were sent down, but when they had got half-way they were recalled for fear of a sortie, and Sir Colin did not like the risk of driving the enemy out, having only Turkish infantry, who though good behind walls, could not be trusted for an attack. I hear Lord Raglan has given positive orders that no engagement should be risked at Balaklava, while the siege is going on, and I think he is quite right. We were kept out all day and ready to turn out all night. I think though that it is but postponed for a few days, for at last we must I think fight this army, reinforcements are continually coming up. Perhaps we shall meet them for a final farewell after Sebastopol is taken before we re-embark.

Sunday, October 22nd. The day before yesterday we were all put in a state of excitement through a false alarm: we were turned out about 4 p.m., some enemy having made their appearance over the hill beyond our outposts. There were eleven battalions of infantry, and some cavalry; they must have been in great force, for it soon grew dark, and we could hear them marching in with their band playing, and when dark the reflection of their watch-fires could be seen in the sky over the hill, and seemed like the lights of a large town. They came near enough for the Turkish batteries to send a few shot among them, and some rockets after dark, to try and discover their position, the H. Artillery also sent a few shot at them. It being quite dark the cavalry and guns were moved back, nearer to Balaklava, and then formed two lines and dismounted, and a wretched cold night we had, standing to our horses, ready to mount. Sir C. Campbell sent twice to Lord Raglan to get some infantry, and towards morning some came down, but were called back when on their way, for fear of an attack in front from the town.

At about 9 p.m. one of the Turkish forts commenced to fire musketry, and the shape of the earth fort in which they were could be distinctly seen by the bright flashes sparkling out all round it. I immediately jumped on my horse, making sure the enemy were advancing up the hill, if they had we should have been in a bad way, having no infantry except two or three regiments of Turks (who of course are not to be trusted much in the open) and half the 93rd Regiment. Cavalry, of course, are no match against unbroken infantry, and of course nothing would be easier to put Cavalry in confusion, than an attack on a dark night. Soon the fire ceased and we thought they must have been firing on our patrol by mistake. About an hour or two later I was just going to lie down, being very sleepy when a bright flash lighted up the horses. I at first thought it was lightning but on turning round saw that the sailor's battery in our rear on the hills above Balaklava had opened fire. Of course I immediately mounted again, thinking the enemy were close upon us, in the meantime the shell came tearing up the ground and rolling along and bursting very prettily in the dark night, the round shot too were making a tremendous noise as they went through the air. The Turks on the hill, seeing the Artillery open, immediately commenced to fire, at what they knew not, then a fort with Turks, on this track where the enemy were supposed to be coming opened their musketry fire also. You may imagine that this soon ceased and we waited till morning not knowing what had happened. We afterwards found that the Turks, who keep a very sharp look-out, discovered some drunken foot-guards, who had lost their way, they puffed off some powder (their mode of giving an alarm) which the sailors saw, and taking it for the Russians advancing, they opened on them as I told you, supposing their front clear; it is well we were not further out in the plain. This shows what a little thing puts an army on the alarm. We were turned out again yesterday; the same story, 'They are advancing,' but soon came back. It is dreadfully harassing work, and is telling on the men, most of whom sleep without any shelter at night.

Our new surgeon from the 2nd Life Guards has joined, he seems a nice fellow. The army is still hanging on our rear, waiting I expect for a reinforcement. I shall not say much about the siege which is still going on, though the place was taken by *The Times* ten days ago. I expect you will hear the official report by the time, or before you get this, which will give you more correct intelligence than I can. Everyone you ask tells you a different story. One says 'Oh we have it all our own way'; the next tells you 'The Russians are firing two guns to our one,' and so everyone tells you what he thinks, and of course you hear fifty different accounts, nor can you tell much better when looking on, you see the place covered with smoke, and the sharp flashing of the guns, while the shot make a tremendous noise in their course. Now and then comes in Lancaster, and you hear this gun projectile hissing and puffing, as it seems like an express train, owing to the twisting of the shot in its course. Two of their guns appear to be doing well, though there was much doubt of this at first.

Lord Dunkellin, Foot Guards, was taken prisoner last night in a sortie. I have just heard that Major Willett of the 17th Lancers died today of cholera. I believe there are not many cases now, but he had diarrhoea some days which he could not get rid of and the other night out finished him. Their colonel is gone home on sick-leave, very ill: the 5th are doing very well, though a good many men have gone sick from the work. Kilburn is unwell from Crimean fever, I don't think it is much, I hope not, he has been so well all along. I often see Watson but have not called on him for some days owing to having so much to do. Nicholls is gone to Scutari sick. McNeile and Burnand still at Scutari sick.

I believe you think in England that every preparation has been taken to make the sick and wounded as comfortable as possible; such is not the case, indeed anything so disgraceful as the whole department it is impossible to imagine. The other day I was told on good authority that 500 men went to Scutari after Alma, sick and wounded in one ship, and attended by *two* surgeons and *five* men, one of whom died on the way, and the poor fellows had no one to assist them or look after them. On their arrival no preparations for their reception had been made. There are 1,200 wounded at Scutari, and 4,000 in hospital altogether there. I heard from one hospital sergeant, who went on board one of the ships at Balaklava the other day, that the state of things there is just as bad or worse, the ship crowded with men shouting for water etc., and no one to attend to them, even when the decks are washed they get wet with the water, there is no other place for them. Of course numbers die, while the ship is waiting for her full cargo.

I could tell you more and worse cases, which I think cannot be known at home, they want attendants and doctors, certainly this should be exposed. Wounded men from the trenches pass here daily for Balaklava, though there are not a great many wounded, one hears no end of narrow escapes and brave doings. Captain Peel of the *Diamond* the other day picked up a lighted shell which fell among his men and threw it over the parapet. The sailors fight, or rather work their guns right well. Several regiments have volunteered for the storming party, and I suppose it must be taken by assault at last; an officer who was at Malkins with me (Irby) carried the colours of the 47th; they were shot through and splashed with blood. We get lots of salt pork and beef here, the latter hardly eatable, especially when one is not very well. I shall be glad when the place is taken. ... There is a particular hill, overlooking the town, from which you get a splendid view of it, always crowded with officers off duty, who sit there and smoke and talk all day, the place is very properly called Gossip Hill.

Your affectionate Son

Camp, Balaklava   *October 26th 1854*

My dear Father — Yesterday the attack* which I told you I thought must take place came off, and here I am, Thank God, safe and sound, though the loss the cavalry have sustained is very severe. We were on parade as usual yesterday 25th an hour before daybreak, and soon after it was well light, a gun from the Turkish forts (their outposts) told us something was going on. The Cavalry immediately advanced across the plain and halted behind the forts on our side the ridge; by this time the fire along the whole line of batteries was continued with great quickness, this time I knew we were in for it.

The H. Artillery and battery soon opened, but the former soon shut up for want of ammunition, and the Captain (Maud) being wounded severely by a shell which burst inside his horse. Soon the unmistakeable sound of the shot over our heads told us they were advancing in force, indeed so fast did they come on, that our out-laying piquet was near being cut off, and the officers on piquet lost their cloaks, a serious loss here. They now began to ply the forts with shell, many of which missing the hilltop fell among us. One could see them drop, and in another moment the fragments flying far and wide — causing one by an involuntary impulse to bob one's head, though well knowing it was of no use, as the pieces whistled and hummed over our heads. Odd to say, though several shell fell within a few yards, neither man nor horse was hurt.

Soon the Turks outside the fort, on their extreme right commenced to fire musketry, and as we were only about 300 yards off, with my glasses I saw everything. Up the hill came the Russian infantry, meeting a warm fire from the Johnnys, who at that moment turned and rushed up again under their fort; on came the Russians, shouting and running up in column in fine order, and giving a heavy fire. The Turks again showed a front, rushed at them, then wavered, and in went the enemy over their works, the Turks retreating down the hill into the plain in the greatest

* The Battle of Balaklava.

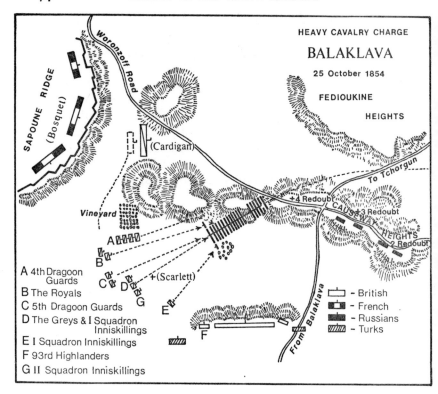

Heavy Cavalry Charge, Balaklava, 25th October 1854

confusion. I saw a few braver than the rest close with their enemy, but only to meet their death, and so in less than half an hour, the strongest fort was in their hands. The Turks all along the range seeing this threw down their arms (at least many did), left their guns, and ran like the rest to Balaklava, so that the enemy quickly got the whole range of forts, and turning the guns on us, peppered us well as we retreated, which we did at a walk, frequently halting and fronting, but what could we do without infantry, against numbers, and the round shot too, much too thick to be pleasant.

The poor horses running about loose dreadfully wounded were sad to see, one with *three* legs, belonging to the Royals, would throw itself into our ranks, till at last I put an end to him with my revolver. We retired to our camp, which had been struck, and everything was nearly packed. We had no sooner formed in rear, than the enemy who had formed all along the heights sent down their cavalry in two masses into the plain, one went at full split at some Turkish infantry, but the 93rd who were lying down, jumped up and gave them such a volley that they wheeled to the left, and rode off as hard as they could go in good order, the artillery pounding them all the way. They never expected to meet English* there I am sure. At this time a large mass of cavalry came over the hill in front of our camp, and would in a few minutes have been in our lines, and have cut down the few men left, when we got the order to advance.†

The Greys and Inniskillings went first, then we came in support of the Greys, their (the enemy's) front must have been composed of three regiments, and a very strong column in their rear, in all I suppose about 1,500 or 2,000, while we were not more than 800, however the charge sounded and at them went the first line; Scarlett and his A.D.C. well in front. The enemy seemed quite astonished and drew into a walk and then a halt; as soon as they met, all I saw was swords in the air in every direction, the pistols going off, and everyone hacking away right and left. In a moment the Greys were surrounded and hemmed completely in; there they were fighting back to back in the middle, the great bearskin caps high above the enemy.

This was the work of a moment; as soon as we saw it, the 5th advanced and in they charged, yelling and shouting as hard as they could split, the row was tremendous, and for about five minutes neither would give way, and their column was so deep we could not cut through it. At length they turned and well they might, and the whole ran as hard as they could pelt back up the hill, our men after them all broken up, and cutting them down right and left. We pursued about 300 yards, and then called off with much difficulty, the gunners then opened on them, and gave them a fine peppering. It took some little time to get the men to fall in again, they were all mixed up together of course, all the regiments in one mass.

* Not 'English', of course, but the Argyll and Sutherland Highlanders. This was the 'thin red line' which stood between the Russians and Balaklava.
† This was the successful Charge of the Heavy Brigade.

The enemy being gone, and we all right, had time to look round, the ground was covered with dead and dying men and horses. I am happy to say our brigade lost but seven men dead, but had a considerable number wounded, some mortally. The ground was strewn with swords, broken and whole, trumpets, helmets, carbines, etc., while a quantity of men were scattered all along as far as we pursued. There must have been some forty or fifty of the enemy dead, besides wounded, for I went over the ground today to look at it. All the wounded were of course immediately taken off. Lord Raglan who was looking down from a hill close by sent an A.D.C. to say 'Well done the Heavy Brigade.' This is some satisfaction after all we have gone through this summer.

The Russians seemed very steady and well disciplined, but our men made fearful havoc among them with their long straight swords. The Russian swords were much more curved than ours and very sharp. Scarlett was wounded in the bridle hand, but not much, he and Elliot were in the thickest, and his helmet was battered in, and the skirt of his frock-coat sliced down. Poor Elliot did not escape so well, he got a bad cut in the face, and a very severe one in the back of the head, having lost his hat. I hope, however, he is not dangerously hurt, he is better today. He is a very brave fellow and fought very hard — so did Scarlett who is as blind as a bat; Swinfen was run through the hand, and poor Neville being a *bad* rider, and too weak to use his sword well, was soon dismounted and had it not been for one of our men who stood over him, Private Abbot, he must have been killed. He was wounded in the head and in three places in his back, and they fear that his liver is injured, in which case he cannot recover. A corporal of ours was killed, and one man, and another must die. We have nine wounded besides, and have lost about fourteen horses.

It had been well if this success had been all the cavalry did — but some infantry having arrived we advanced, and owing to a mistake in an order which Captain Nolan brought from Lord Raglan, the Light Cavalry then charged down a valley,* under a fire of Minié rifles† and guns on each side of the valley and a battery of, I believe, twenty guns in front. They drove all before them;

---

* The Charge of the Light Brigade.

† A muzzle-loader, rifled, with a range of 1,000 yards but not very accurate; used by both sides.

took the guns, cut down the gunners and killed an immense number. They then retired but were perfectly annihilated by the cross-fire, and the brigade major told us that directly after, the brigade numbered under 200, having turned out that morning 600 or 700 strong. It was a terrible sight to see them walking back one by one and the valley strewn with them. Our brigade came in also just then for a heavy fire, and the Greys alone lost forty killed and wounded, all for nothing.

The Russians still have possession of two forts, and spiked the guns of the other. Today they attacked our right, close to Sebastopol, but they were totally routed with tremendous loss. The siege, I believe, is progressing favourably. I see the Russians have got up the hill over Balaklava, and I expect to see a fight there tomorrow, but *we* cannot be engaged in that — I expect they will get a good beating. I got a bruise under my right wrist, which makes my hand stiff, and I cannot write quite so well, it was a sword cut which went through my coat, but not the thick woollen jersey I had on. I had the luck to find a Russian officer's coat, a famous warm one for sleeping out, all lined with fur, I had not time to pick it up after the charge, but an artillery man got it, and I gave him 10s for it.

The men are in excellent spirits and only want to meet the enemy again. We have some English infantry and also some French come down here now; had they come before we should not have lost those forts. I shall sleep better at night, we are certainly safer now. We have terribly hard work, I have neither had time to undress or wash for two days. The weather continues fine and cool, in fact most delightful. I am quite well and the troops in fair health. My box not yet arrived. Love to all.

Your affectionate Son

Army before Sebastopol   *November 2nd 1854*
My dear Frederick — The post goes out tomorrow so I must just send you a line. We have had a tremendous cavalry mill since I last wrote to you. On the 25th the Russians (the army in the rear near Balaklava) carried one fort held by Turks, and then the rest ran away, and all our forts and about seven guns fell into the hands of the enemy. The Cavalry were forced to retire, and we were

under a very hot fire from our guns turned upon us. We retired beyond our camp, which we had struck, and our servants were packing our things. At this moment a very large force of cavalry came across the plain at full split at some Turkish infantry near Balaklava but the 93rd Highlanders were lying down, and the Turks all ran away, but up jumped the 93rd and poured in such a volley from their Minié rifles, and our batteries on the hill pounded them so, that they all wheeled to the left and cut as hard as they could go.

I had hardly time to put in my glasses when a cloud of Cossacks came towards us, spearing the retreating Turks, who kept firing at them; with them came a very large body of regular cavalry, supposed to be over 2,000. We advanced, formed line, and by this time they were close to our camp and would soon have cut down our servants. The Greys and half the Inniskillings charged first, but they were so close to our old camp, we (the first line) could not get up any pace to the charge, so they met nearly at a walk. The Greys and Inniskillings were immediately surrounded, which we seeing, the 5th and the rest of the Inniskillings went in with a shout and a yell, and for about five minutes we were all hacking away at each other, pistols discharging, and the devil's own row, then they turned and ran up the hill again as hard as they could go, and we after them. Having called off and formed again, a matter of some trouble for all the regiments were mixed, we had time to look about; there were over forty lying dead and dying in pools of blood, with most fearful cuts. We lost a corporal, quite hacked to pieces, and one man shot; another must die, his lungs came through his back. We lost this day, two officers wounded, two men killed, nine wounded, gone to Scutari, five men were slightly wounded, seventeen horses killed, two officers' chargers missing, and twelve horses wounded.

I had one or two shaves for it during the day, my coat sleeve was cut through and my wrist bruised, but not cut, as I had on some very thick jersies. My coat was torn in the back, which was not done in the morning, I think it must have been a lance thrust that tore it. I was within an ace of being knocked over more than once by round shot, and once I had just galloped up from our rear squadron to the leading one, when a shell came close over my head, I looked round and saw it fall and burst exactly where I had just left, knocking over some four horses. We killed more of the 12th Hussars than anything else.* We were under a terrible fire at one time, grape, round shot, shell and Minié balls, the ground was dashed up all round by them.

Later in the day the Light Brigade charged down a valley, they had no business to have gone there, they lost about 300, but can't get the numbers exactly, they took twenty-five guns and killed an immense number, but were totally annihilated by batteries on each side the valley. The weather is fearfully cold, and if it were not for a Russian officer's coat I found after the charge lined with fur, I don't know what I should do. We lost a man today, the doctor says he died of the cold last night, another is dying. I think we are quite sure of another row. Our Vidette and the Russian look at each other on hills not half a mile apart, there are a great number of them. I hope we may get a real good charge at their cavalry again, but I think they will funk to cross swords with us after their licking. They have never licked the English yet, though they did the Turks.

I don't fear their swords at all, but don't like their lances. Neville was badly wounded, and Swinfen run through the hand, and a lance wound in the chest very slight. Elliot badly cut on the head and nose, he went in a regular mucker — he is now on Carew's yacht.† Our Brigadier behaved most pluckily, went right in, got his helmet smashed, hand cut, clothes cut through, and horse much cut, and a spent ball on the arm, he is all right. I think the brutes must have killed our wounded, they will get no quarter next time. I feel sure we must have another row, and I may not get so well out next time, but unless a bullet takes me off I think I shall be able to do something with them first. We have so few cavalry and they so many, it will be a hard fight if we meet. Lord Raglan in general orders gave our brigade great praise, also the Light Cavalry and 93rd. I fear we shall get no clasp for it, as the Turks lost all their forts and guns.

It is nearly impossible to keep warm at night, there is a sharp frost every night, another man is dead, the doctor says from cold.

* This was one of the Russian regiments in the Charge.

† Carew does not seem to have been in the regiment, unless very temporarily. Rich officers, like the Earl of Cardigan, were able to bring out their own steam-yachts, and there were yachts belonging to rich visitors.

I think the town will be stormed in two or three days more. We shall never take it like this. Don't forget the Trinity Audit*, take it home and keep it. I *may* get home next year, but there is a good deal to go through first. They say we are to winter here. I hope not, it is wretched work, and the cold gives one diarrhoea. We are so far from water we seldom get a wash, and everyone is covered with lice which I pick out every morning regularly, but they come again. We are often turned out in the night and often sleep with our clothes on for fear of an attack. I never take off anything for weeks together but trousers and coat, it is too cold to take off more. The weather is very fine and bright. Our men (the 5th) behaved right well the other day, and their steadiness under fire, and that of the brigade was a matter of wonder to the French General. You may look out for another row and lots of killed soon, if we storm the place, so good-bye.

Your most affectionate Brother

* Most Cambridge and Oxford colleges brewed their own beer, and college 'Audit' was specially renowned for its flavour and strength. Temple Godman's brother Frederick was an undergraduate at Trinity College, Cambridge.

† This account to his brother includes details which would probably have shocked other members of the family.

The successful charge of the 'Heavies' should have been followed by pursuit from the Light Brigade but orders to that effect were not issued. The Light Brigade was thus feeling frustrated when it received its own disastrous instructions.

5

The Winter Siege

Camp before Sebastopol   *November 3rd 1854*
My dear Mother — We have moved our camp within the French
lines, nearer Sebastopol and have given up retaking our late line of
forts. We now hold Balaklava and the line of hills in rear of
Sebastopol. Our wounded are all gone to Scutari; the last I heard
our officers were getting on well. . . .
You say that you heard of the disorderly state of the 5th, and
that my letters confirm it. This if I have, I never intended to do,
nor do I think I ever said anything about the regiment being in
disorder. The fact is we were cut up by disease, and half-starved,
men and horses — and then we met with very hard treatment from
Lord Lucan, who was certainly jealous of the high character the
regiment and our Brigadier have always borne — and like many
others was glad to have a rap at us. Then some wrote home, and
the people read in the papers reports as false as they are absurd,
some to the effect that the regiment was dismembered, and
incorporated with the 4th D.G. True it is we were attached in
general orders to the 4th but have never had anything in the world
more to do with them. Indeed they might, as they say themselves
learn much more from us than we can from them. Everyone said
we had been most unjustly treated. General Scarlett is I believe
going to write to the papers to contradict these reports, and I
hope you will do the same for me, if ever you hear anyone mention-
ing them. Whatever they may say I am sure the men behaved in
the most steady and plucky manner possible, when under a very
heavy fire — and also all through the day. Lord Raglan was much
pleased, and sent for Scarlett to thank him in person for what our
brigade had done, he also gives the brigade much praise in general
orders. The cholera was a far greater trial than any fight can be,
and anyone who saw the orderly and quiet manner in which they

behaved during the cholera, when about half were ill, would never doubt for them afterwards. . . .

Your affectionate Son

Camp before Sebastopol   *November 8th 1854*
My dear Father — I suppose you will get the official account of the terrible battle fought on November 5th.* I hear the enemy's loss is computed at 10,000 *hors de combat*; ours very large, they say thirty-eight officers killed, and ninety-six wounded. Neville has lost his brother in the Guards, a sad thing for the family, one killed and the other wounded. The attack was made on our extreme right, near the valley and castle of Inkerman, the enemy came on under cover of a thick fog, it was some time before supports could come up, and our men were near being beaten. We lost Sir G. Cathcart, one of our best leaders, Brigadier Goldie of the 4th Division, and Brigadier Strangeways, H. Artillery killed. The tents of the 2nd Division are riddled with bullets and cannon shot. The enemy were in tremendous force, part of the army of the Danube having arrived, also the one from Odessa, and the Grand Duke Constantine, and Prince Menschikoff are said to be here also.

Everyone seems to say we are doing nothing with the siege, and there are great doubts if we shall take the place. With such a tremendous force against us we ought to have large reinforcements, especially if the Russians pay us such visits often as November 5th. They are said to muster 150,000 men; this, however, must be over the mark. We were not engaged though we could see and hear the battle raging, and an intensely anxious time it was. It began when we were turned out in the morning about seven, and the worst was over about 3 p.m. There was a large force near Balaklava, no doubt for the purpose of drawing our troops from the true point of attack, I saw 300 or 400 cavalry alone, and there were many more at the point of the attack. Owing to the nature of the ground our cavalry could not be used. An officer of the 17th Lancers was killed, I believe from a shell from the ships in harbour. We were in the rear of the fighting but not under fire. The field of battle is a terrible sight, near a battery round which there was a

* The Battle of Inkerman.

great struggle; the bodies lie so thickly one can hardly walk. Some poor Russians yesterday were still on the field wounded, and made signs for water; they were so thankful when we gave it them. They are mostly fine stout men, but their faces are broad and flat, and betoken great ignorance. They say their Generals tell them never to spare the wounded. The consequence was they bayoneted all they came across. I wish they could see our men giving them water and their own rations of rum and biscuits. Our officers are much too conspicuous, the Russian officers can hardly be distinguished from their men. The right flank has been strongly fortified which will I hope make a great difference in case of another attack. These horrid Turks ran away again, they are of no use. As a Russian officer said the other day 'What a pity two such nations as England and Russia should fight over such brutes as these Turks.'

There have been two councils of war since. We must trust to our Generals to lead us right, but things look rather bad. I wish we could get more French — they fight right well. The weather has been warmer since I last wrote. We can buy warm clothes sometimes, on the ships, from which also we get hams and soups and potted meats, in fact nearly everything. The *William Pitt* has not arrived; I hope she has not sunk with my box. Burnand and McNeile sent us up some eatables from Constantinople in the *Himalaya* but we could not get to the ship, and now she has run aground, and has to go to England to repair, our parcels and all. If you hear of her in England, and she is coming out again, I know Captain Killock, or Mr Lane the purser would take charge of any parcel for me.

They say we are to winter here, and they are going to put huts up. In fact, I suppose we must take the place, for I don't see how we could re-embark in the face of such an army, and if we did we must lose all our siege train. Watson is all right, I saw him the day before the action, and some one told me they had seen him since.

I hear Lord Lucan has put in his dispatches, that the 4th and 5th Dragoon Guards were led to the charge on October 25th by Colonel Hodge of the 4th Dragoon Guards. This is perfectly false: the 4th were not anywhere near us, nor was Colonel Hodge. Lord Lucan is determined the 5th shall never get any praise, but he got the brigade into such confusion that day, it was fortunate Scarlett was there to put us straight when the moment came. The French gave us much assistance in carrying off the wounded men. The enemy had an immense quantity of artillery, and very large guns too.

Your affectionate Son

Camp before Sebastopol   *November 12th 1854*
    My dear Father — As I wrote to Joseph by this mail I also enclose a letter to you. You will see by the official dispatches that we are still far from taking Sebastopol. I fear it will be a much longer and more difficult task than they had any idea of. Poor Sir G. Cathcart is a great loss, he is supposed to have been a very rising officer. Had his advice been followed, they say there is no doubt Sebastopol would have fallen long ago. He proposed to follow up immediately after Alma, while the enemy were in confusion and disheartened, and he even volunteered to go alone with his division. Instead of this we gave them time to assemble more forces and to fortify the town, nor as events have proved did they make a bad use of their time. Our Regimental Sergeant-Major has been recommended by the Brigadier for the vacant cornetcy, without purchase,* in which case he will be gazetted as cornet and adjutant, vice me, so you will most likely soon see this in the paper. . . .
    I have just seen Sayer of Marshall's regiment, he is out as an amateur on four months' leave, he does not seem to envy our position. He says the last news is that Nicholas† at the head of 100,000 picked troops is on his way here from Moscow, but I can hardly believe this, certainly things look anything but bright. However, I suppose Raglan has made all his plans, and has better information, and they say he seems very cheerful and not apprehensive of any disaster. Then we have some good heads amongst the French Generals. The 46th marched in a day or two ago and were greatly cheered by the French who brought their bands out to play them by. We are glad to see reinforcements arrive, and they say that about 5,000 have arrived within the last week, and many more coming. We have from this a good view of the Russian valleys before Balaklava, and they often seem to move and get uneasy, then we saddle and expect they are going to make some

* Promotion on active service could be made without purchase.
† Nicholas I, the Russian Emperor.

attack. I expect our weakest point now is from where we are down to Balaklava, but the whole line is entrenched, and where they cannot dig they have made a wall.

The *William Pitt* is arrived, and my and Halford's parcels on board; they are to be landed, and we can get them tomorrow. My second parcel I have not heard of. I must write to Grace about it. I shall send a list of things I shall want as we are likely to be here for the winter. Each regiment is going to send a sergeant directly to Constantinople to get clothes and necessaries for the men to last six weeks. I shall send for a lot of my warm things by this means which I left at Grace's. Our regiment is increased to 450 men, seventy-five per troop, and 372 horses, sixty-two per troop, so are all the regiments on service. I suppose if the war lasts they will be made up to 500 men, but then out of this number only four troops are on service. We have lost four men of cholera since we came on this ground; it is not like the cholera we had in Turkey, though the men died in about ten or twelve hours. The doctor says it is produced by extreme cold, which they cannot get over. It does not appear at all virulent, as no other regiment in the brigade has lost any, and we have had no cases for some days.

It has been reported to Lord Raglan that officers on sick-leave at Constantinople are abusing their privilege, and numbers are there quite well, so I believe a commission is instituted, and the names of officers absent is sent in by every regiment; this I expect will have the effect of sending some back, and others who cannot serve must sell out. This is but fair on the working part of the regiment, I am sure some officers would go, if it were not for leaving just now. Burton and Inglis both want to quit the service, but they wish to get their money and no one will pay a price beyond regulation out here. I wish we could get some to go, the Duke of Cambridge is gone on board ship, and I believe is going to England. He is said to be in an extraordinary *state of excitement* since Inkerman. He seems much liked by the soldiers, I hope there is nothing wrong with his mind. It is dark here about 5 p.m., and about 6.30 p.m. we go to bed, as it is cold sitting up and nothing to do. I find arrowroot with ration rum a fine thing to warm me before going to sleep. We get up before daybreak. My horses are as well as can be expected in this cold and wet. . . .

I get on tolerably well speaking French, and often get a chance.

Sometimes the French bring us bread to change for our biscuit, and excellent clean sweet bread it is they bake here — it is better bread than we got in Turkey. The French under all circumstances always seem so merry and happy, no matter how many Russians are near; nor what the weather is, they are always jolly. They are much better made up for this work than we are: in the first place they are used to camp life, and second they are not made up of lace and white belts, and polished brass and steel as we are. Their uniform does not show dirt, whilst we look filthy; on this account they turn out much as usual. I have a better opinion of them than I had a year ago, and how the English drove them out of Spain, and beat them, appears a miracle to me. They fight well.

I suppose all the Militia will soon be doing permanent duty for we shall want all our regulars. The pens came all right but I have no time to draw. There was tremendous firing last night by the French batteries, evidently strong musketry, which lighted up the sky for some distance, and the shells came one after the other some half-dozen at once. I have not heard the result but it must have been the Russians making a sortie. It lasted about three-quarters of an hour. A deserter has come over who says Nicholas has arrived; I cannot believe this. Last night dreadfully wet. An attack on Balaklava daily expected. . . .

Believe me your affectionate Son

Camp before Sebastopol   *November 12th 1854*

My dear Joseph — I am glad you have had such good sport and that the chase promises so well; I only wish I could be with you to enjoy it too, but my winter's occupation will be of a very different sort. I hope that next winter may see us all together, and a brighter prospect before us than the present one. I can only scribble for my hands are so cold I can hardly hold the pen. We hear it is settled we are to winter here, but how this is to be accomplished I cannot imagine. We are to have huts but it must take some time to build these, and they say we are to live in tents till the beginning of January.

The winter is setting in and we have just had two days' rain, the misery of which you can hardly realize. The horses up to their fetlocks in mud and slush, through which one must paddle to get at them; the saddles soaked; the tents so crowded that the men have no room in them for their arms, which must therefore lie in the rain. In our tents everything is wet, except what one can wrap up in a waterproof; mud outside, and mud within. The men of course are worse off, most having no change or only one of clothes — of course their clothes get wet in the daytime, and their cloaks, and these they must sleep in as also their boots, for if they pulled them off they would never get them on again, no wonder we had twenty-two cases of sickness this morning. Dysentery is on the increase. If we are left like this the horses must soon die, and men be knocked up. I must say I do not see the use of our being kept here, for we are shut up inside a fortified line, out of which we must keep the enemy, and it is not likely we shall stir to attack them. Unless they make us and our horses huts soon we shall be quite useless by the spring, even if we get through the winter. I do not yet quite despair of going to Scutari some six weeks hence. Of course the infantry are better off, inasmuch as they have only themselves to take care of.

I suppose you will soon see the account of the Battle of Inkerman, and a bloody affair it was as you will see, worse than Alma. They say the Russians tell off ten men a company to shoot the officers. We sent them a flag of truce, to tell them they had better not kill our wounded next time or we should have to do the same. Just fancy, one of their *majors* we caught killing all the wounded. They are perfect savages. One of their men being wounded, long after the battle shot at one of ours (also wounded), hit the breast-plate, and the ball glanced off and went through his shoulder, so he crept up to him, and with the only arm he had left, he pinned him to the ground with his bayonet, served him right. The enemy are far superior to us in number and weight of their artillery; ours mere useless popguns compared with theirs. The enemy have hardly any tents, and if the town were entirely invested, I expect those outside must starve. The wretches fired on our men taking off the wounded after the battle. They have been quiet since then, and we have much strengthened our position on the right, they have about 7,000 or 8,000 cavalry here: all idea of storming the place is abandoned, and I don't suppose it will fall for two or three months, if so soon. We continue a mild fire at the place, not that we *do any harm*, but only keep them in check. I believe heavier guns have been sent for from Malta, which Watson tells me will destroy the place if anything will; it must be long before these arrive. They say the enemy can send no more men till the spring. I hope large reinforcements will arrive for us first, and that the place will fall before then, but no one at present seems at all sanguine about it.

Lord Lucan, who received the nickname of *Lord Look on* from his having so often led us near the enemy without letting us have a go in at them, quite retrieved his character at the action of Balaklava, when he showed he had plenty of pluck, but I fear not much besides necessary to qualify a General. The greatest dissatisfaction is expressed at the inactivity of the fleet, who don't help us at all. The Admiral has received the appellation of 'Admiral D — d Ass'. We hope he will be recalled and Lyons put in his place.

Your affectionate Brother

Camp before Sebastopol　　　　　　　　*November 17th 1854*

My dear Father — Your letter of the 29th reached me yesterday, before the post, having got into Lord Raglan's bag. The pens came safe, I don't want any more at present, as I have no time to draw. I have enough wafers, but you may send more from time to time. This mail will bring you a bad account from the seat of war. On the 14th soon after our morning parade was dismissed, a violent hurricane accompanied by tremendous rain broke over the camp; in a few minutes every hut was levelled and all our things drenched, while we, turned out of house and home, had to weather the storm as we best could. Away went cooking kettles and all kinds of things — one officer's air-bed I saw flying high away over the Turkish camp, hardly a tent was left standing. When my hut came down, away went the *Illustrated* you sent me, and of which I had only read about one page. After a little the wind moderated, but the rain continued and then snow, till the ground was covered an inch thick. Of course no fires would be lighted, there we had nothing but biscuit and rum and water all day. At last we got our tents up, and rolled ourselves up for the night, everything as wet as it could be, having been rained on all day. The next day was fine, and so it has been ever since though very cold.

I could see about six ships on shore near the Katcha River and

6 The harbour at Balaklava, photographed by Roger Fenton, showing the dense overcrowding that made Godman so anxious about fire

7 Ships unloading at Balaklava, one of the earliest of Roger Fenton's photographs

8 Officers and N.C.O.s of the 5th Dragoon Guards, photographed by Roger Fenton, showing the wide variety of dress adopted when off duty

9 General Scarlett, painted by Sir Francis Grant. When war broke out he was 55 but had never seen active service. Nevertheless he commanded the Heavy Brigade with courage and distinction. Temple Godman described him as 'the best man in the Division'

I fear some were men of war. I hear that a million and a half of damage has been done to the fleet. At Balaklava, even in this landlocked harbour, surrounded by high steep hills, the vessels were jammed together and most of their masts gone, while those outside which could not get to sea, were driven on the rocks and went down with nearly all hands. There are said to be about 500 men lost at Balaklava alone. The *Prince*, a fine steamer from England, sunk with all the warm clothing for the army, the *Polytechnic* man and diving apparatus, and two large mortars, etc. The harbour is full of hay, rum barrels, etc. The *Prince* had been in ten days, so there is no excuse for not having her unloaded. All the rice and sugar are used, the former a most necessary article with so much salt meat, we are getting much infected with scurvy in consequence. Some of the troops I hear are worse off still, and there is no saying how soon the biscuit or anything else may be stopped.

All sorts of rumours about here. The Commissary General is positively stated to have told Lord Raglan that he would not undertake to forage the cavalry, but he said not a soldier should leave the Crimea till Sebastopol is taken. Some talk of storming again now that large reinforcements are arriving; all seem to expect an attack on Balaklava daily, in which case I suppose we should take the enemy in flank. I expect soon to be engaged again. Many say we never can outlive the winter in tents, but I hear no huts can be built for us, so we must do our best. One thing is certain: if we stay here we shall be quite unfit for service in spring, while the French heavy cavalry will turn out fresh from Bourgos. It is out of the question for an army to take the field, without the branch, when the enemy are so very strong in the same arm, besides guns are nearly useless without cavalry. It is all very well for Raglan living in a house with plenty of coals. We and all the cavalry, and I may say all the army have an immense number of sick, and I am sorry to say I am too frequently called on to read the burial service. We changed our ground on the 16th a short distance, as our late encampment was like a ploughed field, and knee-deep in mud, saddles and all buried. Thompson has arrived in harbour, but we have not seen him yet. I think very likely he will get the majority this time, in fact perhaps it may be better to get promotion, than to be again thrown over, and we must trust to some other way of getting rid of him.

I am sorry to say the Duke of Cambridge is reported to have gone quite mad, he was on board a man-of-war which was near being lost in the storm. I send you a medal from the field of Inkerman, please keep it for me. My box has come safe and only one of the bottles of Zest broken, it is all most acceptable. I think the soup will be the most useful of all. I must send you by my next a list of the things I should like sent. I had the mutton yesterday, as we had salt beef, such stuff! The mutton was very good but rather fat. My horses very well considering all things; the chestnut does not turn out a very good charger, though a useful handy horse. I don't want a better mount than my brown in action. I can manage him so easily and his mouth is so good. I have no time to look over my letter — the post is just going. You will see in the papers the account of all the damage.*

Your affectionate Son

Camp before Sebastopol   *November 22nd 1854*
My dear Father — Since I wrote to you last I think things are looking up again. In the first place, though the weather still continues very cold and wet, yet it has not been so severe as the last week I wrote, and we have had some fine days. Then we are in hopes that our life on the 'Tented Plain' will soon be changed for a more suitable habitation for this time of year. Huts are being marked out, and stable huts also, though when they will be done I can't say, and I fear most of the horses will be dead before they get them under cover. Glanders, farcy and lung complaint are killing a good many.

The Turks are to be set to work to build us huts; this sort of work and scraping the mud off the roads is all they are good for. Everyone out here (in spite of what *The Times* may say to the contrary) hates the name of a Turk, while a Russian is certainly the more noble and a braver man. I can't think how the Turks ever beat the Russians, for they seem to fight well and to be well led; they are most determined-looking fellows, while all the former I have seen (which are not a few) are the most rascally-looking rabble in the shape of an army that any nation could produce. French and

---

* The storm described in this letter destroyed the stores which would have alleviated the hardships of the winter.

English look at them with contempt. The Allies are busy building winter houses dug out in the earth, and roofed over with sticks and then earth, anyhow they will be warm and dry, while now the rain pours through the tents on our beds. Fortunately I have a waterproof rug, which I pull over me and so sleep, as it were, under water. Then the damp out of the ground wets even the saddle-bags through and rots one's clothes, so one is forced to keep on one suit and wear them for a month. It requires pretty good health to stand this work, but I am thankful to be able to say that as yet I have stood it out very well, with only a touch now and then of diarrhoea, which indeed is universal.

I saw our brigade major just now, who told me he had been to breakfast with Canrobert.* He was in excellent spirits, and said that now the reinforcements are come, we shall soon have another pound at the town and be in it before Christmas. Also that now more French cavalry have landed we are going to attack the army in our rear and give them a regular licking. What pleasure it will be turning them out of the huts they have built, but they have many heavy guns in position, and it will be a tough job, however the French know what they are about. Now this is not a *shave*† like the generality of their reports, but I think you will allow it comes from a pretty good source. Perhaps before you get this we may have had another fight. Everyone here says that November 29th is to be the day for a grand attack of the enemy on us. Leiders is reported to have arrived with another division.

I will try when I have time to send you a map of the position of the Allies, and of the position held by the enemy in our rear. The 97th near 1,000 strong have just marched in all clean and new, the French bands welcomed them, and received them with tremendous cheering. These French are very jolly fellows, I get French bread now nearly every day, only they require us to give them such an immense lot of biscuit for a loaf, but we generally settle it somehow. You will be sorry to hear poor Neville died of his wounds on November 11th at Scutari. I suppose the lung was touched. I think he must have heard of the death of his brother in the Guards at Inkerman, he was very fond of him, and this must

* General François Canrobert had replaced Marshal St Arnaud as commander of the French army in the Crimea.
† Hoax.

have taken much hold of poor Neville's mind, a sad thing for his family, the two killed in one week. I sent home a medal from the field of Inkerman, did you get it? The parcel was most acceptable, the mutton rather too fat, the brandy is invaluable. I send a list of some things I should like sent out as soon as you can get them. I have sent to Grace by our sergeant who is gone to Constantinople, to see about my other parcel, they are so careless I am sure the delay is with them. The essence of ginger is very useful, the portable soap would be invaluable on a march, and very useful anywhere, I don't care so much about potted meats as we can often get them here. I have bought a fine thick greatcoat lately, and also a quilt for my bed, so I am pretty well off now, and I hope to get up all the winter clothes I left at Scutari, by our sergeant. I may very likely tell you of something else to send in my next letter. I am very anxious to get a Cossack lance and accoutrements to send home, and if I can I will. Some carry very handsome accoutrements; perhaps I may get a chance soon. I paid 15s for my box. I got the Hampshire paper you sent. I can't see how we are to open the campaign next year without a sufficient force of cavalry, but where are we likely to be, I can hardly fancy we shall take the Crimea, for if we did a large army must go to Perekop to keep it, and they would be more useful elsewhere. There are some beautiful spots under the mountains near here overlooking the sea, and vineyards are very plentiful. Near Yalta on the coast I believe the scenery is lovely, and very mild, what a pity to be in a country like this, and only able to see so little, but perhaps we may see more of it next year. North of Simferopol I hear is flat and ugly. The report of the Duke of Cambridge having gone mad is quite untrue, he is still on board ship. My map came all right and seems a very good one. The sea people tell us we may look for south winds all the winter — I hope so.

Many officers have lately sent in their papers which have mostly been returned. Fisher, 4th D.G., sent in his after the gale, but I hear they were refused and he withdrew them. For my part I shall stand by now for better or worse till we get through. Many here say that Lord Raglan is far too old and slow, and in fact he does not appear to give satisfaction, still he has a game to play and ought to be allowed to play it out; there may be more in him than there seems, certainly our head people are very slow. All the

French have had warm sheepskins served out to them, and now our heads of affairs begin to think that such things might be useful to us, so I suppose we may get them towards spring, the same may be said of the huts. We lost three or four men the other day from positive cold, nothing else, so did some of the Zouaves, and also some of our other cavalry regiments. The men were frostbitten in the trenches and had to be carried out just like the wounded. I saw Watson yesterday, he is quite well.

Thompson has joined us — he is as great an ass as ever, and perhaps more consequential; as to consulting him on matters connected with the regiment, I might as well talk to a post. He always says 'yes' or, if he does not, 'I don't mind'; in fact I do pretty much as I like with the direction of affairs. He makes sure of getting Le Marchant's vacancy; I hope he may, as being the less of two evils, for if not we shall be thrown over again with respect to promotion .. but I fear we shall be done. Campbell has been laid up for a month with a bad leg (an old affair) in a little tent . . . not a very lively state of existence as you may imagine, and no wonder he has made up his mind to go, he does not want the price we give for troops at home, though what it is exactly I don't know. He is engaged to be married, too, which is another reason. Now Halford I rather think won't give much over regulation, as I suspect he is waiting for Scarlett's step to go without purchase, as the Brigadier must be sooner or later promoted. But I must talk to Halford seriously about it, for it won't do to lose a step if it can be avoided, and if he does not get his vacancy perhaps Campbell might exchange to half-pay, bringing in a man to serve, which would completely do us.

A letter from McKinnon says that when Thompson went to the Horse Guards about his promotion, a friend of his told him to apply for the majority and Lt.-Colonelcy, which he promised to do, just fancy such a fellow. McKinnon also says Le Marchant's brother told him that Le Marchant had been to a levee at the Horse Guards to retire, but that they advised him to take a little time to consider about it; I can't believe this, I think he is staying on with the chance of getting Scarlett's Lt.-Colonelcy, and then he would sell out, making a lot of money by the transaction. It cannot last much longer, and it is a shame he is not made to sell directly. I think McKinnon would like to come to Park Hatch, when he has settled his affairs, he is trying to get on half-pay, I hope he may succeed — his leave expires the end of this month. I suppose Fred will be at home by the time this reaches you, tell him I got his letter, I have also received all his and Joseph's also.

Your affectionate Son

Camp before Sebastopol   *November 27th 1854*

My dear Father — I believe the wood for our huts has arrived at Balaklava, but as we are to hut ourselves, I expect it will be long before we get under cover, as we now have hardly sufficient men to carry on the duty of the regiment. The Cavalry look worse every day, and are half-starved, I mean the horses; they die off fast, it is quite melancholy to see the state they are in to anyone who takes the interest I do in it. But how can it be otherwise? Up to their knees in mud, and cold and rain every day. I got the paper you sent me, the idea of sending cavalry out here now is absurd, if they were here, about three weeks would make them as bad as us, and they have the greatest difficulty to forage us.

No news about the siege, if such it may be called. I was up at the front today, the French seem very near the town, but hardly any firing is going on, and what there is, is all from the enemy. I don't know what we are doing, but suppose we are obliged to wait for a stronger force before anything more is done, as we are not strong enough to show two fronts at once, which we should have to do, in case of the force in our rear attacking us while we were working the town. I believe the Generals are sanguine, and I hear Canrobert says the Allies will soon muster at least 85,000. For some reason or other the enemy have been very quiet lately, perhaps the rain, which has been nearly continual the last week has damped their pluck.

This wet is very disagreeable; for the last two days there has been about two inches of mud and water in my tent, and frequently at night I am roused by a regular waterspout right into my face, through the tent. However I am happy to say I am quite well. Thompson had a letter from someone in England to say that Le Marchant is not going to leave the regiment. He has good interest, and has I suppose managed to do us somehow; I can't think he can stay long, I don't believe he has the pluck to come here, and if he did hardly anyone in the regiment would speak to him. You may fancy the feeling against him when I tell you the men have been heard saying that 'He would not come here, because he would not like the noise of the cannon.' McNeile wrote for three months' leave and then to sell out, but was told to join or sell directly, so he I expect will soon be out of my way of promotion. I shall be sorry when he goes, but his health could not stand this work. Burnand's leave expires this month; I don't know what he will do. I must say it is hard on me and others who have gone through the hardships of the campaign. If we went home tomorrow Burnand would get his troop before me, and perhaps keep me back a long time. All who have the misfortune of ill health ought to retire.

Our surgeon from the 2nd Life Guards is much too great a swell for me, he does not like this rough work and has been before a board to get a medical certificate, a regular case of shuffle. I don't like such chicken-hearted men, and the sooner these go home the better, especially the doctor, who ought to stick by one to the last, when affairs look bad, and his services are likely to be wanted. The other day in the gale, his tent like all the rest came down, he was in bed, though half-blown out of it, and rain coming down on him in bucketsful. I, though turned out of my house and home too, could not help standing by to admire the scene, while he was shouting for help and for his servant, and when I asked him if this was as pleasant as Knightsbridge Barracks, he seemed to think I was joking and did not half like it. I could not help laughing in spite of our mutual misery.

I find the preserved mutton is much best cold, just as it comes out of the tin it is excellent, not too rich. The tous-les-mois is very good, I should like some more instead of arrowroot; don't forget the jam or marmalade. If you can send some cherry brandy, I shall be glad of it. I also want another drawing block, double the size of what I sent, but usual thickness. When we get into huts I hope to do something this way. Also send some chocolate powder, I like this better than the paste. The preserved soup is excellent, and if we were marching would be still more valuable. We hear the missing dispatches sent back to Malta in mistake, the post-master here too I believe neglected to send the letters of the Cavalry Division the time before last, so it is not my fault, as I write by each mail if I can. You seem to wonder I can find time to write, but being constantly near the enemy and danger, one becomes used to it like most other things.

The papers seem very confident of our success; I suppose it is a case of slow and sure, no doubt we shall get in after a time. We are always most anxious to hear the opinions and feelings of people in England, so mind and tell me when you write. We are sure to winter here now. Allow us time and I expect we shall give a good account of Sebastopol, of course we cannot expect to take such a place without great loss, but once down it will be a heavy blow. The credit of the two nations is at stake and fall it must. I have not seen Watson for some time. My horses are tolerably well, they are always piqueted to a post. I always ride the brown when there is a chance of a row. The chestnut is hardy, but not so handy or easy as the brown. I shall never get a better mount than him. The troopers are piqueted to long ropes fastened along the ground. If you happen to be going by Gibbys & Haines, you may tell him to be sure and give me good leather and strong work for my overalls, as some he has turned out have been bad in both ways. Kilburn is all right and takes good care of me and my horses; he was seedy about the time of Balaklava action, when we had to bundle off our ground so quickly with all our traps, but was not obliged to go to hospital. I gave him quinine which did him good. I have lots of quinine but the bottle is broken. I hope you got my letter about Balaklava action. The servants were very near all being speared when taking off our traps, only we advanced and charged just in time. I wish we could get Sidebottom out, I think he would soon have enough of it. I fear Campbell has changed his mind and is not going yet. I was disappointed at not seeing the proper account of Balaklava action by last mail. Love to all.

Believe me your affectionate Son

Camp before Sebastopol   *November 27th 1854*

My dear Fred — I suppose you will be at home before this reaches you, where I hope you may enjoy Christmas, please let me know all your good runs with foxhounds and ours, and next winter may I be there too. Scarlett has bought some huts which the Turks had nearly made when they were ordered off to Eupatoria, they are warm and comfortable. Tell Duckworth if you see him his

brother's horse is looking very bad, indeed so are all. I fear he will
never live to see England, tho' every care is taken of him. I am glad
D. has given up coming out to Turkey.

I went to bed tonight soon after five, for it is the only place to
get warm. I am writing in bed. Your letter of the 9th reached this
the 26th as you say, there is very exciting work here sometimes, but
the intervals are dreadfully dull and we have a great many dis-
comforts to put up with. We get plenty of salt meat now; I find a
lump of fat pork day after day for a ration is not very agreeable.
Somehow, though by no means particular I can't eat it. Then we
can seldom wash either ourselves or clothes, and the consequence
is that livestock abounds. Carew is, I think, going home again; he
came out one day on a small pony, determined to have a go in, we
all expected the Russians to come on, but were disappointed. He
wanted to bring up his three guns and help at the siege. Fancy a
man going into action on a little pony, but he said he did not come
out for nothing, he was unfortunately absent the day of the fight.

I have had no more Cossack hunting. One day I am sure the
party I was with would have made a good bag, but an A.D.C.
spoiled our sport, it *was* very exciting trying to stalk them. Next
chance we have, I will try and get the lance and arms of one of
them to send home. I sometimes wish you were here, but after all
it is a great comfort to have no one to think of, I mean no near
relation out here. Elliot is on Scarlett's Staff, and wherever our
brigade is, he is, and wherever there is a fight you will find him in
the middle. He was doing great work the other day till his hat was
knocked off and he got three cuts — one bad one, right into the
bone at the back of the head, one on his forehead, and his nose
nearly cut off — but he has got it stuck on, and it has grown up
quite a good job.

Fisher, 4th D.G., sent in his papers the other day and they were
refused; he is not much of a soldier, he made a bad business of that
piquet when his men got speared, for which he got tremendously
blown up, only don't say anything about it. I believe his piquet
was surprised when watering, and the men dismounted, so report
says. Elliot is all right again. The General has got a lot of Zouaves
to finish his huts for horses, and all. . . . Some of the huts that the
infantry are making are very comfortable indeed, I do not think
any more troops can be coming up now, the roads must be so bad.

I think we shall finish off this place after a time, but it is a tough job, and no saying how soon we shall be engaged again. Tell my Mother I have enough boots for the present. I see they have again put that lie in the papers about the 5th being incorporated with the 4th even though now we can turn out as strong as they can. Write sometimes.

Your affectionate Brother

Camp before Sebastopol   *December 3rd 1854*
    My dear Caroline — Though I have little to tell you, I don't like the post to go without my usual dispatch. Things are going on much the same, and as everyone has a different story, I can't tell you when the town is likely to be taken. Some say it will fall before Christmas, though why it should I can't see at the present rate of proceeding, for we never fire a gun hardly now. Others say that the place must be entirely invested first. There is generally a tremendous fire of musketry and artillery for about five minutes every evening soon after dark. I believe the French rifles annoy them much and make them savage which causes this. Raglan is never seen about, and people seem dissatisfied with him.
    If my parcel is not gone by the time this reaches you, I should like a waterproof coat sent, long and loose, and a hood to button on, it must not be one of those very thin ones as they melt in the summer. We cannot get good ones here, and what we do get are about three times the proper price. Some potted meat would be very acceptable, not preserved meat, but I have asked for such a lot of things it will give some trouble to get them. I should like some of those floating cork wicks, not the very small ones, they will be useful in a hut. The best way to send is by Messrs Oppenheim; they send by steam and have agents at Constantinople and Balaklava and seem more attentive than Grace. Halford has things coming by them.
    By the time you get this it will be near my birthday, I shall spend this in a very different way and place to the last — may the next be at Park Hatch. I am very well and happy though much troubled with chilblains on feet and hands, the former being always wet. I have also got rheumatism in all my fingers, not very pleasant, though of no great consequence. The horses are dying fast of cold

and starvation. Lord Lucan has reported the Division unfit for service. All the horses that are left are mere skin and bone, quite bad to see. I believe we are going to Balaklava in a day or two, when sheds will be built for the horses; this should have been done long ago and not begun in the middle of winter. I shall with the help of Kilburn soon make a hut for myself. . . .

The Russians have just given us the usual volley of I don't know how many cannon. One takes all this now as a matter of course. I got Mr Rennell's letter, also the one from home of November 9th. The account of Balaklava action is not bad, but one would think the Greys and Inniskillings were engaged ten minutes at least before we came up, whereas the whole thing was the work of less than ten minutes, and we went in just behind the Greys and one squadron of the Inniskillings with us, only half their regiment was in the first line. . . .

     Believe me your most affectionate Brother

6

Building for Survival

Camp near Balaklava   *December 7th 1854*

My dear Father — What a change in the language of *The Times* since the Battle of Alma, they seem now anything but confident about the taking of Sebastopol; but I think things look much better, and I expect that it is all right. The weather, though very wet, has been extremely favourable when we consider what Christmas might have been, for people here say that long before this time there is frequently six feet of snow. Certainly the wet is bad enough, but we may be thankful it is not snow, for that would have been death and starvation to us. They say such storms never took place here before, and I can fancy this, as numbers of trees are blown down and buildings unroofed.

The place where we were being so far from the depot of forage etc., being much exposed, and up to our knees in mud, we have been moved down to within a mile of Balaklava and are now in a sheltered gorge inside our lines, which run from Balaklava to the heights before the town. We are much better off here, for beside the place being sheltered, we are close to the harbour and can easily go there to buy provisions, which before was a day's march in the present state of the country, also our horses have not so far to go to get forage. The state of the cavalry is melancholy; the Light Dragoons *led* their horses here, and I don't think there are six horses in the brigade that could trot for quarter of a mile, the most miserable starved horse you ever saw on an English common, is nothing to the horses here. Our brigade are better, but very bad. I don't suppose they will save ten horses out of each regiment by spring at this rate. They are starved: an officer told me he saw two troop-horses eating a dead one the other day.

Lord Lucan has reported the Division ineffective, and I think Lord Raglan must be to blame, he never seems to stir out of his house, nor to care how things go, I suppose he looks down on this branch of the army, but I should like to see him take the field and make any head against the enemy without cavalry. They still *talk* of building huts for the horses — it will not take a very large one if they wait much longer. I don't care about *my* comfort, or that of the men so much. *We could* put up with the cold and wet, but I cannot bear to see such shameful waste of horses, when we well know how scarce they are, and what a cost to the country, when a little foresight or energy might have provided huts for them. You see what a pretty state we are in, not a single General of Division left, but Sir G. England. I believe Sir de Lacy Evans told Lord Raglan before he left that he intended to represent to Parliament as soon as it meets the great neglect before Inkerman; he and the Duke having several times represented to Lord Raglan the weakness of our right flank.

The Turks are making a road (the only use we can make of them), I suppose to bring up the immense guns just landed. They expect a frost soon, when they hope to get up these guns, and after three or four days' constant bombardment to storm the town. This is the *on dit* and the guns have come as I have seen them. I expect we must finish the place now *very soon*. This morning a great smoke over the Russian encampment led us to suppose they were burning their huts, and they have withdrawn their Vidette and piquet, and are said to have retired on Sebastopol. There was much firing this morning, and I heard that the 2nd and 4th Divisions had a go in at them, as they went into Sebastopol. I believe two steamers came out this morning to play on the French lines, but very soon had to put back again.

Campbell is gone away very ill, I expect he will sell out, he says he will and I hope he may. Burnand rejoined but immediately laid up again, as he might expect, coming out of a house to a tent this time of year; as for that greatest of all humbugs Le Marchant, it is very easy to get your doctor to tell you the Crimea climate will kill you, when one does not want to come back, but if he did die it would be of fright I expect. However so much the better for us. I am sure we don't want to see him again. McNeile still at Scutari, I believe going to retire; Burton would gladly leave, but can't afford to lose the extra money; Inglis also wishes to go, he is no soldier, and would be as well out of the way. I am delighted to hear the cavalry out here are to remain, and be made up from home. We shall I hope soon get rid of all the home *soldiers* and get really good and zealous ones in their place. I hope they will not be so insane as to send out more horses till the spring, if they do, they send them to certain destruction. We have all gained much valuable experience this year, tho' at some cost. Never I suppose in any war were cavalry treated as we have been.

Send old Henley some more pheasants before the season is out, I don't suppose he has any news from the regiment. We write to him sometimes, but the news he gets is old as yours. Please keep me the newspaper accounts of the action of Balaklava. The *Illustrated* news account is a very bad one, they put in the Royal Dragoons as having charged. They were not in the fight, all the men they lost were hit afterwards, when we got under the batteries in support of the Light. The 4th Dragoons were *hardly* in it, they executed a flank movement. The Greys got much most spoken of, being so easily distinguished by their bearskin hats and their horses. They and the Inniskillings and 5th D.G. were the only regiments in the thick of it.

You want to know more particularly of the 25th: there is not much to tell you. I rode The Earl, an excellent mount for anything of the kind, he has such pluck he will go anywhere, while I can easily manage him with one hand. He is much faster than the Russian horses; two or three times I just slacked my hand, and in about three strides he ran alongside any of the fellows going as hard as they could. I can't say I saw the man who hit me, we were all in a crowd cutting and hacking at each other, and I did not know till some time after that I was touched when my wrist got stiff, then I found the cut through my coat, it was only bruised for a few days. The Russians shot some of our men with pistols. I don't care about their swords, they use them so slowly and only cut, but I don't like their lances. The part where I was engaged were all the 12th Hussars, in long grey coats, and I don't remember seeing a single lance though a whole regiment was there. The wounds our long straight swords made were terrible, heads nearly cut off apparently at a stroke, and a great number must have died who got away. Our corporal who was killed was nearly cut to pieces, his left arm nearly severed in four places, I suppose there must have been a good many at him at once, as he was very strong and a good swordsman. All the Russians seem to cut at the left wrist, so many men lost fingers, and got their hands cut. Please buy me a map of the position of the besieging army, and keep for me.

The Russians seem to sneer at us for the Light Brigade charge, but next time we meet we shall settle accounts for this too. It had been better for them that day if *their* light cavalry had shown one-tenth the pluck; however now they know what our cavalry is made of — and what they may expect. There are a good many too, who won't have a very pleasing remembrance of the fellows in the brass hats, as the Irish used to call *us*.

My horses are in very fair condition considering the exposure; it is very bad work this, for a horse, and likely soon to knock the strongest up, but mine have stood it much better than I expected. I expect the Russians in our rear were half-starved and half-drowned by the rain. At all events the more troops in the town the better, as our shot will tell more when we open with our big guns. I am very well, and in spite of the constant wet and exposure I have never had a single cold or cough. The climate near the sea is mild, but the exposed heights near the town are very bleak and cold. Last winter was unusually severe, so a mild one is expected this year.

Elliot is at his duty again nearly well; Swinfen has recovered his wound, but is very ill at Scutari, his wound was very light; Montgomery is ill on board ship. Our doctor could not pass the medical board and will have to return to us, he got well snubbed too. Kilburn is all right. I have broken my little quinine bottle, and the other also, I have plenty of it left. We are well off for tents now. The infantry suffer much, it is well Charles Darrington is not here, the night work in the trenches is terribly hard duty. We have had no fresh meat for a week, and shall not get much more, I have had no meat for two days. I find biscuit soaked in water and then fried in salt butter, which we get in Balaklava, very good. I eat this instead, when I can get fat I fry it in this, which is better. I gave 16s for a cheese today, which you could get at home for 7s. I hear today 18,000 sheep are come, which will last a few days. I expect Scarlett will have the Division next year, I hope he may. Cardigan gone home.

I shall stay as long as I have my health, glad as I shall be to see

England again I will not desert while any fighting is going on. No fresh adjutant is appointed yet. I expect to keep it on for some months longer. The Russians are now firing very sharply from Sebastopol, as I sit here I can distinctly hear the shot whistle, though so far off — a splattering too of musketry is going on all day at the walls. The best way to send out things is by a steam transport if you know of any one coming, you pay nothing, and I could easily get it when the ship comes in. They are giving as much as £40 for troopers now in England. Good-night and love to all.

Your affectionate Son

Cavalry Camp, Kadikoi　　　　　　　　　　　　*December 10th 1854*
My dear Mother — Thanks for the parcel you have sent. If I had been with you, you could not have selected things I am more in want of. You will see I wrote for knife, fork and spoon, etc. a letter or two ago. The sergeant we sent to Scutari for necessaries for the men has not yet returned, but we expect him daily, and by him I hope to get some warm things I left at Constantinople and some boots. You say you have sent me some cholera belts, I think they are most useful in summer and have now left them off, they were served out to the troops, flannel ones.* Woollen things are certainly most healthy, but they harbour the creeping things of the earth very much, and in the way in which we are obliged to live it is impossible to avoid this, however it is a less evil than being cold, and there are few things one cannot get accustomed to.

You seem very anxious about Kilburn: he is very well and will no doubt appreciate your present of the jersey; he is an excellent servant, and always makes the best of everything without complaining, which is what I like. The only thing I don't want is the nightcap, a thing I never use. The saucepan will be most useful, only I wish the kettle could have been made to go inside it. I am afraid I shall not have much time to study Italian, but it is as well to have the book out here. There is a good deal to do one way and another, but it is wonderful how quickly the day passes. I expect to

---

* Cholera belts were designed to keep the stomach warm. They were useless against cholera but were probably some help against diarrhoea.

10 The Charge of the Heavy Brigade during the Battle of Balaklava, painted by G. D. Giles

12 Major A. W. D. Burton of the 5th Dragoon Guards, often referred to in Temple Godman's account

11 Major Abraham Bolton of the 5th Dragoon Guards in full dress, painted by William Buckler, 1853

get my second box by our sergeant from Constantinople. We are going to give up Grace & Co. — they are so dilatory — and Oppenheim seems more civil. Grace had a box here for Halford, and though our agent, never landed it or sent him word, and so the ship took it away again. It is much best to send here, and not to consign to Constantinople; there must be people in London who would do this.

The Earl and Chance both have rugs, and the Cob has a Russian do, which I got off the horses which broke into our camp one night, a very good one too. I expect to get the horse clothing I left at Constantinople besides, so they are pretty well off. We get our forage much more regularly now, so my horses are very fairly off. We have plenty of water, though it is sometimes muddy, but the infantry near Sebastopol are very badly off in this respect. Our men have had some warm clothing given out; so we are better clothed now. Since I last wrote we have had beautiful fine clear weather, which they say will last till the snow comes, about January 10th. We have actually had dry feet for a week, a great blessing, for we had many men laid up, from being unable to stand, their feet being so bad from the constant wet, and being unable to get their boots off for days together. We have had two or three very severe nights, and a tent is little or no protection, any water left in the tents was frozen.

I attribute to Lord Lucan chiefly the blame of our not being housed, he is in a house, and does not seem to take any trouble about us. I wish we could get rid of him, he is not fit for the command he holds, besides which he has a most horrible temper, and is often most abusive, which I call anything but gentlemanly for a man in his position. Everyone hates him who has anything to do with him. We have had fresh rations about twice the last fortnight, and we also get potatoes and onions. The officers generally manage to have some preserved soup on salt meat days. I can manage the salt beef though it is tough and stringy, but I can't eat the hot salt pork, which is none of the best. We have been getting rice again lately. Numbers of ships come in full of jams, hams, preserved meats, etc., which are very soon all bought out, they are always very dear.

I think ladies are very much out of place as hospital nurses, however kind their intentions may be; it is better left in other hands.

I must say I should not like a lady to attend me if I knew it. I look upon it as a sort of fanaticism. . . .

I saw Watson yesterday, he is quite well; he tells me the Russians are building new and very strong earthworks round the town. If this dry weather continues perhaps we shall be able to get up the big guns; some large mortars drawn by about twenty horses have already gone up. The English have got as near the town as they can, the assault must be made from the French side. Drafts are constantly coming in, and two or three fresh regiments have arrived. Doubtless the place must fall in time, and this side taken we could, if we don't lose too many men, still hold the heights and let the town alone, especially if we could get our shipping into the harbour — we could easily hold the only approach, which would be from Inkerman. I don't know if the forts on the heights the other side command the harbour. These would have to be invested regularly, and to the eye they don't seem to afford anything like the chance of so prolonged a resistance as this side has done — they would I expect fall to the systematical attack of our engineers. Besides the town would then be entirely surrounded, and all resources cut off, and when we get inside this ridge, good-bye to the Russian fleet which has done us so much harm.

It is not likely we shall get round the other side without fighting this army in our rear. They seem inclined to attack us again at Inkerman, and we were ready this morning as they were fully expected today. The Cavalry were not engaged at Inkerman, their casualties were all caused by shells from the enemy's fleet. I believe the two steamers which came out the other day have rather opened a secret to us, as we now know the way in. You may fancy the state of the Light Brigade when I tell you that they could not muster horses enough in the Brigade (besides those that bring the daily forage) to bring down twenty sick men who were left at their late encampment, but had to come on the Heavy Brigade and they were provided by my regiment. Commissary Fielder declares, in order to get the blame off him, that they must have sold their forage, *because* the same regiment did so in the Peninsular; by the same arrangement it might be added that Mr Commissary General F. ought to be hanged, because General Picton threatened to do so in the Peninsular.

I think Lord Raglan's promotion somewhat premature, they

might have waited till this place falls. I don't think he has shown any great Generalship, certainly the march on Balaklava is the best and only thing he did, but who with his eyes open would not have taken advantage of so strong a natural position. I think all these reporters, though satisfactory to the people at home, anything but politic; they must inform the enemy of much more than Lord Raglan would have them know. Then again all our movements and all our resources are so accurately laid down in the public papers, that the Czar knows exactly what we are doing, and what the extent of the requirements necessary to meet all our resources.

I think it a very good plan that the Militia should take all the Colonial duties, and so send us all the regulars, but I should hope the Government will never allow them to take part in the war. I think that is at once putting them out of their proper place as our reserve, and also rather derogatory to the army. If they come out it will be time for us to shut up and go home. They will have quite enough to do to furnish volunteers. I am anxious for Parliament to meet to hear what is to be done, and the campaign discussed. I suppose it cannot be long first, for if the Militia are to relieve the Regulars in the Colonies I suppose the act must be altered. Certainly I don't see how they can very well be sent to the seat of war, for though very efficient and valuable troops in themselves, yet so many of their officers, and frequently their senior officers, having always led the life of civilians, it cannot be supposed that they have, or could easily acquire, the knowledge requisite for any command on active service, where colonels and even inferior officers are often placed in positions where the experience of years is often necessary for safety and success. Do you hear it talked of in England that they are to come out?

I think this part of the Crimea must be very healthy, and the climate is said to be beautiful. The order for the two augmentation troops, seventy-five men each, reached us today. I should think the regiments at home will be very savage at having to give up their men and horses to come out here. I expect as soon as Sebastopol falls, we shall go to Scutari to refit; all our saddlery wants renewing and so much to be done. I think we shall make a better business if we get a fresh start from Coolaki (?) Barracks, and it is only a day's steaming from here. We hear 40,000 Russians are on their road from the Danube, can this be true? I hear the Turks have refused to make roads, or do any dirty work, I wish we could get rid of them, the brutes won't work, won't fight, and eat up all our stores, besides stealing all they can put their hands on.

I think I can see a deal of promotion, and if all goes well I ought to be a captain before next year. The Brigadier we hear is made a Major-General, at all events he is sure to get it soon. This is one step without purchase, he will lose nearly £15,000, but this I don't suppose he cares about. Then I suppose the *un*worthy major gets the Lt.-Colonelcy, he dare not join again, and will probably sell or exchange to H.P. with a man to sell. This gives another step; he has such influence that he is able to perpetrate any amount of rascality. Thompson will stick and I suppose he will soon be Lt.-Colonel; perhaps it is better to have him promoted than to be again sold by him. Then we must get rid of him as best we can. Burton wishes to leave, but can't get his money, as no one will give more than regulation, nor can he afford to lose it, so must stop on, but he could not go now during a campaign. Campbell gone away sick, must be invalided home, and he has promised to sell out immediately. Sidebottom can't stand this work, and I suppose he and Henley are soon to be ordered out, I expect he must sell out. The Brigadier said the other day he should write and advise him to do so, he is a very bad officer. Henley I should think would soon go for regulation, for to come out would put him to much expense to provide for his family, and would probably be the death of such an old man. These two augmentation troops, we will say one only will go in the regiment. Swinfen I don't expect to stand another campaign, he is away very ill now. Elliot will probably get a troop in some other regiment, as there are plenty going now, and he has lots of interest with Lord Harding, and some claims too. Halford will stay, he is a very good officer, but I forget Inglis, he will stay, a very bad officer does not care about it. McNeile has sent in his resignation from ill health; though not much of a soldier, he will be a loss to the regiment. Burnand does not care to serve and wishes to get out of it soon, he says he can't stand another summer.

Next comes myself, you will say I have disposed of a great many very summarily, but suppose two-thirds go, and then the casualties of another campaign. It is no use to go lower down, but you seemed to want to know how promotion was likely to go. We have several very indifferent officers I wish we could get rid of. Did you see in the *Chronicle* that Robbins our late adjutant through a letter from me has contradicted all the false reports about the 5th. We have received orders today that we remain here the winter, so tomorrow I begin my hut. Monday a beautiful warm day as warm as spring, but no sun. When do people in England think next year's campaign will be? As long as I am still well I shall go on, I don't dislike this life, and a regular campaign will be much more exciting than a siege. Among other shaves, we hear the enemy will give up the town, if we will let the fleet out — a likely story. There was great firing there last night.

December 12th. Our mail arrived: I received a letter from Caroline and Frederick, have hardly had time yet to see the papers. Did you see a letter in the *Chronicle* of November 20th from a corporal of ours, quite a lad, to his Father an old 5th man. They have now given us orders to carry up all stores for the infantry, this really is too bad, it will soon finish our horses. Our ambulance is so defective that we have to borrow that of the French to bring down our sick from the front. Lord Raglan's dispatch about November 5th is thought very bad and incorrect, in fact he was taken quite unawares and it is useless to conceal it.

Believe me your affectionate Son

We hear the *Jason* having met with an accident was landing the baggage at Constantinople, the boat upset and lost all — we have all more or less on board. The paymaster had £100 in it.

Cavalry Camp, Kadikoi   *Sunday December 17th 1854*
My dear Caroline — The mail is not yet in, though it has been due two days, so that I have not received any letter from home since your last. I have been very busy this week making my hut or rather digging a big hole, but now comes the most difficult part, the getting wood — every tree without our outposts has been already cut down, and though Balaklava is full of timber, which has been brought there for the purpose of hutting, they will neither give nor sell us any, so that my excavation seems more likely to become a pond than a house. We had our week of beautiful weather, in

which everyone seemed to forget all the miseries we had experienced, but this state of things was too good to last, and we have now gone back to mud and rain with sometimes snow by way of a change. However I don't despair of getting wood, and hope soon to be under cover, for a tent is not very pleasant in snow and rain. If I could only finish my hut I should be as jolly as possible, for we are now very fairly off in the way of food of which we can buy plenty at Balaklava.

Meantime the siege is still going on, several large guns have been got up, and now they are busy carrying up pills for the Russians in the shape of immense 13-inch shells which take two men to lift and four make a good cartload. A new battery is nearly ready to open, which they say must nobble the ships, for if they run from it they must get under the other batteries. Many are ready to bet ten to one we are in the town before Christmas, but I think hardly so soon, though it must be all up with them before long. Reinforcements are constantly coming in. Some French are said to be marching up from Eupatoria to take the Russians in rear, while we have a go in at the town. Then a large force of Russians is coming up whose vanguard 40,000 men is already this side of Perekop; I wish them a pleasant march of it. Such are the shaves here, but for us it is enough to believe as soon as we see their ugly faces.

You would not recognize the British soldier again were you to see him here, unwashed and unshaven, covered with mud from head to foot, some clothed partly in Russian garments, an old sack, or some original dress made out of an old blanket, tied on with bits of string. Then alas! The Heavy Dragoon and smart Hussar, what if some of our lady friends could see us now; I don't think they would ever care much about soldiers again, with uniforms torn, and hardly to be recognised, legs bound up with hay and straw bands, some without shoes or socks, etc. The Johnnys are made to do all the dirty work, that is as much as the idle rascals can be forced to do. Everyone pushes and cuffs them, especially the sailors, who make great fuss of them. They work now in the trenches and when Jack* sees a shell coming, he picks up a stone which he lets drive at Johnny, just as the shell bursts somewhere near, who feeling himself hit drops his spade,

* Jack Tar (sailor).

and runs about howling, to the immense delight of Jack and his comrades.

The other day the French sent out a party to reconnoitre, so I went with them in hopes of seeing some fun. But we saw nothing except a lot of Cossacks who came near us — and then galloped off again when the guns were unlimbered. The French brought back a lot of wood, so did two jobs at once. I took this opportunity to ride over the late field of battle, as it is rather too much outside our outposts to be very safe. The whole plain is strewn with dead horses (now picked clean by the eagles), saddles, Russian caps, etc., while the numerous cannon balls about still black with powder, mark the ground of our late action. The ground where we charged is still covered with jackets, belts, pouches, horses etc., tho' visited by so many people from the ships who have carried away most of the relics. There are several graves here, where the less fortunate actors of the 25th lie, while here and there a white skull looks out partly uncovered by the birds and rain. While looking at these things I had got some way from the French who were going home, and I found several Cossacks coming after us, so thought it wise to make off. The rascals evidently thought they were going to catch me, as they came quite close into our outposts. There were two other officers of the mounted police who have just come out, they are great swells in their own estimation, and nothing would do but they must have a shot at the Cossacks, which however they did not get and were very near being caught for their trouble. I wish they had been quite for they are my great aversion, two horrid snobs, and think themselves regular cavalry men.

I hear McMahon is put in, in place of Le Marchant, what a shame, thrown over again, it is too disgusting* — at any rate we have got a gentleman this time. More news this afternoon. The Turks have landed in force at Eupatoria, and they say French too. Tomorrow is Nicholas day and they fully expect an attack on the plain again. They say 70,000 enemy are behind the hills, orders were sent down to finish disembarking the troops today, which looks like work. Sir C. Campbell at Balaklava said they had only these fellows to beat and then go home; no doubt they will get a precious

---

* Difficult to know if this is a joke or a reference to Burton. Lt.-Colonel McMahon from the 9th Lancers took over command but went home almost immediately; however he retained the command.

licking if they come. If they do come the cavalry are sure to be in it also.

Your most affectionate Brother

Cavalry Camp, Kadikoi   *December 21st 1854*

My dear Father — Soon after your letter of November 28th arrived I heard that the *Royal Albert* had come in also. She did not come inside the harbour and has disembarked all her troops today, and is I hear going round immediately to join the fleet. I did not know the troops were disembarking so did not not go down, and as she is some way outside the harbour I fear I shall have some trouble in getting my box out; but hope to be able to do so. It is very kind of you to get me such a lot of things. Indeed everyone in England seems to take the greatest interest in our comfort and welfare, and it is no small satisfaction to see that our work is duly appreciated and that the spirit of the nation is so unanimous, and heart and hand so ready to support the vigorous prosecution of the war, certainly this is the only way to peace. I am so glad to hear Austria is now in earnest on our side; she must prove an immense hindrance to the Russian designs on Turkey, with her vast military resources, and will cause a most important diversion in our favour, in case of a Crimean campaign next year.

We have had some most delightfully warm weather the last week, they say this month is very often fine, but after Christmas we must look for a cold hard time of it till February. I hope to get my hut finished before this, and I think I know now where to get wood. There is an order that all officers as well as men are to have an issue of warm clothing, to consist of a sheepskin coat, fur cap, gloves, two drawers, two socks, two jersies, but it may be spring before we get them they are so slow. The *Jason* came in the other day, and I found my saddle-bags cut open and some of my things stolen, your warm things will be very acceptable. Washing is rather difficult, and to dry things more so. Moreover I have only had three shirts all the campaign, tho' I have plenty at Constantinople, which I hope to get very soon. As it is not safe to more than half-undress at night, a change of clothes is not very common.

The charges in the *Illustrated* are not the least like, it is too bad making so much of the Greys. I know our Brigadier will give the

5th the first chance next time. I think all the Commanding Officers that day will get a brevet rank most likely. McMahon has been on Lord Lucan's Staff as Adjutant and Quartermaster-General,* a very gentlemanly person. He is gone home ill, has been nearly all his life on the Staff; I believe he has hardly commanded a troop, we don't expect he will ever join. I don't know who will get the step, at any rate we get rid of that *Snob* as the Brigadier calls Le Marchant.

We are much better off here than at Balaklava, where fevers prevail, and the houses are bad and filthy, and Turks die in quantities. My horses are wonderfully well, though of course low in flesh, and not up to any very strong work, still they would do well anything I might want at present. The brown has stood out well and is quite saucy at times, the other two are well and hardy; as for the Cob he is as round as a barrel, and does nothing but shout for his food all day as Kilburn says; we get forage regularly now. We have only eighty-five effective horses left, and forty sick; they die off about five a day. They use us now as pack horses to take biscuit to the front. I don't suppose we shall save fifty horses out of 250, and they will be useless. We are ordered to dig stables, but this is slow work, as every man is employed every day in other ways.

People express much discontent at our Field Marshal — who is never seen and seems to take things precious easy. He got his promotion for nothing but his negligence, he did not turn out at Inkerman till long after the battle began (I am told) and as to commands, not one was given. Regiments, companies and small knots of men fought like devils to keep back the enemy, and all acted independently in a thick fog without orders. Such was Inkerman won *only* by the bravery of the troops engaged,† and at one time we were as near beaten as possible, quite driven back and the enemy in our camp, and had they not been driven back by our men, they would soon have been able to bring the whole of their force to bear at once (which they could not do on the point of attack) and then it was all up with us. . . .

I have told Scarlett I will keep the adjutancy for some time, as

* AQMG: Adjutant and Quartermaster-General, usually abbreviated to AQ. The Staff officer responsible for information about the supply of men and stores.

† Inkerman became known as the 'soldiers' battle' as they were taken by surprise and fought without orders in some parts of the field.

I expect I must get a troop in a year — and there are some advantages though more trouble and responsibility than for other subalterns.

Yesterday I was riding out and saw some French cavalry going across the plain to reconnoitre, so of course I went too and never saw a prettier soldier's sight, or better done. We advanced, covered by skirmishers, drove in the Cossack vidette and piquets and were soon skirmishing sharply with these fellows. A distant fort on the flank fired a few guns but too far off for the shot to hit us, and on we went, the firing coming sharper. At length we got to Kamara and reached a high rocky hill to the left of that place, the French made the best of their time, and the General and his engineers soon sketched the whole of the Russian position, for they could see the whole valley of the Black Water, from Inkerman to the mountain pass leading to Baidar valley. There were the enemy entrenching themselves, making a very strong position. The sketch was soon made and all they wanted effected: just at this time a column of infantry came up the hill, and we were obliged to bolt. Meantime a very smart fire was going on below the hill with the swarms of Cossacks to whom we were nearer than usual. The trumpet now sounded to retire and they began to fall back skirmishing beautifully. The infantry had now gained the top of the hill and were sending their Minié bullets pretty fast over us, making a most peculiar noise like ping-ping. The Chasseurs d'Afrique at the foot of the hill returned the fire very smartly, and though so many Russians were blazing at them from the hilltop, not more than 200 yards, I did not see one hit. We soon retired out of range of the infantry, who did not follow, but our skirmishers were pursued up the plain by numbers of Cossacks.

It is great fun to see these rascals work, they gallop as hard as they can split for about twenty yards, then circle and turn quite short, and when there is a small rise in the ground, they dash up, and only their head appears above till they see the coast is clear, they take advantage of every inch of ground, firing behind hills, etc. In the open they dash up as near as they dare, and stop short, fire, turn round and bolt at best pace. A considerable body of cavalry was advancing, but never got near us. When arrived on the plain, the skirmishers were called in and on came the Cossacks, hallooing and yelling; I suppose thinking we were driven back, but the rascals knew better than to come further. I wish they had that we might have caught some — they are so impudent. The French had a man or two wounded, I don't know if any Russians were killed.

The Russians as I told you have left the Turkish forts they took and have retired a bit to the rear — they had been hutted very snugly, but had destroyed all before they left. They dig a hole about six feet square and three feet deep, fence it over with thick sticks tied at the top, thatch with brushwood and cover with mud — makes a very snug warm house. We saw in the plain some skeletons or nearly so, in spite of the Russians having said all were buried. It seems so odd to be on ground which five minutes before or after would cost you your life to visit — though one sees it every day. We were not able to bury all the dead of Inkerman, many are there still. Today the Russians have fortified the hill up which the French went. I could see them at work with my glasses. Our force was a Heavy Dragoon regiment — four squadrons, about 400, and about 200 Chasseurs d'Afrique, first-rate Light Cavalry. The enemy inspired by the *bottle* as usual, got into our trenches last night, killed about thirty-five men, took two officers and killed another, but were driven out again. They say we shall not take the place just yet, but we are so very close now. I expect we shall be in before very long. We, i.e. my mess, are going to get a plum pudding off some ship for Christmas Day. I hope my next may be spent at P.H. I wish you all a happy Christmas and best love.

Your most affectionate Son

Cavalry Camp, Kadikoi   *December 29th 1854*

My dear Father — We have lost another of our number, poor Campbell, who died a few days ago at Scutari — he owes his death entirely to the disgraceful mismanagement of our medical department. They would not let him go away till he was so ill he was nearly insensible, and in this state sometimes wet through in his bed, as the water comes through our tents. He died of dysentery; a very sad thing indeed, a man who had already gained three Indian medals and several clasps and had been all through this campaign to die like a dog through neglect. He was a very clever and agreeable man, in fact very superior and had seen an immense deal of life. Unfortunately he was engaged to be married to Miss Mansel, daughter of the General at Cork. We shall miss him much, he was so cheery (though not a first-rate officer) all through the cholera and bad times; he always cheered one up with his stories and anecdotes, he had served all over the world.

Seven months ago we sailed from Cork nineteen officers in all, out of which ten only are left, five being dead, and four gone home from ill health. An officer I knew in the Greys who was taken very ill after October 25th went on board ship, and being too ill to stir; the ship sailed with him to Scutari, the authorities sent to put him in arrest for going away without leave, the medical man though knowing him to be as ill as possible took the message to him, the consequence was the shock killed him in a few hours. Fancy too, a man so ill as to be nearly dying to be ordered to attend a medical board two or three miles off to which he must either walk or ride, but this I have known done, and many other instances I could tell you which perhaps you would hardly believe. There is someone come out from London to inquire into the medical department. It is certain if an officer gets ill here, unless strong enough to stand the attack, he *must* die, and the doctors seem rather to hasten this than otherwise. Certainly the army Staff could not be worse. We might as well have an old woman to command us as Lord Raglan, then our commissariat is nearly useless. Our ambulance totally useless, and our medical department very bad. . . .

There are great reports here of peace, surely none can be made till Sebastopol falls. The credit of England and France is at stake, and we must take this place. People seem pretty confident about it now. We have got up our mortar and lots of shell, etc.; they say when we open again the whole place must be burnt. The French got into the outskirts by the Quarantine harbour the other day and hold it yet, I think it will be taken before spring. The whole of the cavalry (they say) have left the Crimea for want of forage. *We* are now totally useless as cavalry. I don't think we could muster a squadron in the whole division, at least one that could meet the enemy; the horses are skin and bone, and most regiments reduced to about fifty effectives (as they are called); we lose sometimes seven or ten a night. They work us very hard to carry biscuit to the front, or to take sick to Balaklava, work which the ambulance or commissariat ought to do. The French carry lots of our sick for us; one trip they brought down 1,500 — see the difference between us. The ground is very heavy and every journey averages from ten to fifteen miles and we usually have three or four horses drop dead on the way from hard work.

I see we are to get a medal for the campaign, a clasp for Alma and Inkerman, the latter we shall get also. I wish they had given one for Balaklava. Did you see Halford has got one of the augmentation troops without purchase? I suppose the other will not go in the regiment. I think this rather hard when the regiment is on active service. Simpson is gone home ill, I suppose he will get Scarlett's promotion, and so get his troop for nothing. I hear Scarlett is Major-General though I have not yet seen the gazette or who gets his step. Elliot has applied for a troop in *any regiment* and is very likely to get it, having plenty of interest; but if not gazetted before Campbell's death is heard of I suppose he will get that. McNeile gone home, and his papers are gone in. Burnand says he will not stay another summer, so you see I am nearly first for my troop which perhaps I shall get without purchase. I don't think Swinfen will come out again, I dare say he would sell out if he could. I expect Sidebottom must come out now, I hope so, we shall be more likely to get rid of him, as he certainly will not like campaigning. I would not give a farthing more than regulation out here — once senior subaltern there is always a chance of promotion without purchase.

I have not yet finished my hut for want of something to cover it with. I hope to get it done before the very cold weather comes. We have had fine weather and some very hard frosts, so hard as to freeze the breath on one's blankets at night. I had Fred's letter from Cambridge and also one from Joseph and Caroline.

December 1st. Tell Fred I always look to see where the foxhounds went, and should like to know the runs they have. We had fresh meat Christmas Day and made a pudding after a fashion — our rations now are always salt.

Your affectionate Son

Cavalry Camp, Kadikoi   *January 2nd 1855*
My dear Fred — I have just been reading *The Times* correspondent's letter of the gale of November 14th. It certainly was the

most wretched day I ever spent. What a difference from my position this time last year — spending then a life of enjoyment and luxury in such a house as P.H. with nothing to do but to amuse myself, while this year finds me digging a hole in the ground for a house, and plenty of duty to occupy my time, and the dull routine of camp life. However I am just as well satisfied, though I don't mean to say I would not rather have spent my Christmas at home, instead of the Crimea, but next year I hope we shall all spend the winter together. I see there is a picture in the *Illustrated* of the position of the Allies; it is not correct: the cavalry were never encamped where they mark it.

The railway* is come out here, but will not be finished for some time, it is not yet begun. I hear the French have 190 guns ready, and are waiting for us, and in great fear lest a sortie should be made, and their batteries destroyed. Old Lyons intends to have a go in at the sea batteries at the next attack; they say our force here in spite of all these new regiments does not increase the least. The 9th have been here about three weeks and have already buried 200 men. The 98th landed about a week or ten days ago, and have already buried fifty men, and out of 850 they could only muster on parade 350, five days ago. This gives you some idea of the sickness. Our men are pretty well now, though we still lose and send away some. . . . The Russians have been pretty civil lately, the army in our rear has nearly disappeared.

I went out again on December 30th with a French 'reconnaissance en force' about 10,000 men, and 1,000 cavalry, to have some fun with the Cossacks. The piquet bolted very quickly. On getting to Kamara in the valley to the left, a little beyond, there were a lot of regular lancers and Cossacks. These were charged by the Chasseurs d'Afrique, and after a plucky resistance were obliged to bolt, the French being too strong. Several Chasseurs were wounded, and an officer got a lance in his stomach, which I fear must have settled him — he was with the other men carried off by the ambulance, of which there were a good lot out. Some Russian prisoners were taken, among them a Cossack officer; some of these fellows got more than they bargained for and several sore heads were made by the swords of the Chasseurs. One Cossack I

---

* The light railway, built by specially imported 'navvies', linked Balaklava port to the siege works, and transformed the supply situation.

noticed on the ground wounded, his head cut open; with a pair of English artillery trousers on. The head of the column advanced, Chasseurs, in skirmishing order leading, and the infantry following up; after a bit a battery on our left began to annoy us by shelling our men, several were wounded.

The artillery now came forward and brought up four or five guns to the top of the hills on our left — at the same time the Zouaves and other infantry took up a position on the top of the hills, just out of sight of the enemy. I went up with the guns which unlimbered, and soon showed their muzzles over the hills. As soon as the enemy saw them they immediately let fly, the shell came hissing, and the first stuck in the hill. Bang again, this time I could tell by the hissing that they were nearer their mark, and the shell burst behind the guns, unpleasantly close to our heads, the pieces whizzing all round, and making me and the colonel of a Zouave regiment which was coming up, bend our heads close to our horses' necks, while the pieces knocked up the leaves and buried themselves in the ground close under the Zouaves' feet. Having no duty here I thought it was now time to mizzle* but a precipitate retreat was not in the question before these Frenchmen, so I had to look pleasant, and get away quietly, while the enemy who now had the range, sent their shells right among the men, though I did not see one knocked over. I now got behind the hill where I thought I was all right, and was dismounted and pulling up my saddle girths, when a cannon ball came there into the hill, and bounding clean over pitched close to my horse, and nearly made him break away, which would have been an unlucky thing out so close to the Russians. The French having opened their fire soon silenced the enemy's guns in about twenty shots. It was very pretty to see the Zouaves skirmishing up the hills in their picturesque dresses, and taking occasional shots at the retreating Russians.

We had now secured the hills at the entrance to the Baidar pass, so that they could be held against any force which might come up the Black Water valley from Inkerman. Fires were now lighted, and in three minutes all the men were hard at their dinners as jolly as possible. General Maurice had his lunch too, and his A.D.C. asked me and the other English officers to come and have some also. Lunch being over we started off with the cavalry, and a

* Decamp.

few ambulance mules for the wounded up the pass, and trotted on for some way; the scenery was wild and very beautiful, the road cut out of a mountain side with a deep ravine on our right. Having proceeded about eight or nine miles, we emerged into a beautiful valley, with woods and villages, fields, etc. surrounded by hills, very like parts of England. Here we halted and dismounted, and having seen no enemy did not go any further. Some Russians had been encamped in and near the village, and so we thought we would just leave our marks, by burning all their huts, which in five minutes were all in a blaze, this was about two miles from Baidar.

On our return we found the Zouaves had plundered all the Russian huts, of which there were a good number, the enemy had left them in a great hurry as we came up, and their fires were burning and dinners cooking. Lots of pots, pans, axes, etc., and many other useful things were taken by the French, and then all the huts burnt. This sort of thing the Zouaves delight in. They are dreadful robbers and plunder for the mere sake of mischief; many things they take cannot possibly be of any use to them, such as pictures, looking-glasses etc. I rode off with an officer of the Inniskillings to the back of Kamara where was a regular village of huts, near which the French had not been, so we were obliged to keep a sharp look-out, for fear of the Cossacks. We went into many of the huts, I should have gone into more, only my brown horse is so restless and hard to mount in a hurry. Presently out bundled two chicken which my friend ran after while I held his horse. We were obliged to be quick, so after a short hunt he succeeded in transfixing one with his sword, but the other unfortunately escaped, a bad job as these creatures are both scarce and dear here. We found an axe, billhook, etc. which were most useful to us. I got a cooking pot, which however I was obliged to drop, it was too heavy to carry. I also found a Cossack lance leaning against a hut, the fellow had evidently been in too great a hurry to take it. Inside was his loaded pistol, valise, etc., we took them all, I shall bring home the lance-head. After ransacking the huts and upsetting their food (such beastliness as it was too) and doing all the mischief we could we rode off.

Ever since our fight at Balaklava, immense flights of eagles and vultures have been very common all about, and here they were so tame and gorged that we could ride right among them before they flapped out of our way. I think I am not over the mark when I say they were three feet high as they stand. I could easily have shot them with my revolver, but did not like to make a noise. The French all come home at night.

January 3rd. It has been raining and snowing ever since yesterday morning. All today I have been working at my hut, and have nearly roofed in, I hope in another week to inhabit it. I fear I have made the roof too flat for the rain to run off. It will require a fire for three or four days before I can get into it, as it is very damp of course. Our horses are overworked and die fast, we have got the glanders too; so have another regiment. We lost fifty-seven last month, I don't expect we shall save a single one. We are making stables but without help and very slowly. They gave the officers clothing like the troop horses have, they are Turkish and cannot cost many shillings each. Now we have had them some days the authorities find out we are not *entitled* to them, so are to give them up again, really it seems that everything that could be thought of in order to annoy and put officers to expense is done.

January 6th. There are now five or six inches of snow on the ground and a cutting wind from the north-east. They say that sometimes the thermometer goes down below zero, and that with this wind no one could live in a tent. . . . Last night was the most severe we have had yet; our tents frozen as stiff as boards, so that this morning the door flaps could hardly be undone. Everything was frozen, my boots and trousers quite stiff, and my waterproof bedcover, my cold pork for breakfast quite hard, and ink frozen up, even now it freezes in my pen — this accounts for the writing. Today bright and sunny, but frost very sharp. Our poor men suffer much, their blankets were frozen on them last night. I can't see how we can hold the trenches in this weather, and shall not be surprised if the siege is raised.

We get charcoal which will I fear cause many fatal accidents. Swinton of the Artillery was found dead in his bed from its effects, and our doctor and a major of the Greys were nearly killed by it. I shall burn roots as there are plenty to be dug close at hand. Swinfen is sick at Malta. The Heavy Cavalry don't get the clasp for Inkerman, tho' the custom of the service is to give it to all troops present under arms. Lord Lucan has written to Lord Raglan to remonstrate. I would not care about this but something I think ought to be given for Balaklava — not a clasp, but something of which we should be equally proud. Certainly it was more a victory for the enemy than for us, but we could not help those horrid Turks running away, and this the only chance *we* have had, we certainly gave them a licking, and if we deserve the Queen's thanks, we might have some reward more lasting than mere praise. We hear and see in the papers no end of clothing, huts, etc. come out, but where they go we never know, we never see them. If they don't give us any clasp, I fear some will not wear the Crimean medal, as every thieving commissariat man will be able to get the same.

Your most affectionate Brother

Cavalry Camp, Kadikoi   *January 8th 1855*

My dear Father — Yesterday having heard the *Leopard* was arrived I went to Balaklava and found my box in the office, for there is one now established for the reception of parcels. All the things it contained were most acceptable, the boots are extremely warm and comfortable, and if I had any piquet or night duty would be invaluable, they are the *admiration of the camp*, and I expect to find them most useful, the socks my Mother made me fit very well.

We have had some severe weather the last few days, and snow six inches deep; some days however have been beautiful, such a day as one never sees in England, nevertheless very cold. When it snows you can't fancy anything more dreary than it looks; tents and the hills round our camp covered, while in the plain it drifts very deep, and the mountains round for miles look awfully cold. It is the north-east wind that is so bitter here, it drives I suppose over such a vast extent of ice and snow, that when it arrives if at all strong, it is enough to cut one in two. They say that with this wind and the thermometer at zero as it sometimes is, no one could live in tents. I am now, thanks to you, well supplied with everything warm; would that all the men were as well off.

I believe the infantry suffer much and am told that the 63rd, who have been here about six weeks, turned out to parade the other day six men and a corporal, such is the story. The French do everything for us, they make our roads, carry up our shot and shell, and bring down our sick, it is really sad to think that through mismanagement we should come to this, and if this is the way we are to help our Allies, they will soon wish to be without us. Our troops certainly are first-rate, but are useless, and become utterly destroyed for want of proper Staff and management. Where the fault lies is not for us to say, but I do hope time will bring us more competent leaders and a better system. It was the same at the commencement of the Peninsular War, and in time we had a good and efficient General and Staff there; let us hope it may be the same now. People in England seem most anxious about us, and certainly Government have the universal support of the country, and I can tell you it is a great comfort to us to see how everyone at home seems to feel for us, and wish to help us in all we have to endure. A French officer who was in our tent today told us that about 3,000 of their men are daily employed for the English — of course they do not like it, and I should not wonder if much ill feeling was the consequence.

Take for instance our Cavalry: we lost about a third from mismanagement in the field, and for the last six weeks we have been doing the duty of ambulance and commissariat. Of course we have lost many horses through this extra work which is severe, and often when the men come in half-starved with cold and disgusted with such usage, one hears them say they wish they had been shot and put out of the way at once. If we had not been doing the commissariat duty, we should long ago have had our horses under cover, and perhaps men too. We and other regiments have got the glanders, from bad and short feeding, hard work and exposure. We have only ninety-nine horses left, and some of these I hope we may save, as we have got some sheds nearly ready for them. We have had Turkish clothing for about ten days, but this gets wet and freezes on their backs as hard as a board, no wonder they die. They talk of courts of inquiry into the destruction of the horses, and no doubt Raglan & Co. will try and put all the blame on the regimental officers.

Today we were selling poor Campbell's kit and horses, which by the by only brought about £20 each, though costing about £100 or £150, while the clothes etc. brought absurd prices. I was going to tell you in the middle of the bidding we heard a gun fired, but not from Sebastopol — everyone looked up and left off bidding. In the plain we saw three Cossacks and another horseman in front, evidently pursued, all getting through the snow as fast as they could, which was not very fast, as the snow was very deep. Presently the horse of the pursued fell, and the rider ran on foot as fast as possible, but would soon have been overtaken and killed, but for the shell from our batteries, which burst right over the three Cossacks, and made them turn tail. It burst just too soon, or I think would have knocked some of them over — another shell soon followed, which buried itself in the snow close to them. It was a deserter from the enemy's piquet, who on being seen was pursued and had his horse shot under him, but managed to get safe over into our lines. . . .

They told us the winter here does not commence till January and does not end till March. We are much better off here than we should be in Balaklava which is dirty and unhealthy, full of fevers and dead Turks, indeed every house is occupied by officers of one sort or other — and there would be no room for our horses. The valley we are in is sheltered north and south. The whisky in my tin bottle is rather black, but seems none the worse. The cheese very good; don't send too many as they last a long while. What is the tin box full of holes for in which I found my leather socks? I saw a good letter in *The Times* about two more troops for the cavalry, this would be a good thing for me. We are to have six troops only out here, consequently two troops and two captains must stay at the depot. I hope Sidebottom will soon have to come out. We shall want six lieutenants and six cornets out here next year. Our new cornet Sir Edward Hutchinson was formerly a lieutenant in the Inniskillings, and would now have been near senior captain. I know him as we used to see a good deal of him in Dublin, he has a younger brother a captain in the Bays.

Our piquet does not go out now as the snow has been too deep, and since the thaw it has been a regular bog to get to the place. The piquet remains near the outskirts of Kadikoi, and comes in at night. The Cossacks still keep their place, though they look very cold perched up in the snow. I get off much unpleasant and hard duty which saves me many a wetting, and as we have only three subalterns now for duty, it comes very often, still I have much bother and many annoyances as adjutant, but this can't last long.

The snow has brought the wolves from the mountains round our camp.

January 12th. I received your letter of the 23rd today, and have seen the article in that day's paper about Lord Raglan; it is quite true that the most disgraceful mismanagement is destroying our army, but I don't think we shall ever do better with our present Commander-in-Chief. He rode through our camp the other day, the first time we have seen him since we came to the Crimea, except in the action at Balaklava. The *Malacca* not yet in. I see Elliot has his troop so I am now second for mine. Burnand must get Campbell's which will leave me first. I should think McNeile would be much annoyed when he finds how soon he would have got his troop for nothing. When you see Mr Watson tell him, I think when they are talking about medals in the House,* he or some other public-spirited individual might propose something for Balaklava, we feel it very hard to get nothing for the only chance we have had. . . .

Please send me a teacup, you can get strong ones which will not break, made of iron and glazed over with something like china. I don't like metal cups. Also send me the *latest edition* of *Cavalry Regulations* drill-book. I have the brown horse in a stable, and when my own house is finished I shall stable the other two. I made a hut dug out of the ground, but the rain came through, so I could not live in it. I have now nearly made another on a different principle which I hope will answer better. I cannot answer all your questions this time, but when I get into my hut I shall have better opportunity of telling you everything. Kilburn has cut his hand badly so cannot help me, but I have nearly finished the hut without him.

I am very well, I have frequently had brow ague, a very disagreeable malady, but the quinine seems always to take it away. Wonderful stuff is that quinine. This is a very cold day with a cutting north-east wind. The fur cap is very useful, and the boots in the evening to sit in as good as a fire for one's feet. I think we are going to have more snow. The 19th is said to be the day our batteries are to reopen. There was a vigorous sortie the other night; I believe we made 600 prisoners, and the French lost a great number of men. The Cossack deserter I told you about, who was

* House of Commons.

pursued turned out to be a Frenchman who missed the road and got quite close to the piquet when he discovered his mistake. Give Sergeant Jackson 10s for me, I usually do when I am at home, and remember me to him.

Believe me your affectionate Son

Cavalry Camp, Kadikoi   *January 18th 1855*

My dear Father — Having at length exchanged my tent for a hut I am much more comfortable and better able to write to you. The first hut I made was a failure, I dug a hole in the ground and covered it over, but did not give the roof slope enough, so that when the snow melted it all came through. I therefore commenced another, which with the help of my servant I made in nine days, in spite of the weather which was very unpropitious. I did most of it myself, and really it is a very snug little house.

I must tell you how I made it. First I dug a hole in the ground four feet deep, and eight feet broad by nine long, then I made the Cob draw up planks, of which a great number have been landed at Balaklava, and some rafters with which I roofed it over cottage shape, having two gable ends, in one of which I put a window, which I got out of a house in Balaklava. I have not quite finished stopping the holes and cracks, which I am doing with mud, tow and tar, so that very soon it will be quite airtight. I have a stove and chimney which keeps the place very warm, and the ashes scattered on the ground make a good floor, we are allowed charcoal besides which we get wood and roots to burn. I have slept here two nights, and found it very comfortable, and one can write now without the fear of your letter blowing away. The pegs you sent come in very well. The last night I had in my tent was anything but comfortable, for it was frozen so hard I could not shut my door, and when I woke I found the inside of the tent covered with snow which was about an inch thick, also on my bed. I cannot help fancying myself very like Robinson Crusoe with my fur boots etc. and in this primitive house.

I have now been over seven months in a tent, and never slept under a roof but once in that time, which was on the floor in a house at Shumla. I have indeed seen a good deal in this time, and hope to stay here as long as the army and there is anything going on. We hear a report, that in consequence of our losing so many horses, fresh regiments will come out to relieve us, then they say too that men from regiments at home will not volunteer. I hope such may not be the case, for having gone thus far I wish to stay till the war is over, or at all events as long as anything is going on here. . . . How glad I shall be to see home and you all again, and I hope this may be accomplished, perhaps in the present year. Who knows? But if the regiment is ordered home, and others come I shall try through Scarlett to be allowed to remain out. Depend on it, the wisest plan will be to reinforce the present regiments as now intended. The men and officers left have learned that experience, which will take long and cost much for fresh regiments to attain.

The snow has been about eighteen inches deep and in many places deeper. The troops suffer much especially in the trenches, the infantry are on short rations, and what is worse than all, I am sorry to say are deserting in numbers from want and hardship, many I am told have been shot in the attempt, many have blown their brains out, rather than desert or live longer. An officer on piquet last night told one of our officers that two double sentries deserted, that is four men. One fellow deserted from Balaklava, and was met by a Cossack to whose piquet he was running, and shot dead — served him right. I hear our battery opened today, but as the wind is high and contrary, we cannot tell if ours or the enemy are firing. Many talk of storming in a few days, about 30,000 Russians came into the town on sledges a day or two ago, and lots of stores. I hope the place may fall soon, for towards spring we shall certainly have to meet Russia's best troops in numbers. It would be a great thing for us to take the place and recruit our forces, starting with the first sign of spring for Perekop before the enemy could bring down more troops, for I don't believe their present force *could* stand before us in the field, however they must bring a *very very* large force to put us out of this position we are now in.

My Regimental Sergeant-Major, my right-hand man, has got his commission, subject to H.M. approval, it is dated November 5th so he is already senior cornet, and likely to get his lieutenancy for nothing on poor Campbell's vacancy. I think I shall most likely resign the adjutancy to him, being now near the top of my rank, and most probably so soon to get my troop. I hear in a roundabout way that McNeile, though his papers are gone in, intends to try and wait on for the troop, as it will go without purchase. This I can hardly believe he would do, even if he could, I shall be much disgusted if he does. It is bad enough to see Burnand get the troop without purchase, when one considers he is only one month senior to me in the service, and that he was taking his ease at Constantinople while I was going through the fighting and hardest part of the campaign. When on board a ship yesterday an artillery officer told me Watson was gone to Scutari with a fever, but not very bad, that he did not think he would return, as his proper company is in America; great talk here of peace, tho' I don't see why.

I hear Russell, *The Times'* Special Correspondent, offers to bet ten to one of there being peace in two months. I believe we have now about 11,000 effective men here, and between 13,000 and 14,000 sick. The 63rd I heard could *not* muster one man the other day. It is dreadful to see the poor wretches brought from the front, they come down on our horses wrapped in their blankets on the coldest days, in all the snow; many have frostbitten feet and are otherwise ill, perhaps they have never been on a horse before. You see them with their feet, just with a bit of rag round them. Sometimes the horses fall in the snow and tumble on them, many seem almost senseless, too ill to hold the reins, and fall off insensible on the way, perhaps frostbitten, and require to be rubbed with snow, many cannot stand and are *held* on the saddle. A sergeant was found the other day still in the saddle, on his arrival at Balaklava, but quite dead. Two days ago one of our horses brought a man into our camp quite insensible, he had strayed from the rest; and the horse came to his own camp, the man was wounded and very ill, and we put him in our hospital. It is such treatment as this that causes men to desert and commit suicide, for the former crime if taken they must be shot.

I put no stamps on my letters as none can now be bought; they say the letters go as well if 3d is paid the end of the journey. I see Lord Grey proposes to make non-commissioned officers captains at once; this would be most unfair on all officers of a junior rank. Our lines are now so close to the enemy that one may almost pitch a stone into the town. The sentries are so near that they are always firing at each other. I expect the places the enemy have left are well mined for us. People here don't seem to object so strongly to the Foreign Legion as in England. I must say I think it shows rather unnecessary misgivings on the part of the Government when one sees how vigorously enlistment is going on. They will certainly require considerable trial ere the same reliance can be placed in a new body as would be in British troops.

My brown horse has been in a stable some days but has conducted himself so badly by eating all the boards and rafters within his reach, that the officer to whom the stable belonged is going to turn him out. I am making a stable of my old hut and shall get all three in, in a day or two. Some rascal stole my rug off Chance the other day — a common practice here — I was obliged to give him my waterproof rug off my bed in consequence. The huts are come, but few can be taken to the front for want of transport, some are up near Balaklava. I suppose many will be useless. I am sorry to hear the poor are so badly off. How are they about us? Ours tho' poor always seem contented. I hear McMahon is stopped on his way to England very ill, they say he is likely to leave, perhaps Thompson may get the regiment. Many of our men wounded at Balaklava are useless for further service, and must go home. Our men are well off now for warm clothing, most have two greatcoats and they require it, not only for the day, but for night covering.

I think the present system of promoting Staff officers and officers commanding regiments for any action is most unfair, while regimental officers who generally are in much more danger and fighting get nothing. Major Lowe of the 4th Light Dragoons got brevet rank for killing so many men at Balaklava, he himself says it is most absurd, but that article in *The Times* did it for him. It is not the duty of an officer to see how many he can finish. Lowe was not the only one. I know several officers who killed four or five men that day in self-defence. Please send some ground coffee. We have had sheepskin coats given us with wool inside, they are very warm. The greatest luxury one gets here is bread, which is made in the town by a Frenchman and very good, 2s a loaf. There is only one shop and the bread is seized as it is drawn out of the oven — and the money gladly paid for it; the rush and crowd to get it is incredible.

We have made about fifty yards of stables, having dug down

about six feet, built up a wall in front and roofed it over, of course it is but rough work, as we have had no assistance, the wet comes through now it is thawing. I fear the few horses we shall have left will be little use in the spring. The men too are nearly broken down and worn out. We cannot expect to see spring weather till the middle or end of April. . . .

Your most affectionate Son

Cavalry Camp, Kadikoi   *January 22nd 1855*

My dear Father — Having written so lately I have not much to tell you. We don't seem to progress with the siege at all. There is a report that we cannot take this side and are going round to the other; but if true we must have a larger force to do it, as we should certainly be obliged to draw on supplies from Balaklava. Our papers which come very irregularly seem most bitter against Lord Raglan, I thought his promotion would be found to be premature, he got it dated from the day of a bloody battle, which would not have taken place but for his want of care and foresight. . . .

Fitzgerald, our new cornet, does not wish to take the adjutancy, as he says he is not capable of performing its duties. Of course a new man must soon be appointed, as they cannot stop my promotion on this account. I have just been speaking to General Scarlett, and he says if he had anything to do with it, he would not recommend any officer who had been away sick so long, he would recommend those who had been all the time with the regiment. I wish this were done: I should then get my troop for nothing. McNeile has arrived in England. There is in *Blackwood's Magazine* an article entitled 'The History of the Campaign' rather well told, except the action at Balaklava, which is totally misrepresented, and I think I must write and contradict it. It was in orders the other night that we are to have the new dress in the April issue of clothing, and officers are recommended to write home for theirs directly, I shall not do so yet. My boots, gloves and cap have been most comfortable during the late cold. The snow has nearly all gone, they say it never lasts long here. Fisher, 4th D.G., has come back from Scutari looking very well. Has Gobbey sent my regimental trousers yet? My hut is very warm and comfortable. Inglis has bought a wood house from Constantinople for about £50 putting it up and all — mine cost nothing — and is much warmer than his. We very seldom get fresh meat now, about once or twice in a fortnight. Many men cannot bear the salt beef and pork. The latter is pretty good cold, but of the former a little goes a long way, very salt and strong, no fat, etc., often only half-cooked from the state of the weather and want of wood, many men prefer going without it. We have sent away numbers from bad legs and feet, consequent on cold and wet, and salt provisions. All the shop people in Balaklava are to turn out in a day or two to make room for the commissariat, so I suppose then we shall be as bad off as ever, and the boxes now on the road will be doubly acceptable.

Your affectionate Son

Cavalry Camp, Kadikoi   *February 2nd 1855*
My dear Father — Edward Bradshaw left me yesterday — I find I was mistaken in supposing him to be John Bradshaw; what a nice little fellow he is, his ship was to sail this morning to the fleet, and thence to England. He took a Cossack lance and whip home for me — the same I got at the reconnaissance party. I gave him a queer brass thing which he must show you — I got it off a sergeant of Hussars killed at Balaklava — he also took home some buttons etc. He went to the front with some infantry friend of his, and slept in a tent, last night he dined with me in camp, and then went back to his ship, he seems very well and happy.

I got my box off the *Malacca*, and presume it is the one Aunt Jane so kindly sent, I am really now well stocked with provisions. I fear I shall not have time to write and thank Aunt by this mail, but will do so by the next. I do not think I shall want a box every fortnight, we are really now living in comparative luxury, being so near the ships, and with so many parcels.* I fear my last letter was late for the mail, but Thompson would keep the orderly till past the time. I dare say the acquaintance of naval officers might be of use to me, they are always very civil to officers. If I knew any captain well I might get a sack of coals, for firewood is very scarce, and one has to collect wood and dry roots to burn. I have been

* Indignation at home transformed the Crimean supply situation and soon more than was needed — or wanted — was dispatched.

thinking of writing to Watson, but most likely you have heard of him before this — if not you can write in my name to Doctor O'Flaherty at Scutari Hospital, and he will tell you all about him, he is a very nice kind man, this would not be losing time. Our doctor tried to get medicines here the other day, but as usual there was none but opium to be had — so the men must go without. It is just the same with the horses.

The Grand Dukes are said to have arrived with reinforcements. A large sortie was made yesterday between the English and French lines, they got the crossfire and their officers could not persuade them to come on, but they went back (an officer of the 50th told us) tumbling one over the other and roaring most furiously. They say there are now 90,000 in and round Sebastopol, and a general action is daily expected, some think it will be a sortie made straight at our lines and camp before the town. Sir Colin Campbell who has command here, expects an attack on Balaklava. He seems I think one of the best officers we have. He expects they will not cross the plain, because of our batteries, but will come from Kamara at night under the foot of the mountains, and make a dash at our extreme right at daybreak, perhaps with about 50,000 men; if they attempt it there will be a sharp affair. We are ready to turn out at daybreak and dusk daily about 250 cavalry, we should doubtless be engaged. Balaklava and its stores would be a good prize now, but they won't get in as long as any of us are left, and the Marines and Highlanders will make a good stand no doubt. The railway is begun. Weather fair, but looks like rain.

Your affectionate Son

7

Bombardment of Sebastopol

Cavalry Camp, Kadikoi   *February 3rd 1855*
My dear Father — I got your letter of January 18th yesterday. I dined and slept last night at the General's, some time since I slept under a house, and a few months ago I don't suppose I should have passed a very good night wrapped in some cloaks on the floor, but I can sleep anywhere now. I am going to board the inside of my hut, for it is four feet under ground, and the sides are always damp, and I have never been quite well since I came into it, having had sore throat and low fever, nothing serious, only I can't shake it off; no doubt when boarded it will be all right. The Russians have not paid us a visit here yet, we are getting up a new battery for them at the entrance of Balaklava, one gun is already in position. We are pretty strong now too, having the 93rd, 42nd and 79th Highlanders, some Marines, some Rifles, and the 14th and 39th and 71st just come, the two last about 800 strong. They are all in huts round Balaklava, so no doubt will keep in good health. Then there are Turks besides, so I expect the Russians will catch it, if they come here.

Did you see Hampton's father had been writing to *The Times*, and now *Punch* has taken it up? Of course his son gets much laughed at, though it is not his fault. What nonsense *The Times* prints in the shape of letters etc. from the Crimea and half of them are false. Did you see the article on the 17th about the Cavalry? They say that the French and our Artillery do not lose their horses. This is false, for I know the French 6th Dragoons lost over seventy horses in one week. They want to make out it is want of care that causes our loss, but will find it hard to establish this fact. I shall be very glad of some bacon in some of my boxes, this is always useful.

I think I see the commencement of a slight improvement in affairs here. Some of the patriotic fund has arrived. The navvies are hard at work, but would not work yesterday (Sunday) though the soldiers set them the example. They are much disgusted at finding themselves subject to military law, and they don't like the commissariat, so their own steamers are to keep them supplied with food while here.

Believe me your affectionate Son

Cavalry Camp, Kadikoi   *February 7th 1855*
My dear Caroline — The Russians are firing a good deal tonight, they have been very angry and uneasy all day, if one may judge from the noise they have been making. You see as yet they have not paid us a visit here, perhaps they are waiting till there is no moon, and their evil deeds can not be so easily seen. A soldier remarked the other day, he thought the reason they came at night, was they were so ugly, they did not like to show by daylight. We are ready every evening to turn out during the night. If they come I hope it will be by day, for cavalry working by night is very awkward, as we have found more than once. I see we have got a new vet. He is son of a man who was a long time in the regiment. Our horses are improving, what are left (about sixty) and I hope we shall save these. The snow still remains on the hills. Aunt Jane's box was most acceptable, and a very good selection. The railway is commenced, and the navvies work well, it does one good to see them. Did you hear that when Dundas sailed the other day, he saluted Lyons with the signal, 'May success attend you.' He answered 'May *hanging* await you' the signal having by mistake been hoisted wrong, and '*hanging*' substituted for 'happiness', this is no *shave*, but a fact.

The men are much better clothed now, and much good has been done by '*The Times* fund' and the others are arriving. Our men have had cabbage (preserved), a very good thing for them, and the sick have had several comforts from this fund. The sickness in the cavalry, and also much in the infantry is scurvy, and bad legs and feet, from salt meat, even with the officers if one gets a knock or a cut, it will not heal for some time, and we live now better than the men can. We have over seventy men sick at Scutari, and have had in all about sixty deaths since we came out. I hear the French have been fifteen days without hay, and sometimes we have given them a day's forage for their army, so you see they are not always well off.

February 9th. I hear there are 30,000 Russians at Tchorgun, a village just in the hills, and about four miles from this. The troops here and at Balaklava are often turned out at night, and are always ready. They say there is to be a reconnaissance in a day or two. The 20th is the day named for our batteries to open, and the last shave is that 25,000 French are to be landed somewhere in the harbour close to the town. We hear the enemy lost 35,000 out of 60,000 in the snow coming from Odessa. I am much better now, nearly all right again.

Your affectionate Brother

Cavalry Camp, Kadikoi   *February 16th 1855*

My dear Father — The box which was shipped on board the *Esk*, and transferred to the *Clyde* reached me on the 12th, everything it contained is most useful. I fear the kettle will not stand camp fires long, the handle and spout being put on with solder. Nothing new here, they say a flying division with 50,000 men under General Bosquet is going up the country when the weather is finer. One English division with them. I believe the object is to drive the Russians back on the Turks. It is also stated that Sebastopol can never be taken till invested. A large number of French moved up yesterday towards the right, and some say they are determined to carry the round tower, and its mud batteries at any cost, until then nothing can be done. They are getting on fast with the railway. To the great delight of the Division Lord Lucan has been sent home by Lord Raglan. I believe they had some quarrel about the October 25th business, at all events Lord Lucan resigned in great wrath, and declares he will show Lord Raglan up when he gets home.

We have been in quite a sea of mud again, with occasional snow-storms, but the last few days have been fine, and the ground is drying nicely. Many of the huts are put up, and a considerable number are up at the front. Fancy the way things are managed, all the huts are landed without order, and are issued just as applied for, a piece of one and a piece of another, fortunately they are all one size. Instead of marking each hut and giving it out entire, of course a number will be found incomplete at the end, it is well there are so many. I have not yet got my box by *Royal Albert*. Yesterday we had a strong sirocco wind, the heat of which was just like a blast from a furnace. When you send again please put in some pieces of whipcord. Do not send too many boxes; I am well supplied now, and if we had to move I don't know what I should do. I yesterday saw a large number of French troops marching up, and all along their march were groups of four, five, or six men, quite tired out by their loads, and fast asleep. So much for the croakings of our Special Correspondent; don't you remember when we were in Devna what a fuss he made about the number of English who used to fall out when marching in that hot sun. . . .

I have not seen any huts for officers except for colonels of regiments — we never expect any advantages of this sort. In fact you can never rely on any public property said to be for the use of officers; these latter are a very minor consideration. Even in Government tents, one is likely to be turned out at any time, and put some half-dozen into one, so that there is no room to lie comfortably. Having been thus treated once, I shall get a tent of my own from Constantinople, if we go up the country this year.

Your affectionate Son

Cavalry Camp, Kadikoi   *February 19th 1855*

My dear Mother — You will be glad to hear I have got my box with the waterproof boots, they are none too large, but will do nicely. I can wear them with one pair of *thick* socks on. I believe you thought I could get three or four pairs into them, they will be very useful good boots for wet weather and riding. Runciman should have sent hunting spurs with them instead of putting in boxes, but it does not matter.

We hear the Russians attacked Eupatoria, and got beaten, no doubt you will hear of this nearly as soon as we did. I hear 16,000 French are gone up the country, but tho' on the spot it is curious how difficult it is to get at the truth. They say the enemy is very badly off up the country. We have had beautiful weather for a week or more, though with cold winds, there is no weather that hurts the soldier so much as wet. The ground is nearly dry, and I think on the whole things look better. I think this year it will be our object to keep a large army up the country to communicate with Eupatoria, and so cut off the garrison of Sebastopol, and fight any army before it arrives before the town.

I have kept the green and red mittens, who made them? I have kept one of the knitted jersies, and given Kilburn one, and Burnand asked for the other. The men have got the mittens etc., if they had been three months earlier, they would have been more useful. . . .

Believe me your affectionate Son

Cavalry Camp, Kadikoi   *February 23rd 1855*

My dear Father — Everyone here for the last two days has been talking about General Forray,* whom we hear has been detected communicating with Menschikoff for a long time past. I hear that when brought before Canrobert the latter was so angry, he would have run him through, but was prevented. I believe he is sent home in chains to be shot, his reason is said to be spite against Canrobert, who got the command over his head. I fear it will turn out to be true. A paymaster sergeant of a Zouave regiment who speaks a little English, told our non-commissioned officers yesterday it was quite true.

On the evening of the 19th all the cavalry were ordered to turn out at twelve at night, no one knew why. When we mounted it was a *fine mild* night, but a few drops of rain warned me to put on my waterproof coat. We remained on parade till 2 a.m. when it had become colder, the night was so dark you could not see your own hand, but at two we marched off, the wind now north-east, the coldest quarter, blew very strong, and snow began to fall. It was a reconnaissance going, which was intended to surprise the enemy. When it began to snow the French would not go on; and the A.D.C. sent by Lord Raglan to tell us lost his way and never found us. Well on we went for about ten yards, and then quarter of an hour halt, the guns in front constantly sticking in the mud, and on the wretched uneven roads by Kadikoi. At last we reached the plain, and turned to our right under our batteries, then after a time halted for some of the party who had lost their way. The cold was more intense than I ever felt it, and never did I suffer so much as that night. The wind very high and from the coldest point, blew snow,

* General E. F. Forey was the commander of the French 4th Division.

hail and lumps of ice into our faces. The horses could hardly be made to face it, and whenever we halted all turned round like weather cocks.

At last morning broke, and we found ourselves near Kamara, not a Frenchman to be seen. Again we stood still for an hour or two while the Highlanders went to the front. The enemy now showed in numbers on a hill some way off. Presently up came the French, as they heard we had got into a scrape, and came to get us out; we then all retired. Many of the men got their ears frozen. I fortunately discovered one of Halford's a quarter-frozen, the other beginning, some snow brought them to life again, but frozen parts always burst afterwards. The ice hung from our eyebrows and lashes, and those who had beards and moustaches found them one solid lump of ice. I think the reason my ears did not freeze was from a natural propensity they have to stick close to my head. I fortunately had a very thick pea-jacket on, or I should have been half-frozen. It was a pity the weather came on so bad, as we had quite surprised the enemy, and should have walked into them nicely.

The fever and diarrhoea I had were of course much worse for we were out ten hours, and I have been in bed ever since. I am better today and sitting up, but very weak, as I may only eat portable soup, it is lucky I have plenty of it. The snow is not gone and it is very cold. I hope a few days will put me all right again. Did ever any of my letters reach you open, as I hear some have done I have sent to other people?

Your affectionate Son

Cavalry Camp, Kadikoi   *February 26th 1855*
My dear Father — I am still in bed and not much better, though the fever is going, still I can't get rid of the diarrhoea, which has made me very weak, especially as I eat nothing but portable soup and a bit of toast a day. It is the common Crimean complaint. I get up for two or three hours every day. The doctors talk of sending me on board ship for a sail to the Bosphorus or elsewhere, which would I think do me good, but they make so much delay and difficulty about these things that I hardly expect to get away. I have got another box, I suppose by the *Cluster*, but I have so much already I have not unpacked it. I believe it is certain we stay out

here, and are to be reinforced the beginning of April. The report about General Forrey turned out false, though we were informed of it by so many Frenchmen. I hear the French got a bad licking the other night attacking a battery somewhere, they were betrayed and the enemy let them come on, and then fell on them with much larger numbers. They were driven back and they say lost 500 Zouaves, the attacking regiment. Their supports are said to have behaved badly and made a bolt for it. The Zouaves got into the battery and ditch before the enemy fired. The weather has been cold and frosty since I wrote last. McNeile is going to leave the service, but they won't let him sell till they can appoint a successor, so he must join the depot for a time. I found the leather jacket both warm and comfortable. I have not worn the drawers.

Your affectionate Son

The Walmer Castle, *Balaklava**   *March 8th 1855*

My dear Father — Here I am still the same, not getting on quite as fast as I might; had I been sent for a sea-trip for the same time, no doubt I should be better but they won't allow this. The harbour is crammed with ships as tight as they can be packed, and the stench of harbour and town is horrible. Not content with this they put bad cases of typhus fever with us, as I told you an officer died, and now they have brought another who I fear can't live long, for he is quite insensible, and screams and roars day and night like a wild animal. All our cabins are close together, and last night none of us got any sleep: this morning the captain and officers on board, and a captain of another ship, went to Captain Christie the naval agent, who promised us to see to it. This unfortunate man disturbs everyone in the ships near, it is too bad crowding us up like this.

I was ashore yesterday, the weather is warm as May and very fine. The railroad is getting on, and I think on the whole things seem improving much. I fear the heat will cause sad disease, there is so much putrid flesh about, fresh graveyards where lie sometimes half, sometimes nearly an acre of Turks and of English, and the former only a few inches under ground packed as close as possible. All the nurses here are sick. The other day I saw the sister of the Duchess of Somerset, one of the head nurses, they say she is *quite*

* He had been sent on board for ten days' leave and convalescence.

cracked, she seems very odd. I met a doctor yesterday just up from Scutari, and asked him if he knew Watson; he said he did and described him, telling me he was getting about again nicely.

I can't think why they crowd this place so with ships, should a fire occur they can't possibly escape, and some are full of shell and powder and the sailors often drunk, I fear some accident will happen. There seems no management whatever. Since I came on board the ship has discharged *all* her cargo, and is now taking it *all* in again, this is not a single case, there are shiploads of warm clothes going home again. For this ship alone the Government pay £10,000 a year, half of which the owner Mr Green gets, clear of all expenses. Great news or shaves here the last two days. Nicholas is stated to be dead on the best authority, everyone believes it, *I* should like to see it in the papers first. Then we hear Parliament is dissolved, riots in London, etc. They say we are to commence firing in a few days, but not going to storm. Our advanced trenches are already armed. I can't write very well, my hand being unsteady and pen bad.

Lord Lucan has left this some time. Some think much of Cardigan, I am not quite so well satisfied with him. He nearly got into a similar trap as Balaklava in Bulgaria, before Alma. When reconnoitring he saw some Cossacks, would have charged them *up a hill*, but was fortunately ordered not. At the top were strong columns of infantry, and a lot of cavalry, and his men would have been cut to pieces. He and Lucan were always fighting. I don't care about my old coatee, more than that if the men get them and we have to go into action in the old ones, the officers will be unpleasantly conspicuous. . . .

Your affectionate Son

Cavalry Camp, Kadikoi   *March 15th 1855*

My dear Joseph — By a letter I have just received from Caroline I hear you are sending me out some tobacco, for which thanks. Fisher, 4th D.G., gave me some Turkish tobacco today; I don't like Cavendish, it is too strong, and good cigars are not to be had, nor is Turkish tobacco except at Constantinople, so now I am set up for a time. It is a great comfort here, and I think good Turkish the pleasantest thing I ever smoked. I came from my ship last

Monday (12th); I am not at all well and can't get right. The General wants to get me off for a trip in some ship, I should like it much, but I don't suppose I should be let go, so must try and get here. I will not go down to that horrid harbour again, I shall stay on and hope soon to get right again. The ship I was on was also used for typhus fever patients, raving mad, so of course there was no sleeping, and a very good chance of getting the fever, which I am sorry to say is already beginning to do its work here. The winter is beginning to tell on me, I have rheumatism in my legs and arms, but should not care a pin about this if I could get well in other ways. The last year has taken a good deal out of me and I feel to want strength now to stand the summer.

There was a *sharp fight* last night with the French, no satisfactory results. I rode to the front today, our sailors were making beautiful practice at a new earthwork, not a shell missed and the distance was immense. We are running our saps so close in now, that soon there must be an infernal row, the enemy throw up fresh works well and quickly. It is quite disgusting to look clean into the town and harbour, and see all close under you, and yet we can't get it. Many here think the Chiefs have their hands tied and we are not trying to take the place. The railway gets on like smoke, and when they get up the hill (which they nearly are now) it will soon be done.

How do you get on with the Militia, and how do you like it? Remember they now play a very important part in the war, and I hope the officers will do their best. McNeile tells me the Militia in the north of Ireland are either old fools or boys, but whatever they may be, I think *one* county can turn out something worth having. Let me know what you think of them. When you are encamped, I advise you to get some amusement if possible, and books too, otherwise you will find camp life very stupid. I have always found too, that knowing my duty well, or badly, makes just the difference of comfort or the reverse in one's life.

The morning after I came back we had an alarm, the Russians came in force into the plain, we saddled, the infantry got into their trenches, and we thought *now for it*. I examined my pistols etc. and got ready for the fray, but like two dogs we each showed our teeth, but did not wish to fight, so they went back. I was precious glad of it, being so weak, I could hardly have cut a flea in half. It seemed a working party of ours frightened them, as they thought we were coming on to attack them. Next time we have a chance, I hope please the pigs, to have a regular go in, if one could get mentioned in dispatches it would be a grand thing. I hear Cardigan is coming to command us, I hope not, I doubt his discretion. I am sorry you have been seedy, but hope now you will get all right again. I know where are the hoofs of a Cossack horse on the plains killed at Balaklava. They are curiously shod, I think of getting them, and sending them home to be polished. Tell me if you have any hunting.

Your affectionate Brother

Cavalry Camp, Kadikoi   *March 16th 1855*
My dear Father — My hut is now crammed with clothes and eatables. Kilburn declares I have enough to feed me all the summer and does not know whatever we shall do with more boxes. You had better not send more now, for we shall be moving before I can finish what I have got. The weather is beautiful, quite hot in the middle of the day. I have had a visit from Campbell, lieutenant of the *Leander*, his ship is in Balaklava, being a sailing vessel she is no use outside. He asked me to come and dine with him. I was delighted to see confirmed by the *Sun*, the evening of the day you wrote, the news of the death of Nicholas. Surely this will alter the aspect of affairs. I am rather better, and try to ride off my indisposition; yesterday I was at the front, there certainly are an enormous quantity of French here, there can't be far under 100,000 men. Our soldiers were making beautiful practice at a new earthwork at a great range, not one shell missed while I was there. The Zouaves (the best fighting men the French have) say they will not attack again unless supported by English troops, they can't trust their own. The other night the Marines in support of the Zouaves *ran away*, and the former seeing this sent a volley into them, killing many.

We have had races here, a very pretty sight so many different uniforms. The *Illustrated* man was sketching, and said he had never had so pretty a subject. . . . I met Lord Raglan yesterday, he is grown quite fat and red in the face, and looks quite jolly. Lord Lucan I see demands a court-martial, he is a clever fellow, and I should not wonder if he gets the best of it. He was however wrong, for instead of *following* the enemy 'to try and *prevent* their *carrying off the guns*' as the order said, he charged smack into the whole Russian army. Poor Nolan I expect was much to blame. I hear we are to go to Scutari to meet our drafts. If you think there is no chance of peace and of our return home, I must have a pack saddle sent out, for we may soon be on the march now. Love to all.

Your affectionate Son

The ground is covered with snowdrops, crocuses and small wild hyacinths in bloom.

Cavalry Camp, Kadikoi   *March 23rd 1855*
My dear Father — There does not seem to be much chance of peace, indeed I hope not till this place falls. We hear Menschikoff is dead. The Russians are said to be rather panic-struck. They have finished a splendid fortification on the north side of the harbour, said to be a most perfect piece of work. I am better, but still so weak. I ride about and take exercise but can't get strong.

Yesterday I was at the front, the enemy was firing but little, we were peppering them rather more than usual. While I was there we fired two mortars near the piquet house, a new battery. It is most curious to see the operations, it takes a long time to place the mortar, they were firing 13-inch shells. One shell is as much as two men can lift into the mortar, when suspended by a rope to a stick, a man has hold of each end of the stick, so you may fancy the weight. Presently you see this enormous thing flung into the air like a cricket ball, with tremendous force; you see it rise till it gets clean out of sight, and then you see it explode near or at the object. They were firing over 2,700 yards, and making good practice. They did not shell us in return as we expected they would. There was a sharp engagement last night, we lost some men and the Russians a great number, they are twice as much afraid of us as they are of the French.

Our horses have had the mange very badly, mine are quite well, and very fresh, the brown horse looks much better than I expected. I tie them up outside all day and take them in at night. As soon as the Cob is untied he bundles off to the stable alone as hard as he can go, and disappears like a rabbit in his underground stable. I have had offers for Chance, but won't sell, horses are very dear here now. . . .

I am sorry Cardigan is to have command of the cavalry. In no one instance has he proved himself a good commander. The speech he is said to have made about the '7th and last Earl of Cardigan' was I expect made for him in England, at least I have not heard that any of his brigade ever heard of this speech. The ham you sent I had cooked on board ship, it is excellent and will last me for breakfast for some time.

Your affectionate Son

Cavalry Camp, Kadikoi   *Monday 6 a.m., March 26th 1855*

My dear Mother — Our rest was disturbed this morning at three by an order to be ready to turn out at 4.30. — what for we don't know, for as yet we can see or hear nothing unusual, though it is light, so I just write you a line tho' I have not much to say. The *Himalaya* was off the harbour Saturday night; I suppose she will land her troops today, and I shall no doubt soon get my box. She cannot come into harbour, the ships are so numerous and she is so long. We don't expect much peace till Sebastopol falls, which will I fear be a long time first. The place seems to get stronger and apparently we are not making much progress, however I suppose in time fall it must.

On the night of the 22nd there was a great sortie, you will see our loss in the paper. An Albanian, a very brave fellow who has led most of the sorties was killed; he fired into our powder magazine to blow it up, but failed or he must have been blown up with it. The Russians suffered severely and are supposed to have lost 1,000 men. On the 23rd there was an armistice for two hours to bury the dead, which was extended to three hours, not being long enough time. The sight was a curious one, close to the round towers the Russians had very large parties to carry off the dead. English, French and Russian were all mixed up together, talking as friendly as possible, each picking out their dead, the men exchanged tobacco, snuff, etc., and our men gave the Russians some grog which they did not like. The officers were all in deep mourning for the Emperor, and talking to our officers one asked, 'When we were going away', and was answered 'Never', so he said we should never take the place. Another said the siege was a great nuisance, and they inside were tired of it, supposed we were tired too, on which the English officer said 'It certainly was rather a bore.' Another was offered a cigar which he declined, saying he had taken to smoking pipes now as they could not get cigars in Sebastopol. The officers are very coarse-looking fellows. The men looked well but dirty.

When the time was nearly over both parties began to withdraw; soon after down came the flags and the fire again opened, bullets and shot and shell hissing and rattling about on both sides. War is a curious thing. General Jones got a good view of the fortifications, as they were *close* to the Malakoff Tower. No doubt he made good use of his time. I unfortunately got there just as the flags went down, not knowing of the armistice in time, I hope at the next I may be there, there are sure to be more, we are now so close severe engagements take place almost every night.

I am getting rather stronger but very slowly. The firelighters are most useful, lately it has been so warm I have not had much fire. I hope my coatee will be made *loose*, for everyone seems grown stout here, men and officers. . . . You would be surprised to see how we have improved in our cooking, a roast leg of mutton would astonish you or a turkey which are to be had sometimes. We make ovens of the large tins the preserved potatoes come in, knock out one end, put it on stones, and a fire underneath. They answer admirably, will bake meat or rice pudding well. Some keep chicken for fresh eggs and have regular hen roosts. Round our huts and tents many have small gardens, with juniper trees, snowdrops and crocuses. If I had thought of it in time I would have got some mustard and cress seed, a few days of this sun would grow it, any green of this kind would be very wholesome. Lord Raglan on seeing some *flowers* round a hut said, yes it was very well but he should have had *cabbages* instead; I know not where he would have got them, perhaps he thinks the preserved cabbage would grow. Kilburn makes a good cook in a plain way, you may fancy it enough to look after me and three horses and cook too, the horses having a mile to go to water.

I can't think what is up that makes us ready to turn out, it is evidently something sudden, all as yet seems quiet. I send some violets from the heights of Inkerman, they were very sweet when I picked them. They are from the very spot where the Guards suffered so much, plenty of shot and shell were all about them.

Your affectionate Son

Cavalry Camp, Kadikoi   *March 30th 1855*

My dear Father — Your letters seem to arrive far more regularly than mine, there are two letters a week and I always get one; the last, dated the 16th, arrived yesterday. The *Himalaya* box came today, everything safe, the butter jar had a crack, I suppose from the fall, but was none the worse. I hear the *Himalaya* is gone to Alexandria. A letter from Henley says our draft was to start some time ago, so I suppose they are now on the sea, 140 horses, seventy-four men, Bolton and Sidebottom. The latter we had written to, telling him to bring out plenty of things; we hear he has got enough to fill a small ship and intends to give us a swell breakfast or dinner on his arrival. This was one of his weaknesses at home, he used to have great lunch parties, and everything most expensive, whether in season or not, the more it cost him the better he liked it, and I suppose he never got off under £40. It will be immense fun to see him arrive, but I doubt his seeing us through the summer.

The Chiefs here are in much alarm expecting an attack on Balaklava. More than once it was to come off on a certain night they had got '*certain information*'. Every precaution has been taken, new batteries made, parapets heightened, ditches deepened. We saddle and get ready for a turnout every day before daylight, as that is the most favourite time for an attack. The Infantry are under arms from 3 a.m. till daylight, so I hope we shall not be caught off the alert. I suppose it will come at last, and when it does it will be rough work. One night one is woke up by an order to saddle, another to strengthen the piquet, or some other message which has the effect of stirring me out, being adjutant. Though I sleep through the heaviest firing in front, yet the least unusual stir, or musket fired at Kadikoi is sure to rouse me. We have been making fine practice with our 13-inch mortar lately. They say we open fire again next week. The French are sapping steadily on, and I suppose will in time reach the round tower. They are now close to a fort near it which has done us much harm. Our piquet patrols the plain all night, not very safe or pleasant work when quite dark. We now have a moon, which is all in our favour. I am glad you called on McMahon, he seems a good sort of fellow, I dare say we shall like him.

The electric telegraph is complete from Balaklava, Kadikoi, headquarters and the right and left attack. The railway works all right, it must astonish the Russians to hear the engines puffing, and shows them that we are never all asleep. The trucks run for about two miles out of Balaklava, and much more of the line is near finished. Lime is being thrown all over the camp but not in sufficient quantities as yet. The weather has been very hot, and turbans are coming into use again, the summer will be intensely hot if we may judge by March. There is no grass, and not a tree to take off the glare. The climate is very changeable. The graveyards begin to smell most horribly, and you must pass two to get into Balaklava from here. The condition of the army is wonderfully improved this summer, and the campaign may be said to have recommenced in earnest. I am surprised we have not been attacked before this by fresh reinforcements. The enemy has lost his best director, the Emperor, and the departure of Menschikoff who has so well defended Sebastopol is in our favour. There is a lime-kiln in front which the enemy are supposed to take for the steam of the railway terminus, and they have been wasting immense quantities of shell at it.

General Simpson seems to have quite superseded Lord Raglan, he gives what orders he likes, one is that we shall all wear swords, and he is said to threaten the use of the razor again. It is evident he has not spent either last summer or winter exposed to this climate, or these absurd orders would not have appeared, if this is all he came out for he had better have been kept at home. Even French officers do not wear swords off duty. We have had lots of races at the different divisions to which Lord Raglan has subscribed. The French had some the other day, the attempt at a hurdle race was very fine. I am very well again, but not quite as strong as this time last year.

I have only just had a shine over Lord Lucan's evidence, there seem to be several inaccuracies in it. Burton has written to *The Times* to deny ever having made such a statement to Lord Lucan, he was very angry about it. I am not sorry for his (Lord Lucan's) trouble, he was always *down* on this regiment. He says the 4th lost most men; this is not true, we have lost most, over seventy men having died since we came out. We are now told it is likely our clothing will not be changed *this year*. It is too bad making us get clothes and then not wanting them, nor is it fair to make the soldier pay for his clothes. One suit given every two years is absurd on service where men must often sleep on the ground in them. . . . Lucan, as you say, lost a good opportunity of striking a blow with the Light Brigade after our charge. Of course *we* were broken and took some time to reform, expecting another attack we did not pursue far. Had the Light Brigade charged the retreating column in their flight, they must have been nearly annihilated, for in their flight they offer little resistance. As for this having anything to do with the subsequent disastrous charge, it is absurd, and the report of jealousy between the different branches of the service, which was suggested by *The Times* as the cause of the disaster, is perfectly unfounded.

Your affectionate Son

Our new adjutant is coming out directly. The Photograph man* has taken a picture of our camp, the officers and horses standing about, my hut does not come in well. He has also taken me and my horse (in fighting costume) and Kilburn, the latter likeness is excellent, when I can I will tell you where to go in London for copies, as many as you please at 5s each.

March 31st. General Scarlett is off to England by this mail and will arrive as soon as this letter, and Elliot too. Mrs Scarlett is very ill. Lord Raglan will not accept his resignation, but has given him leave, this shows he thinks much of him. I have just heard on good authority, we commence the bombardment on Tuesday April 3rd.

Cavalry Camp, Kadikoi   *April 3rd 1855*

My dear Caroline — Everyone here is talking about peace, indeed I heard some Staff officers today at the Adjutant-General's office say that everything is settled. I believe that we were to have opened fire this week, but yesterday two shots went smack through the parapet of our twenty-one-gun battery, showing that it is not sufficiently strong, so another week must be spent as the last have

* Roger Fenton. See Plates 4, 6, 7, 8, 12.

been. Campbell and 300 men of the *Leander* went to the front yesterday. I tried to see him yesterday but could not succeed. . . . I went into some of the batteries today at the front. In the ravines near these batteries, the Russian cannon ball and shell are so thickly strewn, you cannot help walking on them. I cannot tell why we do not fire on the town and unearth the enemy — they could smash the whole place — but Lord Raglan will not allow it. On our right attack we were firing a good deal, and the practice on both sides was capital. It is hot work now in our advanced trenches; if a man shows his head now for a moment, he is sure to have a bullet through it. The Russian camp outside seems increasing, so I should not wonder at some fresh attempt to raise the siege. The number of new batteries is extraordinary, and they are still hard at work; they have more guns than we have, but are said to be short of ammunition and artillery men. Time will show. Scarlett left in the *City of London* for Malta last night. Remember me to Miss Bishop. Love to all.

Your affectionate Brother

We are to get the clasp for Inkerman, and so we ought.

Cavalry Camp, Kadikoi   *Easter Monday April 9th 1855*

My dear Father — If the good people have had such a day as we have, I fear Easter Monday will not be much of a holiday for them. It has been raining hard since yesterday afternoon, consequently we are quite in mud again, and it makes one recollect strongly the almost forgotten wretched November and December days. My hut is not very waterproof after the late fine warm weather, which we have enjoyed, and which warped the roof; however I am in hopes it has only been an April shower. Saturday night we were informed a spy had arrived, stating we were to be attacked that night; but it never came off. However we have to turn out every morning at three or four besides which I am generally routed out of my bed in the night by some order or other, so that one does not get much sleep. This morning soon after four the batteries of the Allies opened a tremendous fire on the town, and it has been kept up all day. The enemy seems to have been taken by surprise, as he did not answer for near half an hour after.

I rode up this afternoon well-cased in waterproof, to hear what had been done, the fog was so thick that without my compass I should not have found my way. I fell in with an officer who had been two hours looking for the 4th Division and could not find it, though he had been close to it. Of course I could not see what was going on, nor is it yet known what we have done, but the papers will tell you more about this. I met Lord Raglan riding with (I believe) Canrobert, but as I had no sword on I did not go near him. I hope you will soon hear of something having been done. If the wet is against us in some respects it is good in one, the enemy will have some trouble to bring their guns across the plain to attack us here, and this I suppose would be their plan to create a diversion. We see their piquet fires at night much nearer than they have been for some time.

I am very well now, though not quite so strong as before. My hut seems to agree with me so I shall stick to it while here, it is cooler than a tent in hot, and warmer than a tent in cold weather. I will call on Captain Giffard if he comes here again; I don't think he could have helped me to a cruise, they won't let one out of the harbour as long as there is a chance of getting well, but if not, they seem only too glad of getting rid of one anyhow. I should like to have been with Captain Giffard at Kertek,* it seems to have been a well-executed affair. I could not get an English pack saddle at Constantinople, and the Turkish ones are not worth having. I am glad you did not get me a cart, which would involve my getting a servant to drive, as my servant could not lead a horse besides, and a cart, *even if allowed*, is not always desirable, nor the best thing, especially for a subaltern officer. I shall never march with much baggage, for it is a great nuisance. Of course a colonel is allowed more pack animals, and means of transport than other regimental officers. Burnand has two tents coming, one a marquee I believe. I hope mine is *not* a marquee, they are too large, and too heavy to carry. I have plenty of things left from the boxes, the mutton and soup make my daily dinner. Thank Aunt Margaret and Sophia for the jam, etc. sent. My horses all well and improving. Long boots very useful.

Your affectionate Son

* This seems to be the affair at the Straits of Kertch, when an Allied expedition destroyed large quantities of Russian stores.

Cavalry Camp, Kadikoi   *April 12th 1855*

My dear Caroline — This is the fourth day of the second bombardment, and we seem doing *no good*. The enemy keeps up his fire well, no one is in the least sanguine as to the result. Some talk of storming, but I hardly think this likely, though today they said the scaling ladders were gone to the advanced works. If the bombardment fails, which there is every reason to suppose it will, I conclude there is but one other plan, and that is to wait till large reinforcements arrive, and then to fight this army outside and invest the town. I think before long this army outside must be drawn away by us. I fear we shall never do anything so long as Sebastopol can communicate with the country. The new 32 pounder battery is landing, and will doubtless be of great service in our next engagement in the field. Omar Pasha is here and has brought some Turks of the right sort with him. I am glad to hear Joseph likes the Militia. It is considered in the line *quite the thing* to get the Light Company, and generally it is the smartest men, and the greatest swells of the regiment who are the officers of the Light Company.

I have got a garden round my hut, and if here long enough, I hope to get some peas, beans, etc. out of it. I am quite well again now. Should you hear of General Scarlett, let me know. I am so sorry he is gone, we lose the services of the best man in the Division. I fear poor Mrs S. is too ill for him to return, though he would much wish to do so. Everyone here is disgusted with Lord Lucan, and his evidence before the committee, etc.; he deserves what he got. Cardigan, too, is thought *very very* little of, everyone was sorry to hear of his return, indeed it is said he took more care of himself on October 25th than was becoming. We have had some photographs of our camp done, unfortunately some of the horses would not stand still, but the whole gives an excellent idea of the camp.

Believe me your affectionate Brother

April 13th. This morning for some hours the heaviest fire I have ever heard was from our batteries. The Russians for some reason are firing rather slack, they have shut up our eight-gun battery. I expect some crisis is at hand, most people suppose the storming will come off shortly. About 20,000 Turks from Eupatoria pitched their camp in Kadikoi today. If we are to be attacked here, now is the time we may expect it. I think we are sufficiently strong if the Turks stand, which no doubt they will, Omar Pasha being here, and they bring old soldiers. Tonight about one mile across the plain the enemy's watch-fires are very numerous, more than I ever saw before, even about the action of Balaklava. What it means we can't tell. I was surprised to read in *The Times* '*We had been attacked here* on the 13th and 17th of March last.' I was told today the telegraph was complete from Raglan's to Downing Street, except a few miles near Varna. If so you will doubtless now be in greater suspense than even we are.

Cavalry Camp, Kadikoi   *April 17th 1855*
My dear Father — The bombardment still continues, and we are making more advanced batteries; most people are more sanguine than of late, the Russian fire is more slack, and we have done them more harm than in the last bombardment. Part of the 10th are here — their horses are perfect *beauties,* but the men and loads they carry are rather too heavy. I believe they are 780 strong. They are very vicious animals, yesterday some got loose, and put everyone to flight that came here. They have been four months on the line of march, and a most interesting one it must have been. The 12th Lancers are also on their way here.

We have about 30,000 of Omar Pasha's troops here, I think they are mostly Africans and Syrians, the best troops he has. Omar says he would give all he has for the Russians to attack us, and he says we should give a good account of them. We expect the storming to come off soon. I suppose we can't keep up the bombardment many days longer. No doubt we shall get the place in time, even if we fail now. I hear that rascal Grace has failed, and I don't know what has become of all our things, for we all left things with him. Don't send any quinine, I have plenty of it. I expect we shall rather astonish the Russians this summer when all our fresh troops arrive. We get plenty of luxuries here now in the way of wine, etc. We have not yet got the mail due yesterday. There is a troop going in the Inniskillings, I suppose for regulation. If it were worth while for me to apply for it at the Horse Guards, no doubt I should get it, as they have no subs old enough to purchase.

Your affectionate Son

13 *The Welcome Arrival* by J. D. Luard. The artist spent some months in the Crimea and here shows the unpacking of food and clothing from home

14 The interior of the Redan at Sebastopol, photographed by James Robertson, showing the basketwork defences Godman describes

15 Kadikoi Camp near Balaklava, photographed by James Robertson

Cavalry Camp, Kadikoi   *April 21st 1855*

My dear Caroline — You see the last bombardment has let us about as near Sebastopol as before. I don't know what will be done now: a rifle pit was taken the night before last, with considerable loss on our side — our trenches are so close now, that both pitch stones over at each other, tho' neither dare show, or they would certainly be shot immediately. I should think when reinforcements arrive, the army will take the field. I expect my tent and pack saddle will be just in time. The *Leopard* is come in with troops, and today I think I shall go and call on Captain Giffard.

On the 19th there was a reconnaissance under Omar Pasha, Lord Raglan was out. We did not take all our Cavalry, and as my regiment was on piquet, it did not go, so I went out to see what was done. There were hardly any shots exchanged, but the Cossacks as usual fired at us at an absurd distance. We drove them in with a few rockets and advanced near to Tchorgun. Some way in advance of our skirmishers were some Russian huts just left, and several officers very foolishly rode on to plunder them. While they were doing this two shots were fired at them, which made them run, and then a volley of about forty or fifty shots came rattling all about them. Fortunately no one was hit, tho' they had a narrow escape, for the Russians were only about 200 yards off and in ambush. The mail is in, but we have not got our letters yet. The weather is very fine and I have begun to bathe. The flowers here are very pretty, all sorts that I never saw before, I wish you could see them. . . .

Your affectionate Brother

Cavalry Camp, Kadikoi   *May 1st 1855*

My dear Mother — The last few days the weather has quite changed and it has been rather cold and wet. I don't suppose it will last long. The men and horses of the 10th just from India feel it much, and look miserably cold. Our Colonel has joined and commenced duties, he seems much aged by his late illness, he is now quite grey, and last autumn his hair was nearly black, he looks ten years older. I think we shall like him much. I am also relieved of my duty as adjutant for which I am not sorry, for there will soon be much troublesome and unsatisfactory duty, drilling the recruits we shall get out. I shall now have to go on piquet, but this only comes about once in ten days, and then you are on twenty-four hours from 10 a.m. one day till the same time the next.

The Light Brigade have got a draft of about 250 horses from England, and we expect ours shortly. I hear Sidebottom brings out £1,000 worth of kit and eatables, a pretty good allowance. . . . Lady Paget is here, also Lord and Lady Stratford de Redcliffe and their three daughters — it seems so odd to see ladies riding about. We are very anxious to know the result of Lord John's mission to Vienna. I suppose we must soon know it.

You ask me as to my bed. I have the indiarubber bed still, but one compartment is not quite airtight. I have not used it for months as I don't like it, it is a very cold thing to sleep on, and if it gets damp it hardly ever gets dry again. I have my stretcher still and sleep on the sacking, it makes a comfortable bed. If we march I think I shall not take a bed, but lie on the ground in my waterproof rug, as I used to do when we first came here. I have got most of my horse cloths up from Grace's. . . .

We suppose here Menschikoff is dead, another head gone. It seems a judgement on our enemy, that Nicholas and M. who were the sole cause of the war, and Admiral Nachimoff who commanded the massacre at Sinope, all died during the first campaign.

Your affectionate Son

On board the St. Hilda, *Balaklava Harbour*　　　　*May 3rd 1855*

My dear Joseph — I embarked yesterday with my brown horse in charge of some men and horses of the 4th D.G., some artillery also on board. Kertele* *is said* to be our destination, and few know the truth, but yesterday I was let into a *great secret*, and was told not to repeat it, as however it must be known in England about the time you get this, there is no harm in my telling you. It is that we are going to Eupatoria, and then march on Simferopol wth 35,000 Turks with Omar Pasha, and I suppose 5,000 English.

I have got nothing but a railway wrapper, and my waterproof coat, and a pea-jacket, and expect we shall have to rough it more than we have done yet. I have bought as much grub (portable soup, mutton, sausages, cheese, etc.) as possible and a saucepan. If this is true (and I expect it is from the number of land transport

* Kertch.

we take, and from other reasons) we shall certainly have some very hard fighting, and probably when you get this shall be at it hammer and tongs. There must be plenty of 'wigs upon the green'. However I hope I for one may get safe through. I don't half like our taking so few cavalry — only fifty but they are picked men and will do their duty, and our officers are very good too. I suppose we go merely to support our battery, as they must have cavalry. I am glad we have got the Highland Brigade. General Brown commands us. I expect they will complete the embarkation today and that we shall get outside harbour tonight. We are to be towed I believe by the *London*.

Tell them at home to let Fred know I am gone on this expedition, that he may act accordingly. If he gets to Balaklava, he will find my hut, servant, and some provisions ready for him. This is a beautiful warm day, and I hope our weather may be fine. This will be an exciting time in England, for I believe this move to be a very important one. . . .

Your affectionate Brother

On board the St. Hilda *off Kamiesele*   *May 8th 1855*
My dear Father — We sailed on the 3rd from Balaklava, towed by the *Valorous*. . . . On the 5th we arrived off the Straits of Kertele and, when we expected to land, to our great disgust we were told we must come back, as the expedition was countermanded. It was a great disappointment for army and fleet. No one knows the reason. Canrobert is said to have been the cause of the countermand. The fleet expect we shall go again soon. The place will be sure to be stronger then, and it is a great chance if the same officers are sent next time. I made sure of at least one clasp. We got back to Balaklava the 6th and as it was blowing hard we could not get in, so came here for shelter. We are now going round again to land. It is bad for the horses to be so long at sea for nothing, we have had fine weather hitherto.

Your affectionate Son

Cavalry Camp, Kadikoi   *Friday May 11th 1855*
My dear Caroline — I have just got your letter of April 23rd. I have come up to camp to see our Brigadier, as there is no chance

of our landing till tomorrow or next day. It is all Admiral Boxer's fault, he is so pig-headed; he will not land us, though there is plenty of room, it really is too bad. We have been off this place since last Sunday, and he will not even answer our signals, so we are in without leave, and now he says he has a good mind to send us back again. Such an old ass as he is really deserves to be turned out. I wish I could see Russell, I would get him to put it all in *The Times*. I just send you this line as you all seem so anxious to hear by every post. The Kertele expedition has failed through mismanagement, like everything else we attempt, tho' this time it is all the fault of the French.

Your affectionate Brother

Cavalry Camp, Kadikoi   *May 18th 1855*

My dear Father — Yesterday I got a letter from Fred dated Constantinople 15th saying he intended to leave the next day for Crimea. I am on duty today so cannot leave the camp to look for him; I can make him up a bed in my hut. Montgomery and I had just arranged to try and get leave for ten days to go to Constantinople; he knows Lord Stratford very well, which is an advantage. No doubt we could manage it before the drafts come. Ours have sailed with about 150 horses, and we expect them soon. Now Fred is coming I fear I shall not be able to go, for he would like to remain eight or ten days at least, and perhaps longer. Grace has failed, and lost or made away with all our things, for me to the amount of about £30, consisting of one trunk, and one box of orderly room books etc., and my coatee, two frock-coats nearly new, gold sash, lots of underclothes, and no end of other things. He is a regular rascal, fortunately I got up one portmanteau of clothes during the winter.

We had a Division Field-day this morning, about 1,500 men out; we shall be nearly twice as strong when all our drafts arrive. I expect we shall take the field by the early part of June. I heard Lord Raglan is sending away his heavy baggage, which looks like a move. The summer promises to be warmer than Bulgaria, today the warmest we have had, the thermometer has been all day at 94° in my hut, which is tolerably cool, being so much under ground, and this only the middle of May. We are better here than in tents. . . .

I was glad to hear of Napoleon's escape, there is no life in the world now so valuable as his, especially to England. The other day (*on dit*) Lord Raglan received a message from England by E. Telegraph, and having lost the cipher was obliged to telegraph for it, before he could read the message. It is thought here that Rothschild having taken the whole of the loans expects peace. It is really absurd how people here catch at any chance of peace, the least thing is interpreted into a *certainty*. I suppose the cause is the wish being Father to the Thought. Thank Mary for her letter, but I have not time to write now.

You want to know how the Cossack spear is carried: the foot, or rather the toes, are put through the loop at the end, and the other strap fastens to their right arm when not in use. The whip is also Cossack and peculiar; I have seen many, but never with any point to the lash. Every Cossack has a whip as they don't use spurs. I wish I had sent you a sword and belt, I might have got lots after Balaklava. I have lots of quinine, but don't often have to take it; I have the tin box full and a bottle also. A good deal of fever is about and some cholera. Unless one takes care to wrap up after sunset, and before sunrise one is pretty sure of a fever. Runciman is I know very dear, in fact absurdly so, but I think he is good, it is difficult to find a tradesman who is moderate and good also. Let him wait for his money, I am not sure that it is a good thing to employ a *military tradesman*, as there are plenty of blackguards in the army, who leave their bills unpaid, the tradesmen charge high and we, who do pay, have to make up the loss to the tradesmen. The Photograph man not gone home yet, I will send his address another time.

We bought a *real south down** on a ship the other day — £3. Would you like to part with a few at this price? It was quite a treat to taste real English mutton again, I was quite sorry to kill it. It did one good to see an English sheep, they are as different as possible to these poor skinny Eastern sheep, scarce worthy of the name. They have curious tails, like the Cape sheep, and seem never to have fat in any other part, and this is too strong to eat, about five inches long and six across when fat. Fisher, 4th D.G., lost another horse a few days ago; the sagacious soldier servant fed him on grass for the *first time* for full three hours or more. The poor

* English sheep. This would be the breed kept at Park Hatch.

beast being naturally of a greedy disposition, and not knowing when to stop, ate so much, that he died soon after, a sudden and ignoble death.

You want to know when I ride Chance, he only does second-hand duty, such as when I take a ride, which I generally do every day. The Earl has all the honour in as much as I mount him whenever I expect any work to be done, though if he could understand I doubt if he could appreciate my motive, or think it quite fair. He would no doubt have wished Chance in his place in the *St. Hilda* last week, and so did I as it turned out. Chance is a good sporting-looking horse, and I might sell him well if I wished, I have had some offers for him. All my horses look right well; as for the Cob, he is as fat as a pig, and quite above himself, only fancy this morning I had some trouble to persuade him to carry a barrel of water for me. I suppose he thought like our housemaid Eliza that it was '*too degwading*' to fetch water. I see no great use in water bags on the march, it would involve keeping an extra horse, and they are not likely to send cavalry where there is no water.

We like what we have seen of McMahon, he is no doubt a sharp fellow, and will soon rub the rust off himself. The Sardines* (as they are called) seem very smart soldiers, especially their Rifles, who wear a kind of wide-awake hat and feathers in it. I have got a cellar, that is a hole in the ground, which keeps my beer and wine nice and cool. I am sorry you talk of coachman going, he seems to get on well, and may be hard to replace. I bathe about a mile west of the harbour, one has to climb down the rocks, but it is a good place. We get turbot here for about 5s or 6s each. Canrobert is thought very badly of by his army. Bosquet is far superior. Pélissier is said to be a good General. It was he who smoked the Arabs out of their caves in Algiers.

Your affectionate Son

Cavalry Camp, Kadikoi *May 25th 1855*

My dear Father — Fred† has been here a week and has been making the most of his time. I expect he will leave about next

---

* The Sardinians had been brought in by Count Cavour who felt this might be a step towards Italian unification.

† Frederick, the younger brother, visited the Crimea as did many other 'tourists'.

Wednesday, and I intend to accompany him to Constantinople if possible, but now the French have gone out, as you will see by the papers, it is doubtful about my getting away. Yesterday Tchorgun was taken by the French, and it is said they intend to advance up the heights to turn the Russian flank. I hope we may take the field directly. I really think this is our best chance of taking Sebastopol. I expect within the next month, if not before, a general action will be fought, and I hope Sebastopol may be ours before winter. It is said the 'comic farce' called the 'Bombardment of Sebastopol' will be enacted again on the 27th, *positively for the last time.* . . .

Your affectionate Son

Cavalry Camp, Kadikoi *May 31st 1855*

My dear Father — Fred is still here, nor has he yet decided when to leave, the bombardment is expected to reopen very shortly, and of course he is anxious to see it if possible. I think I have shown him everything here of any note, and he has a good knowledge of the ground. He has been very fortunate in being here at that little business of the Tchernaya, as it enables him to see much more of the country. Two days ago we took a ride towards the Baidar pass, and home by the Marine Heights, it is only just opened, by our late advance on Tchorgun. I think it is one of the most beautiful rides I ever had. The scenery really is superb.

You know by this time the result of the Kertele expedition, which is thought here a blow in the right direction and of much importance. The Russians are said to be in a terrible state all over the Crimea from disease and work. I really think we shall take Sebastopol during the summer, the men only want to be let go at the Russians; things seem decidedly looking up. It is a great consolation to me that there has been no fighting at Kertele, having been left out of the second expedition; certainly I might have seen something of the country, but there has been no honour as yet. Fred could have followed me there had I been gone. It is very pleasant to have him here. We generally start about two every day to see sights, when all my business is done. I was on piquet the day after Fred came, a fearfully hot day on this place without the slightest shelter. The nights too are short and fine, so one does not so much care about the duty. The weather lately has been cooler.

On Sunday we had a thunderstorm, when a regular river came down on my hut, and in about five minutes the water rose about two feet besides some six inches under the floor. The only thing to do was to undress, and try and save the property, and Fred being there we managed to do this without much harm being done, and then emptied it out with buckets. I have now put Fred into Hampton's hut, while I get a shakedown in Montgomery's. My hut will not be safe to live in again, for the wet in the ground causes a bad smell which would perhaps give a fever. I am now writing in my tent which I think a very good one, it is delightfully cool, from the outer fly; the only doubt I have is that this fly might be torn away by a high wind, as it can get under and blow it up, but I may be wrong. Anyway the tent without it is thicker than the Government ones. I am very much pleased with it, you could not have selected a more likely one had I been with you.

Kilburn is delighted with the pack saddle, which I have tried on, the panels on the side might have been a little longer with advantage, but this hardly matters, and they will come down more by use. Everything seems made of the best, and in all respects it is exactly what I wanted. The saddle-bags, too, are excellent. I shall carry my things in them instead of a box as I had intended. I can carry much more now, and with twice the comfort to man and horse than before. Fred wants to try sleeping in the tent. We had a review of the cavalry on the 24th (Queen's birthday) and made a good show. Pélissier was there — he is a very fat, coarse, vulgar-looking man, more like an old coalheaver than a General, however he is one of the right sort. . . .

The young men in the Guards lately come out, are going off fast with cholera, yesterday they buried fourteen men. I wish our Generals would do something now, before they lose too many by disease. They say the bombardment opens on Monday. We are nearer the town, and have more guns and ammunition than ever. I have seen people who have been to Kertele, and am told the Turks have been behaving shamefully, killing children, and committing many other atrocities. We hear our drafts are stopped, as all the ships are required to bring out the 1st D.G. I hear the officer commanding the Division sent all the names of the officers who went to Kertele before to Lord Raglan, but I suppose the reason the 8th Hussars went is because Lord Raglan has a nephew in the regiment. This system of patronage is the ruination of our army.

Your affectionate Son

Cavalry Camp, Kadikoi *June 15th 1855*
My dear Father — Fred left me on the 12th, I went with him as far as the mouth of the harbour, and he had every chance of a fine passage . . . I sent home a box directed to me at L. Square by the *Jason*, please have it opened, and my things put away till I want them, you will find some shot etc. from Balaklava and Inkermann. The *Jason* sailed about a week ago, and was to call at Varna and Constantinople. I am thinking of sending another box home, so as not to leave anything here, as I have lost so much it makes me shy of doing so. My swimming belt has been stolen, like most of my other things. Do you see we have got Colonel Balders's eldest son as cornet, he is very young, being not quite seventeen years old. The *Malacca* is not yet in, don't send any more parcels, as I have as much as I can carry.

Sidebottom came in with seventy-two horses and forty men two days ago; seven weeks from Ireland lost two horses. I am very glad he is come, as I much feared we should be cut out of any fieldwork on account of our weakness. We shall now turn out a strong squadron about 120 horses, there are hardly any of the old horses good for much, and never will be. Sidebottom has not landed yet, but we paid him a visit, and he plied me with champagne, claret cup, punch, etc. *Mr* Webster is with him, and *his* horse, a great swell entirely, nearly equals his master, and does the honours as if all belonged to himself. Sidebottom has brought some cartloads of boxes from Fortnum & Mason, Brook's the wine merchant, etc. and sixteen English sheep. His clothes, etc. will take at least four mules to carry, the first day's march will teach him a lesson. Rickets has just joined. We expect another draft of the same strength.

Fred has left me a few cotton socks as I was short of them. The cholera belts answer well. I did get the parcel by the *Ayrshire*, I thought I had mentioned it. Fred and I had a good many pleasant bathes here, we always ride to the sea, generally about 5 p.m. as the place is shaded. We tie up our horses and climb down the rocks, and the water is as deep as you like to jump into. One has a good many opportunities of speaking French, as so few understand English, I make out pretty well in a *mild* conversation, but can't talk well enough to converse freely. Fred was very fortunate here in being able to see more of the country than we have for the last eight months till now, also in seeing the storming of the Mamelon.* I was unfortunately on duty in camp, but the firing was I suppose the most tremendous that has ever been heard. Of course the spectators were a long way off, and the view much obscured by smoke. He has a good knowledge of the country now, and can give you any information as to position when he gets home.

Most officers and men, lately come out, have been laid up with fever, and some gone home. Hutchinson of the 13th Dragoons who used to own the grey horse I brought from Ireland, is very ill indeed, just come out. Our men are healthy tho' no doubt we shall lose several out of the young soldiers just arrived. The cholera has taken off a few victims, but is not severe yet. The Greys, just divided from us by a bank have had two cases, and one fatal. We are not quite free from it. Poor old Admiral Boxer you see is dead (very sudden) of cholera, only twelve hours. Doubtless he had his faults, but it is not easy to regulate such a port as Balaklava, and already they feel his loss. I know he worked very hard and was about that dirty harbour from 4 a.m. till sunset, which for an English Admiral is pretty good work. I have no doubt but that hard work was one thing which helped to bring on cholera, and that the unjust abuse of *The Times* (as in the case of Captain Christie) hastened his end. If an officer does wrong there is another way of dealing with him than holding him up to public abuse and censure in the English newspapers. I believe Admiral Boxer was once a common sailor, or at all events something very low, and therefore it is more to his credit to have become an Admiral in the *English* navy, and one cannot expect as much refinement as in an officer bred and born a gentleman. There were three infantry officers out here who were at Malkins with me. One was killed, one has lost an eye, and wounded besides, and the third had his leg carried away above the knee the other day by a round shot.

I did nothing more about a troop in the Inniskillings, on second thoughts if I exchange I think it will be into Light Cavalry. This

---

* One of the forts in the defences of Sebastopol.

regiment is so much changed since I joined that I shall not care much about being in it. It will certainly be as well to purchase for *Regulation if I can*, because as a captain in wartime one may get brevet rank, while as a sub., let a man do what he may, he gets nothing, such is the wise rule in our service. . . . I do not think we shall be short of water — all over this country as well as in Turkey, there are lots of fine fountains, with the most beautiful water running out of rocks, etc.

Before you get this, I expect you will hear that this side of Sebastopol is ours. The taking of the Mamelon is a most important step. The French are now making a forty-gun battery on the right which commands the harbour, and the Mamelon is being armed. I suppose the grand attack will be on the Malakoff, and of course we must expect a severe loss, but no doubt it will be taken. The other day the officers could not keep our men back, and some officers of the 88th had to threaten to shoot their men, but they would go on. The Russians have a terrible invention for mines which I give you a plan of.

Note : Sulphuric acid will ignite gun-cotton.
A. A tin tube inside which is glass tube, full of sulphuric acid.
B. A tin tube joining the other tube, and full of gun-cotton, which communicates with the powder.

Dodge: The soldier treads on tube A (not seeing it) breaks the glass, the sulphuric acid runs into gun-cotton.

Result: Soldier is blown up.

One blew up eleven men the other day; they are set all over the ground. They say the enemy is carrying all his goods across the harbour. I suppose they have given up all chance of holding this side. When they storm we shall no doubt try to get round the Russians in rear. M. Soyer* dined with us the other night, he is very amusing, sang some good songs and made himself very agreeable, he is a great swell.

Your affectionate Son

* The great French cook. Soyer produced numerous recipes for making poor food appetising, and designed cooking apparatus, such as the Soyer field stove, which stayed in use for a century. His recipes varied from small elegant meals to cooking for 1,000 men.

8

The Attempt on the Malakoff

Cavalry Camp, Kadikoi   *June 19th 1855*

My dear Caroline — This mail will bring you a full account of our yesterday's proceedings which are indeed very sad. You will see that we attempted to storm the Redan and Malakoff,* everyone seemed sure of getting into the town. Lord Raglan seemed so certain of success that in orders he told the army what to do when inside. There are so many spies about, that I have no doubt the Russians were well aware of our actions. No one had much sleep on the night of the 17th and at 2 a.m. on the 18th the Russians attacked the Mamelon and were repulsed. At about three the most terrific fire ever heard opened, both cannon and musketry, the earth quite trembled, and the noise was like a continual war of thunder. Of course one could not see much.

The French were to storm the Malakoff first, as that commands the Redan. They went up in good style, but could not get over the ditch, which is very broad and deep. They stood for some time firing at the men over the parapet, and receiving a tremendous fire of grape and musketry at a few yards, which mowed them down in heaps; a few got inside the works and were all killed. It is said the signal for us was, when the Malakoff was taken, the French would hoist a flag. It appears the enemy must have heard of this, and to entrap us hoisted a flag. Our men then advanced on the Redan, under a storm of grape, shot and musketry, and placed the ladders. Sir John Campbell, the Brigadier-General, was the first man up, but not a man came back again, for inside were lots of guns loaded with grape, which swept the parapets. The storming party after a desperate attempt, found there was no one to command them, their General, all the Colonels, and most of their officers having been

---

* These two Russian forts were very strong. Capturing them required more skill and courage than the earlier better-publicized battles and charges.

killed or wounded, they were forced to retire. It is a most unfortunate affair.

The French loss we shall never know, but yesterday they said
ours was between 300 and 500 men, killed and wounded, and about
seventy officers. Lord Raglan wished to try again, but Pélissier
would not, Lord Raglan also wished to storm after six hours' firing,
but was overruled by the French. Of course one must expect a
heavy loss in storming, and I suppose it must be tried again. It
makes one feel quite melancholy all this loss for nothing, and we
came back in very different spirits to what we went. No one can say
what will be done now. I saw the regiments coming back from the
trenches looking rather gloomy; all was over by 9 a.m. but the
wounded were coming up in long strings for hours after. The 34th
and 57th have suffered most, nearly every officer being killed or
wounded. The sailors' loss was very heavy. I met Lord Raglan
after, he looked very red, but not much discomposed, he was very
near killed, being under a heavy fire for some time. I afterwards
went to an officer's hut, and everyone that came in brought news
of the death of someone.

A French officer told me the other day that taking the Mamelon
cost them 4,300 men, and over 100 officers. I suppose we shall not
long be idle. I feel sure we could beat them in the open. The
Russians certainly are fine brave soldiers. We expect Scarlett out
here directly, poor Mrs Scarlett is not quite so bad as they say, and
there is some chance of her recovery. All the cavalry were on duty
yesterday at the front. To your tender inquiries after my moustache
all I can say is, it has not taken advantage of the warm weather as
it ought to have done since I left England . . . The French lost two
Generals yesterday. I believe we did not attack with nearly a sufficient force, having hundreds where we could, and should, have
had thousands. I dare say it will cause a sensation in England, but
we can't expect always to win, and such a place must cost a large
loss of life, money, labour and time to take.

Your affectionate Brother

Cavalry Camp, Kadikoi   *June 26th 1855*
My dear Mother — The glasses arrived all safe, but I fancy I
cannot see quite as well with them as with the last. The last week

I have had a host of misfortunes. To begin I went back to sleep in my hut the 22nd it being quite dry; the next evening I was entertaining Fisher at dinner, when the most tremendous storm I ever saw broke over us and made us take shelter under the mess table to finish our dinners, of course all wet. I sent Kilburn down to see after the hut, and he returned saying it was all right. Five minutes after on going again he found it full, and when I opened the door my blankets etc. floated out. We then ran to the stables where the Cob was making a great to do, and found it nearly full, so we ran to the mess, got a knife, and Kilburn plunged in up to his neck, cut the ropes, and with my help got out the horses. In five minutes more I think they must have been drowned, and they would have been had it not been for Kilburn. Nearly all my uniform is almost destroyed, one large bottle of brandy broken, and no end of damage done. All the huts filled more or less. The lightning was one incessant blaze, and balls of fire, and forked lightning with it; all the horses were trembling with fear. The rain seemed more like a waterspout, and tasted salt and sulphury. So partial was it that a mile away they had no rain. The Colonel of the 17th Lancers lost a horse and all his goods. The railway at Kadikoi is swept away, and I fear some people drowned. I had no dry clothes the next day and was obliged to sleep in a greatcoat.

My next misfortune was, I pitched my tent, and there was a little wind but not much, and the brass joints in the pole all broke, so now that is done for, and I am come back to the bell tent. I shall try and get another pole on board ship without a joint, and do away with the outside piece, I am sure it would never do in a wind. The inside is much thicker than Government tents.

General Estcourt and an officer of the 10th Hussars are dead of cholera. Lord Raglan is very ill. General Airey is missing (they say) he rode out towards Baidar, and they fancy the Cossacks took him, this however may not be true. What we are to do now no one knows. The French are sapping up to the Malakoff, we have failed in sapping to the Redan, it being all rock. I rather expect there will be another assault, all that bad business the other day was caused by mistakes. Everyone is much dissatisfied with Raglan. I believe if we had acted according to the plan we should have succeeded. When the *Jason* arrives you had better see after the box as they steal the contents at the custom house. I have made up my mind to another winter here, for if we take this side we shall not get the other before winter. The grass is all gone and we now get none. The weather is very hot. They are very short of water in the front. Did I ever tell you the 'nice young clergyman' Aunt Margaret knew, was soon taken ill here and returned home; he was too great a swell for the Crimea.

Your affectionate Son

Cavalry Camp, Kadikoi   *June 29th 1855*

My dear Father — General Scarlett arrived here today but I have not seen him yet to speak to. I hear Elliot was to leave on the 26th. Poor Lord Raglan as you will see is added another victim to the war. Rather a clearance this at headquarters, in one week Estcourt and Raglan. Poor man I am sorry for him, he was kind and willing to do his best, but was not fit for the post he held. He must have had a dreadful time the last eight months, and that last affair and poor Estcourt's death finished him. Simpson is now in command. Sir G. Brown is sick on board ship, and Pennefather gone home, they say the 'rats leave a doomed ship'; I hope this is not our case. Anyway I think we are in a *fix*. They have reconnoitred as well as they can Mackenzie's Farm and say it is very strongly fortified by the enemy.*

A pair of my boots have turned up in Inglis's saddle-bags which were this day sent up from Grace's, proving I fear that my things have been sacked. I also got two coats back, that I left in a box of Halford's, several officers have hunted for my things, but can't find them. I find Grace has not failed, but lost our things or stolen them. . . . About half the men of our drafts are either ill or gone away sick. We expect two more drafts soon, and three subalterns.

Your affectionate Son

Cavalry Camp, Kadikoi   *July 6th 1855*

My dear Father — I received my box from *Malacca*, which ship has been to Kertele; she did not come in here, and I have seen

---

* North-east of Sebastopol was a farm which had once been owned by a Scottish settler. There were a number of Scots in Russia.

nothing of her. Unfortunately the box got wet, and the vegetable was rotten and useless, the ham soft and musty, and I feared quite bad, but I had it boiled and the outside taken off, and it eats very well, so this is fortunate. The rest of the things all right, the ham, honey, etc. are most useful now, as the only meal I have alone now is breakfast, for which they and the ham come in well. I have as much as I can carry now in the way of food, if we take the field.

We have lost four men by cholera of one draft, and many sick, the old hands are very well. Sidebottom has been very ill: liver, dysentery and fright. He never ought to have come out, he has nearly had a fit, and his resignation is going in immediately, and he is going home if he gets well; he will have to sell for regulation. Montgomery will no doubt get his troop. Burnand has grown tired of this work, and his papers have been forwarded to the Horse Guards, and I am recommended for the vacant troop, he leaves directly for England. He has had the troop so short a time, and never been in action, that I think most likely they will not let him sell his troop as he got it without purchase; he will only get the money for his other commissions. Certainly it is possible they may make us pay regulation for it; mind £2,035 is regulation, don't give more, they will apply to you for the money, if required, so you need take no steps about it. Montgomery leaves today for England, having been sent home by a medical board. Nearly all the new officers are gone away ill. Poor Hutchinson of the 13th Dragoons, whom I knew very well, is dead; he was cousin of our Hutchinson. We have a new draft landing today from the *Oneida* steamer, seventy horses and eighty-eight men. Bolton, Hay and Richards; the latter seems a very good fellow. He was formerly captain in the 9th Lancers, and has one Indian medal. I fear Story will not stand the climate, he is a very good little fellow. Our new cornets I hear are a shady lot. Hutchinson I know and like very well, but Travers I am told is a regular *Irish savage* . . .

The *Oneida* was on fire three or four times coming out, and once the flames on the upper deck prevented one from passing, and the boats were all got out and provisioned, they put the fire out with steam. I hear General Simpson well spoken of. I hope he may be more fortunate than his predecessor. . . .

Your affectionate Son

16 Temple Godman in the uniform of a Major-General

17 Temple Godman was a keen horseman into old age. He is seen here with his four sons, *l-r*. George, Temple, Fred and Tommy, at Highden in Sussex

18 Active to the last, Temple Godman on the moor

Cavalry Camp, Kadikoi   *July 9th 1855*

My dear Caroline — I saw your name in the paper as being at both the drawing rooms, I should like to have been able to go with you. It is very dull work here now, there has been no excitement since June 18th tho' I can't believe we shall be inactive during the whole year. We are of course in a measure ready to march, which prevents one from reading much, or else I should take to my Italian again, but it is of no use to go on for a short time and then break off, for when one only makes a *little* progress, one so soon forgets it again. We don't in the least know what is to be done, though some say we are to storm again soon. The French are still sapping towards the Malakoff. General Simpson has not yet been in orders as Commander-in-Chief, and some think he has refused the appointment.

I am now in command of the troop, I hope to get seventy-four men and forty-seven horses. Such specimens of soldiers as our drafts I never saw, many are quite children and none of them half-drilled. I am fortunate not to be adjutant now. I should have no end of trouble to drill them, then the weather is so hot, we can hardly give them any drill. I don't know what we should do if we had to meet the Russians with such men. I have not heard of Fred since he left me where is he gone? . . .

Your most affectionate Brother

Cavalry Camp, Kadikoi   *July 16th 1855*

My dear Father — In a few days I suppose Burnand's papers will have reached the Horse Guards, if indeed they are not already there. In order to *save time* will you either go or write to Cox to tell him to pay the regulation for my troop *when called on*, and this will save his applying to you on the subject. The reason I want you to do this is because I *hear* that Elliot is going to exchange into the Guards, and if this be true it is important for me (if possible) to get gazetted first, in order not to leave another above me, in case I remain in the regiment. . . . Bolton is ill of fever and says he will not stay in the regiment, if he can get away.

It is quite extraordinary the way all the new arrivals from England are struck down with cholera, fever and dysentery, hardly one escapes, tho' many have it less severely than others, nor do the old hands escape entirely, though it is in general less frequent and less virulent with them than the newcomers. Bolton brought a private servant with him, who died of cholera of only a few hours' duration before the end of his first week in the country. Yesterday I met Comber, Campbell's friend, he has left the *St. Jean d'Arc* and now commands the *Viper* gunboat. He was up in the Sea of Azoff lately, he tells me the new mortar ships are of no use at all, in his and most other naval officers' opinions; if so what a waste of the public money, no wonder the income tax is increased. . . . We have had much cooler weather lately, with thunderstorms, as yet I think the Crimea not so hot as Bulgaria.

Your affectionate Son

Cavalry Camp, Kadikoi　　　　　　　　　　*August 4th 1855*

My dear Father — As it will take me some time to think of all I shall want for a winter here, I shall not be able to send you the list til' my next letter. I hear today that the Russians are assembling in force on the heights beyond Tchorgun, they say something like 80,000 of them. *If* this be *true*, no doubt they intend to attack us, and I think it will be odd if the year passes without our seeing anything of them.

I am going to set about pulling down my hut, and building it higher up on dry ground, and only sunk a few inches underground. I have applied for canvas and tar to the Quartermaster-General and think I shall get it to cover my hut and stables with. I hope to be housed and my horses too before summer is over, and shall no doubt pass the winter tolerably comfortably. . . . I hope they will bring out stables before the wet weather comes, and the army requires more huts too. We are going to build a stone kitchen for our mess, so that we may be sure of our dinners in the worst weather. We have had such thunderstorms here as one seldom sees, and much rain, indeed the summer though warm enough is not nearly so hot as in Bulgaria. We get here a very nice light wine from Besussa, very like hock. You will very likely not approve of this, but for my part I think it does not matter a pin what you eat and drink in moderation, as far as illness is concerned. . . .

I hardly expected they would give me the troop without purchase. It always happens that men who don't care about the service get more promotion than others, and then give up just at the very time they ought to remain. I thought Powell would very likely advise you to go to the H. Guards about it, at all events I am glad you went as it can't do harm, and may do good. I am glad Elliot is made major, he is the only Staff man I know who *deserved* promotion, and he certainly did much more than many of the C.B.s.*

Your affectionate Son

Cavalry Camp, Kadikoi   *August 11th 1855*

My dear Father — The King's Dragoon Guards arrive today — Marshall's old regiment — and reported the death of Sidebottom; he was buried at Gibraltar a day or two before they passed. This makes the sixth officer we have lost by death. He must have been mad to come out here where a man without a good constitution can't live any time. If I was not gazetted before the day of his death, of course I ought to get the troop without purchase, so you must see to this. . . .

I called on the General a day or two ago; he says it is undecided yet whether we get stables sent out here, or go to Scutari or Egypt for the winter. From what he said I suspect he has strongly recommended the latter, because we shall get plenty of forage and can camp out the whole winter and so continue our drill, which we much want with all our young men, and it would be impossible here. We are getting a very fine cavalry force now. I sincerely hope we may go to Egypt, it would be the making of the Division, and it is but ten days from this. Fancy encamping under the Pyramids. We are all tolerably healthy, and I hope we shall get well through the summer.

The best sergeant in my troop (lately from England) died yesterday of cholera in twenty-four hours. The more I see of this disease the more wonderful it seems, it is frightful to look at, and one would often scarcely recognize the sufferer, though well-known. No news of the siege, we are I believe to open fire again *some time* this year. Since writing the other sheet, your letter of 26th ult. has come. As far as I can make out Sidebottom died about ten days ago, and it is not likely I was gazetted *before* that, so

* It seems that service on a Staff appointment was rewarded with a C.B. (Companion of the Bath).

I by right get the troop without purchase, and even if I am gazetted after his death, and before the news reaches England, they will ungazette me and give me his troop. I know a case in point out here of a cornet in the Inniskillings, who got his lieutenancy in the same way, after having been gazetted by purchase.

Burnand promised to call on you and tell you all about me and the Crimea when he got home. I am sorry to hear you have so much wet. I hope the harvest will be safely housed. The harvest here (what there is) is long since over. They talk of our relieving the troops now at Baidar. They have taken lots of champagne from Russian houses a little further on — they got thirty dozen the other day, but I suppose this will be stopped, for four of our land transport got shot the other day. They wrote to Burnand here not knowing he was on leave and said if he would take £1,740 for his troop he could sell, that is regulation for cornetcy and lieutenancy, and £100 per annum for five-and-a-half years' service for troop. French prisoners who have been exchanged say that the whole country to Sebastopol is a hospital, and the Russians are in a terrible state. I had this from the best authority.

Your affectionate Son

I hear the *Jasper* one-gun gunboat is taken in the Sea of Azoff, having gone ashore.

Cavalry Camp, Kadikoi   *August 17th 1855*

My dear Father — Yesterday we were turned out at 3 a.m. and marched on to the plain; they had information the Russians were to attack us. At 4.30, about half an hour before sunrise, a rocket fired by the Sardines told us our information was correct. We advanced down the valley of the Light Dragoon charge near the river, and had an excellent view, though we were not engaged in the action, nor even under fire. We made a good show in three lines, and perhaps the moral effect of our presence contributed in a measure to the success of the day.

The valley of the Tchernaya is about 800 to 1,000 yards wide here, and hills on either side. The river runs close under our side, and between that and us, a few yards nearer is the Sebastopol aqueduct, about four yards broad and about six feet deep. The enemy planted his artillery on the hills. Under cover of their fire, he threw forward his infantry, who advanced over the river (which is generally shallow), threw wood stretchers which they brought on purpose over the aqueduct, and charged up the hill in the most gallant manner, though mowed down by the storm of grape and musketry all across the valley. They got to the top of the valley. The French received them with a volley and drove them down into the river with the bayonet. I believe the Russians made three attacks, and each was repulsed, but the smoke now filled the valley. The enemy seeing it was no go, retired under cover of their guns and skirmishers. The fight was short but sharp, and we got home by 11 a.m.

I rode over the ground just after; it is a terrible sight when the excitement is over to see men torn into messes by round shot and shell, and then the wounded moaning and dying all round. If kings' ministers could see a few such sights I think countries would not be hurried into war so headlong. Many were killed in the river and were lying half in and half out. They say 1,500 men were left on the field. I could not judge the number myself, they were spread over such a long front. I believe the French and Sardinian loss was small. The Russians certainly got a tremendous licking. We had so many guns in position and lots more to spare. One 32 pounder battery and some horse artillery were I believe the only English engaged. Every hill of ours as far as Tchorgun had guns on it. The French fought gallantly, and the Sardines have quite established their reputation, and have proved themselves as good as they look. Scarlett placed his division admirably. One can't help feeling a little small at having no hand in the matter, but the French cavalry were in the same fix.

I and some of our officers had a little adventure, while going over the ground afterwards. We were looking at the French taking off wounded Russians, when without thinking we got into range of a battery, and they sent three round shot at us. Fortunately they went over our heads and pitched amongst a crowd of French, and must have killed some, and hit the ambulance, taking off the wounded. As we were not paid to be shot at just then we of course galloped off, and a lot more French and English also looking on. The Russians then shelled the place and killed some of their own wounded men, an English infantry officer I heard was also knocked over while looking on. This was just at the stone bridge, half-way between Inkermann and Tchorgun, and the R. battery is on the spur of the hill opposite, so you can see the place at the model. There were an immense number of dead at the bridge. They say the Russians were fighting for a piece of the river as they have no water.

Today the English began to bombard but the French took little part in it, the consequence was our batteries got roughly handled. While Halford and I were sitting down looking at the place with our glasses, a 32 lb. shot came over us, and pitched a little way behind about three feet in the ground. Some men dug it out, it was quite hot. I never saw a shot come there before, tho' I have been there often. I don't want any things till the beginning of November. The butter you sent answered very well, but the summer is too hot for it, so I gave it to our mess. We get very good dinners now, generally a leg of mutton, a goose or turkey, stewed chicken and nearly always soup and turbot; we dine at 7.30. I breakfast alone, it is more for this meal I want things sent. The chickens here are not so good as English, being very thin. We lose a few men still, chiefly the new hands. Some regiments have a great deal of sickness.

Believe me your affectionate Son

Cavalry Camp, Kadikoi   *August 25th 1855*
My dear Mother — Your letter of the 7th and the papers of the 11th arrived together, so that I find I am gazetted to the troop without purchase, therefore that affairs seem settled satisfactorily. . . . There has been nothing particular here since the action on the Tchernaya. There was a flag of truce to bury the dead for two days, and a Frenchman on General Ferrer's staff told me they and the Russians together buried over 3,100 of the enemy. They took the papers off General Rud who was killed — they contain the whole plans of the attack which was to have been made had the action on the Tchernaya been successful. He is to send us a copy of the plans if he can get them.

It seems unlikely that with all their reinforcements the Russians will be satisfied with one repulse, they are expected to attack us every day. We turn out at three every morning and march on to the plain to be ready. I am now just come in from this work. They have nearly finished a bridge across the harbour, it is not known what for, but most likely for their troops to cross and attack our trenches, or to retreat if we take the town. The general impression is that there will be a grand struggle before long, and everyone is pretty confident that we shall get this side of the place eventually. I shall be very glad when it is all over, or when the fall of the place gives us a temporary respite; the constant turning out, and perpetual expectation of being called into action at any moment is very wearing, and the men who work hard all day get little rest by night.

I am commencing my new hut, which I am building on higher ground, and above the level of the earth, though being a flat cut into rising ground, I get the advantage of shelter. It will take some time to finish. Please send me a common knife and fork. I had the misfortune to break the knife you had made for me. We have seventy-three horses and two officers on their way out. Our brigade is about 1,500 strong. Any preserved meats will be very good in the winter for lunch etc., pea soup is a good kind, and essence of beef in little round pots. Nearly every officer who has come out this summer is quite done up, and many others besides. All our four draft officers are *hors de combat*. There is a good deal of cholera among men fresh from England, and some fatal cases of only three or four hours. The old hands escape better. We keep our camps as clean as possible by burying all the rubbish we can. I have got a goat which gives plenty of milk, a great luxury, we are well off now and even get ice sometimes. The days close in fast now, we have had some cold winds just as we had this time last year at Varna, but it has set in again as hot as ever. . . . I should like a lump of putty for my hut, it is difficult to get here, the ships give one some, but they generally have none to spare. I have applied for canvas to cover my hut, and if I can't get it, I will cut up some old tents and tar them, and make them waterproof. I never heard of arnica. We have lots of fleas here which bother one rather. They seem to come out of the ground.

Your affectionate Son

I have got a Russian musket to send home when I get a chance.

Cavalry Camp, Kadikoi   *August 31st 1855*

My dear Father — I was very glad to see by the mail such good accounts from the Baltic, and hope the destruction may not turn out to be less than at first appears. It would no doubt have a good effect on the garrison of Sebastopol if they knew it, but things are kept so secret among the Russians, I don't suppose the men will know of it for a long while. There are no Russians now anywhere near the Tchernaya, and the lines of the Allies on that river have been considerably strengthened since the battle. Many people expect that the Russians will withdraw from the south side, and they are taking all their valuables across the new bridge, over the harbour. I wish the English would send some mortar batteries here, they seem to answer well, and if we took Fort Constantine it would be a good set-off against the French and the Mamelon.

I saw the General just now, and he congratulated me on my promotion. He does not yet know anything about our winter quarters, we are in a measure preparing for a winter here, I am going on with my hut. The regiments in front have made lots of little stone houses like Irish huts; cooking places have also been built. The army wants lots more cover, but anyway I don't see how we can be nearly so bad off as last winter, when there was *nothing* but tents. It is most difficult to get wood, and one has to pay 2s each for very poor planks. Send me a few short, flat-headed nails, for putting canvas over my roof, nails are hard to get here. You will know in time if we stay here; if we do you can send my box rather earlier if convenient. My horses are well, in fact the Earl and the Cob, look as well as if in England, if anything *too* fat. I have an old mule I gave £1 for, who fetches water, the pack saddle is most useful, for this carries a small barrel on each side. The water here is plentiful and good, and I hear of no want of it in front. I should like some pounded sugar sent.

Yesterday I went out to shoot quail, which are just coming in. I and Hampton had a few shots and got some; they are not very plentiful yet, but are excellent for breakfast. I now have a man of my troop to help Kilburn, not that it is allowed, but all captains do it. I get 17s a day pay (with field allowance included) as a captain. Both the officers of our second draft, and one of the last draft which landed a few days ago are ill. Out of six officers who came out from Newbridge this summer only one is doing duty now. We hear there is some hitch about Burnand going, but I can hardly believe it, as he is under a promise. His brother is about to return home, having been here about ten days — they were neither meant for soldiers. We have a new doctor said to be a clever fellow, he is out here with the 50th.

It is quite odd to see how helpless the new officers are, and their servants; they don't understand making breakfast between two stones, and lots of other little things. It is well for them we have a mess now, but we were just as bad when we first came out. We get very good dinners, soup and turbot (the Black Sea turbot are very good), a joint, generally mutton, some fowl and hash, and a tart of preserved fruit or rice pudding. Claret cup (not quite so good as in England) and often ice, so you see we are well off, indeed this is our almost daily dinner. At breakfast we get bread is a loaf, and good bread too, and some broiled ham or whatever one can get, we all breakfast in our tents. I generally stay in all day till about four, and then ride to bathe, or to the front, or round the outposts, and home to dinner at seven, to bed about ten, and we parade every morning at four. I have now given you a minute account of my life, which is not a very gay one, but we look forward to some grand movement some day. If I get books I don't find it dull, and one knows so many officers here. Please send me out my Italian grammar and dictionary, and my *Prince's Parallel History* which are among my books. I had a letter from McKinnon the other day, he says he is doing Militia duty now, and but for that his West India property would leave him a beggar; I think he rather inclines to the dark side of things. Young White from Guildford is here in the 5th Dragoon Guards, he looks such a little snob. I shall not cultivate his acquaintance. Did you ever have a stable man of the name of Phillips live with you? I don't remember him, but am told he is now in the 12th Lancers here, and that he lived with you. I am glad you have got a horse to suit you, and hope you will continue to like him. I had a letter from Fred yesterday from Munich: the 1st Dragoon Guards are suffering much from cholera. I should like a buckle for my medal, but not to be sent out, as I intend to send my medal home when I get it. I should like some candles in my box. We had another draft a few days ago, and have now about 280 horses. I hope we shall get stables out in time for them. It begins to be cold now in a tent at night. Burnand gave his hut to another officer before I asked him, but I think the one I am building will be better than his. The General has *as good* as taken two A.D.C.s in place of the two absent, both *asked* to be taken.

Scarlett has a very fine command now, all the cavalry and about fifty guns. I want some tooth powder. I saw the K.C.B. invested the other day, the *Illustrated* man was sketching it. All the swells were there, and a beautiful address was made by Lord Stratford.

Your affectionate Son

9

The Fruits of Victory

Cavalry Camp, Kadikoi   *September 10th 1855*

My dear Fred — I write to you because I think the family will
be from England, and I wish you to keep it, that I may see it again,
for it is to be a sort of history — I have so much to say I don't
know where to begin. I must however leave the Battle of Tchernaya
to another time, but as you know the ground so well I must some
day give you an account of it. The events of the last few days have
been so many, and so important and exciting (such as I suppose
few living can ever have witnessed) that though I know all I can
tell you, would never give you any idea of the same in its reality, and
while those who were here never can forget, I will try and explain
it as well as I can.

On the 5th about 5 a.m. the bombardment opened in earnest and
continued all day; in the evening seeing a great light over the town
I rode up and saw a ship burnt in the harbour. On the afternoon
of the 7th I saw from the lime kiln another ship burnt, the bombardment still going on. On the 8th we were out at 3 a.m. and then
went to the front four squadrons; I went with one squadron, we
were only there to keep back the spectators from getting too near.
I went in front of the piquet house, and saw all. The fire was heavier
than I ever saw before, and the Russians hardly fired at all. At
noon the French had sapped up over the parapet into the Malakoff,
with (it is said) the loss of only one man. (The Russians were
evidently unable to live under the fire directed on the place.) As
soon as they were in they became heavily engaged for about an hour
in rear of the place, and we saw the Russians run out across the
Redan. The whole place became a mass of smoke, and we saw no
more, except sometimes the immense supports marching up from
the Mamelon.

Nearly at the same time our men stormed the Redan, and the

storming party took it and spiked lots of the guns, but the Russians were in such force in rear, and our supports not coming up in time, our men were driven out again. At the same time the French who entered on the left, near the flagstaff battery were not more successful, but the Malakoff was secured. The wounded men now came flocking to the rear, and a great number of officers, and from them we learned for certain of our repulse. Lots of men who came up with their limbs smashed, stopped and talked to us and seemed not to care the least for their wounds. The number of officers was out of all proportion to the men, these latter I may tell you did not behave quite so well as usual. I only say this as you are sure to hear reports about it, but when the country trusts its honour to *children* who know next to nothing of drill and discipline, it cannot expect such deeds as were performed by old and trained soldiers.

I was told by many that at one time about twenty officers held the Redan for some minutes against masses of Russians, but the men did not support them, and nearly everyone was killed; the fighting was desperate, and when too close for muskets, they dashed each other's brains out with stones. After we were driven back, we kept up a heavy fire on the place. I saw the 97th march home, about sixty men out of 800, and one subaltern, they said that was all left, but more turned up after. The officer had lost his cap and was covered with powder and dirt, and his clothes spattered with blood and torn in several places by shell. Then the 88th marched by nearly cut to pieces, six officers coming back out of seventeen. We saw all these men going down in the morning as cheerful as possible. We got home about seven in the evening having had a very long day.

In the night the Russians left the town and retreated across the bridge, I suppose they saw it was useless to remain when the Malakoff was taken. The town was now on fire in many places, and when I went up early yesterday it was on fire all over the large buildings by the water, the ships, the dock, etc. I rode to the head of Careening Bay, and walked into the town by the garden battery, the strength of the place is enormous and I can't think how we could take it. I walked to a high part of the town towards the Library, you know the place, the large building with pillars. However, when I got some way in, I was afraid to go further, there was so much powder about, and the town being on fire and a lot of

Frenchmen drunk and smoking among it, I thought it best to retreat, which I did. The Russians, too, were springing mines with electric batteries; the French were plundering the town, the houses were riddled with shot, and the burst shell and shot was enough to pave the streets with. I never saw such a scene of havoc, there were hundreds of new guns, not in use, and immense anchors, of course very valuable. Just after I came out a large magazine blew up in the docks, and explosions constantly take place even now. They are keeping people out of the town as much as possible, till it is well searched, for fear of mines.

At one time a number of English and French were plundering when a panic took them, some said a mine was going to blow up, and others that a steamer was coming across to shell them. However away they all went, one over the other, dropped their spoil, and the men on horses rode over the men on foot, such a scrimmage you never saw — they did not stop till quite outside the town.

I then went to the Redan, and it seems to me we should never have attacked it, for it is quite commanded by the Malakoff, and could not be held when we were in, but the French said we must go at it to draw off the men from other parts. The Russians were there in heaps, and the ditch was nearly full of dead English piled one on the other, I suppose five feet thick, or more. The Redan was terribly strong, and bombproof inside. There was not a place an inch large that was not ploughed up by our shot and shell, guns, gabions; and even pieces of human flesh of every shape and size were scattered about, it was absolutely torn to pieces, and one mass of rubbish and confusion impossible to describe. Inside were some field-pieces taken, loaded to the muzzle with grape, which they fired at our men, when they got in some had not been discharged.

The Malakoff too was an extraordinary sight, the French lay in piles, where they had been mown down by the grape from a steamer, and then the Russians too were in lines where the French had brought up field-pieces, and sent grape among masses at a few yards. I could form no idea of the number of dead, which must be enormous — it beats anything I have ever seen before, I think even Inkerman, but it is all over now with Sebastopol, and the three or four steamers remaining must soon be burnt too. The Russians have been seen marching by Mackenzie's Farm, and it is expected (now so many troops are liberated and they need not fear our crossing the harbour) that they will attack us somewhere else; lots of infantry have come down in case they should attempt anything.

September 11th. I rode yesterday into the Malakoff, it is a wonderfully strong place, and has bombproof houses enough to hold some thousands of men. The ditch must be nearly thirty feet deep; the French must have taken it quite by surprise, for they say only a working party was in it at the time. If it had not been surprised I believe it would have stood an attack from any amount of men. The town is still burning. I counted ten steamers left, all under the other side, of course we shall be able to burn them too. The smoke of the town extends for miles up the country as far as we can see. The Fleet say the Russians are retreating but I can hardly believe it true.

A Russian naval officer came over last night with a flag of truce; he took back the wounded men, who of course would only be in our way. He spoke English well, but took care not to say much beyond remarks quite on other subjects than the siege. There was some sort of a demonstration this morning on the part of the Russians on the Tchernaya. It is settled that we go to Scutari in November, the order is come, so I shall not want all the things I sent for, if this is not too late. I have not time to look my letter over, as the post is just going. I have been on parade since four this morning.

Your affectionate Brother

Cavalry Camp, Kadikoi   *September 15th 1855*

My dear Fred — I shall hope to hear from you before long of your sport at Park Hatch among the birds. I have been all over Sebastopol; no wonder the Russians made so good a defence, for the place must have cost them millions to make, and now we are going to blow it all up I hear, the greatest blow by far struck yet. All the rest of the steamers are burnt, but there is one that is useless to them, but still not quite destroyed. The dry docks are splendid, all built of white blocks of stone, they are filled by the water from the Aqueduct of the Tchernaya. Two ships were burnt on the stocks, one a fine steamer; nothing left but her engines, and they must be spoilt. You remember a fine stone fort at the corner of the Pier on this side, half-way down the harbour; it blew up and is now only one heap of stones.

The town is a wonderful sight, cannon balls sticking in the house walls, and not one building but is riddled with rockets, bullets, shot and shell; those large buildings on the quays were hospitals and stores. Some that I went into were most horrible, mattresses soaked with blood and putrid, and dead men all colours of the rainbow, and among them the living. We were taking them away in cartloads, and the smell was such that the drivers were all as sick as dogs. One Hospital I saw, where a 13–inch shell had come bang through the roof, and out at the side wall; fancy the state the poor sick devils must have been in. I was in the building with the pillars yesterday, we thought it was a club, but it was a church, much knocked about. The houses are loopholed for musketry, and there is no end to the batteries and barricades in the streets, I can't think why they did not fight it out, it would have cost us an army to have fought from street to street, and they seemed determined to do this at one time. The Russians fired on the town sometimes at the people in it. They are quite close on the north side, and I can't think why they don't shell us more.

I don't think Joseph will see much if he comes here in October, and we may be away by that time. The cavalry are to go to the Bosphorus or Egypt. Fred Marshall is here, but seedy with diarrhoea, he won't stay long if it is over for this year, he is lucky to have been here just in time. I suppose I am not over the mark in saying we must have taken 5,000 guns, perhaps under the mark and lots of them are new ones. The earthworks at the harbour mouth this side are tremendous. A Russian engineer taken says from our movements they expected us to attack near Inkerman, so withdrew their men from the Malakoff, and could not get back in time. They say they had made such plans as to meet us at any point with 10,000 men.

Your affectionate Brother

Cavalry Camp, Kadikoi   *September 21st 1855*
My dear Father — We all received our medals yesterday. I shall send mine home by the first chance and only wear the ribbon. I

also intend to send home my glasses, the new glasses you sent out don't quite answer, and they want putting to rights. I shall be glad to get them out again as soon as possible. I was in Sebastopol today, and rode round the Fort Paul, which is now a heap of stones. The view of the town must be very imposing from the harbour, the buildings are so very handsome, forts, barracks, storehouses, etc., all built of blocks of white stone. You are so close from where I went, you can almost see the guns in the embrasures of the forts opposite, and of course they could sweep the town but they don't fire a shot strange to say, though we keep shelling them and setting fire to stores and buildings on the north side.

Perhaps it is better that we did not take Sebastopol last year (if we could have done so which I rather doubt) as it has weakened Russia much more than if the place had fallen at first. Some said we should have taken the north side; if we had done this I don't see that it at all follows that this side would have fallen also, and we all know this is the most valuable side. We are sinking many mines to blow up the handsome docks, which will take more than a month to destroy. Sebastopol is certainly one of the handsomest and most striking towns I have ever seen of the kind, and it would have taken several years to finish what was laid out in public works. etc.

I am much in want of flannel shirts, having only three and they are nearly as full of holes as the houses in Sebastopol. We were all much surprised to hear of Burnand's intention to withdraw his papers, as he promised before leaving this he *would* not *do so*, the officers are exceedingly angry at such a proceeding, and we have some of us written him such letters as I think he will not much like, we think he has acted in a very ungentlemanly way, and I feel sure he will find it most unpleasant if he rejoins. McMahon too has written to General Yorke about it. . . .

There is a nice Arab horse belonging to an officer in the 12th Lancers, who is away ill; I have a great mind to buy and send him home, he is a roan with white legs, very quiet and a good charger. If I get him I shall make him more of a show pet horse than anything else, he is very handsome and I have a great fancy to buy an Arab. I think I cannot well improve my present stud for campaigning, and one can't sell horses now, they go for almost nothing. . . .

Believe me your affectionate Son

Cavalry Camp, Kadikoi   *September 25th 1855*

My dear Father — There seems no doubt but that most if not all of the cavalry will shortly go to the Bosphorus; we are pretty certain to go. I believe there is excellent shooting there, so please get my gun ready and everything complete in the case, that you can send it when we get our orders to leave this. . . . You talk of my remaining in the 5th. Such is my intention now, as I would not exchange to a home regiment and every one has been so broken up that came on service, that they are much alike, some rather more than others. The 5th, when I joined, was a first-rate regiment in every way, but now it is no longer the 5th of former days, everything is of course altered and not for the better. There now remain but six out of nineteen officers who sailed in the *Himalaya* on May 27th '54 and only about half the men. I am anxious to know if it is thought the fall of Sebastopol will end the war, I think not, I expect we shall get into a scrape with Austria, through the Sardinians. No news here that I know.

Your affectionate Son

Cavalry Camp, Kadikoi   *October 6th 1855*

My dear Father — We thought all chance of taking the field this year over, but the last few days have removed the idea. The 4th D.G., 12th Lancers and Carabineers are under orders and expect to embark tomorrow, it is supposed for Eupatoria, and also some infantry. It is also said we are to push on from here. If all this is true it must be on account of an order from the French and British Governments. The Russians are still strong on the north side and are throwing up works, this may be a blind. I heard yesterday the French have got round to the Belbeck, they have been creeping round from Baidar for some time, and making a road to try and turn the enemy's flank. A French officer from Baidar told me yesterday that the 4th Division was to march yesterday to encamp on the Belbeck, all this looks something like a move.

We have still three weeks' fine weather to calculate on, so of course could not go far, but might do much in that time. Some people say some troops are going to the mouth of the Bay to fortify it and stop trading. It is generally thought the Russians are retreating in small detachments. Simpson has commenced to give officers leave to England, but this is stopped from home. We could easily knock down the stone forts on the north side of Sebastopol but if we did, they would make earthworks which would be worse, so we let them alone. I heard yesterday young White of the Carabineers has died at Scutari. We had some races here Thursday and then a dog-hunt; the dog ran splendidly and about 150 officers after him, unfortunately Captain Rosley of the 55th fell, and has since died from the effects of his fall, a sad end for a man who had escaped all the fighting. . . .

We have had most lovely weather here, sometimes showery, but we have no idea of the beautiful clearness of this air in our English climate. Yesterday I had a delightful ride towards Baidar, only I struck off towards the sea among the mountains. The autumnal tints are magnificent and so varied, more wild and magnificent scenery it is impossible to imagine. Sometimes one comes suddenly on a valley, when you might fancy yourself in the centre of England, more like a gentleman's park, and generally an old ruined Tartar village, with its people in their curious dresses. The women's dress is very tasteful, the Greeks are generally very pretty, but so absurdly shy, one can only see them by taking them by surprise. We have found an immense quantity of wood cut by the Russians, and they say it will save the country some £50,000. The spoils of Sebastopol are to be divided thus, French 5/10 English 3/10 Turks 1/10 Sardinians 1/10. . . .

You speak of the little yew tree I planted, I got it off the wall, on the left hand side going to Godalming on the road which passes Busbridge kitchen garden just after you pass the gardeners. I think that is where I got it, and if I remember right there are some of the new sort of fir trees there, which accounts for the appearance of my tree. We have heard no more of Burnand, his brother left him without much the matter with him, neither of his brothers were ever intended for soldiers, and the sooner they change their present coats for those of civilians the better for the army.

We rather expect to get leave in the winter for three months, but as I am junior of my rank it is doubtful if I get it unless more captains come out before that. I suppose you would say I had better go home for that time if I can get it. I should like much to be home again, though it would be for so short a time, for of course we must all come out again. We shall soon know more about it, but you must not calculate too much on seeing me. If I had the luck to get home, I wish Joseph could be there too. Fred must be away for his degree. I don't think Joseph will like travelling so far as India, nor would the eastern climate suit him. I don't see how he would get through the summer when he often finds the heat in England too much.

You speak of walking through Sebastopol, it is a matter of some danger as the Russians fire much on it. I have however been in several houses at which I have often looked with a telescope. I have been all over the town, but it is anything but pleasant now, and I generally ride the other way as I don't see the fun of being shot at when not obliged.

Your affectionate Son

Cavalry Camp, Kadikoi   *October 12th 1855 10 p.m.*

My dear Mother — We have not yet heard when we are likely to move into winter quarters. All the large steamers are now employed in taking the Light Brigade to Eupatoria, though very likely after all they may not land there, but go on to Scutari, and we must wait their return. I think very likely after all I may not be able to get leave to England, as I suppose two captains are sure to remain with the regiment, and unless I can get three months it would not be worth while to come home. . . .

I have been reading Russell's account of September 8th. It seems a correct statement, but I think he might have left out part with advantage, it has not given general satisfaction here. If the people of England expect *untrained* boys sent out as *soldiers* to sustain the credit of the country, and to fight like the men of Alma, they will I fear be sadly deceived; nor is it fair to trust the honour of regiments to such helpless children. There are plenty of good old regiments in the colonies and they ought to send them here and let them take their places, I mean all those that have been so much cut up. . . .

Your affectionate Son

Cavalry Camp, Kadikoi   *October 27th 1855*

My dear Father — Your letter of the 12th reached me last night. I am very glad to hear you have almost secured Burgate, the property is certainly worth more to you than to anyone else, and perhaps is capable of great improvement, which will be a nice employment for you, do you think of farming it yourself?

There is a report here now that we are not to leave the Crimea because Pélissier says it is against the treaty to withdraw any troops. It may be only a report, but if it is true it seems a very dog in the manger act of his: because he can't save his own cavalry he won't let us save ours. They will nearly all die if left here and John Bull will lose another million or two. The stabling at Scutari is nearly completed; surely if there is any truth in the report our Generals ought to have found it out before. We have been waiting, we supposed, for the transports and the last time I saw Scarlett a few days ago, he expected us to leave the end of the month.

I have had some very fair woodcock-shooting here, but now there are so many people out it is nearly spoilt near the camps. Burnand, when he came out, found no one would speak to him, but now it is all settled, and we are good friends again, he having been obliged to write a letter to the Colonel promising either to exchange with a man to sell, or else to sell out himself by January 31st '56. We have had delightful weather here; but it is getting very cold indeed at night now. On the 25th the anniversary of Balaklava we had a Division Field-day. My brigade turned out 1,300 strong, and by far the finest in appearance. The Hussar brigade turned out 1,000 strong, and the Light Brigade 1,000 strong is, you know, at Eutaporia, so we had 2,390 on parade and a very fine sight it was. We could have turned out another 200 at a push. I should like my gun sent, whether we stay here or not; and a dog too if one can be got. . . .

Your affectionate Son

Cavalry Camp, Kadikoi   *November 12th 1855*
My dear Father — From your last letter I find you have had wet stormy weather both in England and France, while this year we have the advantage, for up till now we have not had a drop of rain; but the days have been fine, and till within the last few days quite warm. Fancy the beginning of November with the sun almost too hot in the middle of the day, no wind, and not a cloud to be seen, and the thermometer up to 70° in the open air at night. Now it has

become very cold and looks like a change of weather. We hear nothing more of our departure, one regiment after another is embarking but it is slow work, and we are not likely as far as I can see to get away for another ten days. . . .

General Codrington has commenced his duties as Commander-in-Chief. Most people here speak well of him, I hear he is very active. He has been much blamed for the unfortunate affair at the Redan on September 8th but many say he was not to blame for what took place. You ask why we did not sap up as near the Redan as the French did, to the Malakoff; we had these disadvantages which the French had not: first, the ground was nearly all rock, and secondly our sap was enfiladed by the Malakoff and was knocked down as fast as put up. Officers who had been all night working there told me, if they got up ten gabions in a night it was considered very good, and this probably with the loss of twenty men, and to work by day was impossible. It is getting late and anything but warm, so good-night.

Believe me your affectionate Son

Home from the Field

P. & O. Steamer Simla, *Balaklava*   *November 17th 1855*

My dear Caroline — We embarked yesterday on board this ship; part of the regiment went two days ago and we have got part of the 6th Dragoons on board with us. This is a very fine screw-ship belonging to the P. & O. company, and we are very comfortable on board, even *sheets* in the berths, which I have not used for a year and a half and did not half like last night. We sail today about twelve and shall probably be in the Bosphorus in about thirty hours. The sea is beautifully calm; we have been fortunate in having most lovely weather, not a drop of rain, but rather cold. At Constantinople it has been wet and rough. . . .

All the regiments will leave this except the 11th Hussars who are left to do orderly duty. There are only two more regiments to leave now. I fear I shall not be able to get leave for England as I expect two captains must be left with the regiments. I asked the General about it two days ago, and he said he was going to see Codrington to know how many might go home; the General comes down by the next ship so I shall soon be able to let you know. My horses are well except the Cob, who is not quite so well as he should be, but nothing serious. I see during the night the brown horse has bitten a bit out of my chestnut horse's nose, they stand close together. It is not a very good place for sleeping, for the horses over our heads keep dancing up and down the whole night especially towards morning when their feeding time approaches. We are just going to breakfast so good-bye.

Believe me your affectionate Brother

Scutari, Asia   *Sunday November 25th 1855*

My dear Father — We sailed from Balaklava about 11 a.m. the 19th and anchored in the Bosphorus off Bugukdin on Tuesday 20th at 6 p.m. having had a beautiful passage, but rather squally when near the Bosphorus. We could see snow on the high mountains near the Crimea, and it looked like change of weather, tho' till we left it had been fine. I am always glad with horses and soldiers on board to have the voyage over. There is great risk, the men are so careless, especially the young hands, and there is so much hay and fire about a steam horse-transport. With all our care we had two fires on board before we left the harbour, but not bad enough even to cause alarm, though enough to make us extra careful.

Our camp was quite broken up before we marched. We had all given away or sold our huts and they were immediately carried off to furnish building materials for officers in other parts of the army. I gave Tredcroft some wood, and he will be very well off for the winter, he had got a little house. In about an hour the ground which had been our home for nearly a year was left as bare as the day we pitched our camp on it. We dropped down the Bosphorus on Wednesday morning, and anchored opposite Scutari. The views are beautiful all the way, and vary at every turn of the waters, from which it is quite a fairy scene, but the moment you land the illusion vanishes and you find yourself in the midst of the dirty reality.

I hoped and thought that after eighteen months after canvas, that now I should have a good room and a comfortable house — vain delusion. My troop disembarked on Friday and went into stables, the men into half-finished sheds and tents, myself into a house in Scutari, two miles from Barracks, and very dirty. Some houses are very good, but in others there are rooms at which you would look twice before you put your dog in. We are supposed to be two in a room, but the places are so bad that most officers have other houses. I am now in a tolerably good room, being in the house of the senior officers. I am not sure if I shall remain here, for I do not fancy being obliged to live with anyone if we are to live here for three or four months. It has a most beautiful view of the Bosphorus, Golden Horn and Stamboul, which is a great advantage, but the rooms are so low I cannot brush my hair without stooping; there are also lots of rats and fleas, but these you find in every house. Some of the officers' quarters have large holes and cracks in the floors, looking into stables etc. below, and now and then one's foot goes clean through the boards. I shall write again in a few days when I get settled, at present I have not much time and have been frequently interrupted while writing this letter. I hear there was a heavy fall of snow the day we left the Crimea. The stables here are not finished and at present we are rather closely packed, there is one stable which holds 1,250 horses. The cholera has been at work here, but now there have been only two or three cases in three days. Before we came the 1st D.G. lost five men, several doctors died, and Mrs Moore (wife of Colonel Moore who was burnt in the *Europa*), I believe died of fever; she was out here to nurse sick officers.

Your affectionate Son

Scutari *December 5th 1855*
My dear Father — I find the Colonel will not let me go on leave; he has allowed all to go that he can spare, so I must be content to spend my winter here. . . . Some of the subalterns go home, so I shall be the only troop officer who has been out all the time and who can't get leave. We have got more horses now and are going to form our three extra troops to make our proper number on service. The Colonel will apply for two captains from the depot, which will rather stir those places up. As soon as they come I may be able to get a few weeks' leave to travel in the Levant or somewhere. I wish you would send Henley some pheasants if you have enough — I told him I should remind you. Our men and horses not quite settled yet, the former though sheltered from the weather are rather crowded at present, and our men are not yet quite satisfactorily put up: more stables are building fast, and we shall all soon be well housed; and shall doubtless turn out strong and effective in the spring.

Now I will tell you about myself. I live in Scutari two miles from Barracks with Halford and Burnand. We hired a house for a month for £8, rather than be put two or three in a room. We had some trouble in getting it, but at last we did though without any furniture. These Turks are very fond of money, but pretend not to like to let their houses to Christians, and give one strict orders not to cook anything in the shape of pork in the cookhouse, for if we did it must all be pulled down, and we are to be sure and not laugh at the Meusin* who comes out at the top of a neighbouring minaret and howls to the people to come to prayers. The Turks seem a very clean people, our house is nearly all wood, and I think will not stand very long, for it is all on one side now, and one wall leans one way and one another. We are sure to be turned out of this for they have got quarters for us now in the Palace at Hayda Pasha's close to the regiment where we are to be several in a room, to which I strongly object, and if obliged to do it, shall pitch a tent outside; one can't read or do anything when so many live together.

Scarlett is here and leaves on Monday for England, nearly all the Eupatoria cavalry are come down, and only two whole regiments more are to come from Balaklava, we shall soon all be here. Nearly everyone seems going on leave but me. I don't think a house agrees with me; I have a bad cold and am not very well ever since we came here, that is why I did not write by the last mail. I am going to try quinine which always sets me up, and no doubt in a few days I shall be all right. They have made me brigade major here for a few days, till our proper one arrives from Crimea — it is like being adjutant to a brigade and takes one off all regimental duty. We have had cold weather here, lots of wind and much rain, all about our barracks is nearly knee-deep in mud, as bad as Balaklava, but it is all being paved. The weather is very changeable: last night it rained all night; this morning very fine, then a little sun, then rain, all the time very sultry: this evening a thunderstorm and a regular hurricane, which nearly blew our house down, and half-washed us out.

I was all over Stamboul this morning and went into St. Sophia, we could not take off our boots as they were wet, but they changed their rules since the army came, and as we refused they were obliged to make us put slippers over them after a great deal of remonstrance. Beyond the building being very old, and a Mahomedan place of worship, there is not much to see in it. I think it is all up with the Turks in Europe and they know it as well as we do, the young Turks are they say quite reconciled to us, but the old ones do not like the appearance of things at all.

* Muezzin.

The Turks certainly have behaved very well at Kars, I am sure after all we have been much too hasty in judging them, and treat them too lightly. I am told they behaved very well the other day at Eupatoria, when under fire, and did not move an inch when the shell came into them. An officer present told me he saw one bob his head (when a shot passed over, which indeed few people can help doing) but his colonel gave him such a rowing for it that D'Alouville had to send and ask what was the matter. Our officers speak very highly indeed of D'Alouville. He wants to get two brigades of our cavalry next year with the Highland Division and guns, and some of our horse artillery, and heavy field batteries, about the 23rd of March, and before the Russians can get reinforcements, to advance on Sebastopol. I should think this a very likely move for us. I spent some time today in the bazaar, looking at some beautiful embroidered things, and have brought some back for my Mother and Sisters. I shall send them when I can. I hear officers going home pay no duty for a few presents. . . .

Your affectionate Son

Scutari   *December 20th 1855*
My dear Mother — All the cavalry are here now, but we are not so comfortable I fancy as most regiments in the Crimea as regards the officers, however we shall save our horses, which will be a great thing, and shall no doubt be able to take the field in the spring in good order. We hear much of peace, but so we have done ever since the commencement of war, and the papers don't seem to think much of it. Scarlett went home a few days ago; he told me he hoped to see us here again in March, before we start to take the field. I see by *The Times*, two miles of corn stacks have been burnt by our gunboats on the Sea of Azoff, this is a necessary evil of war, but it is sad to think of such waste when our poor people in England are so badly off. . . .

I find there is a great deal to do here at present, and the weather is very bad, I don't see much chance of shooting, and perhaps it is too late to send out a dog, but I should like my gun, as I intend always to carry this with me in future. Send some pheasants to old Henley, I expect he will soon be ordered out here. I hope he will not come, for if he did I think he would probably die, he is too old to campaign again as a regimental officer. As soon as we change our house we shall establish some sort of a mess, there is nothing I require at present so don't send anything out. . . .

Your affectionate Son

Scutari *December 31st 1855*

My dear Father — I am still living in Scutari, but in another house and we are trying to get leave to remain in it. Thompson has ordered his horses to be sold, they are not worth much, he seldom has a good horse, but perhaps he intends leaving. I should not be surprised if he does not come out again. We have had some very fine weather, the last week, really quite like May in England. I see a good deal in the papers about peace, what do they think in England about it? I can hardly fancy the Russians will give in yet. I suppose your friend Teesdale is now in the hands of the Russians. Of course he would rather be free, but I dare say he won't pass an unpleasant time after all: and he is safe out of the next campaign. A good deal is said here about Omar Pasha not having relieved Kars, they seem to think he has not done all he might — I expect we English feel the loss of Kars* more than the Turks. I have met an Admiral Slade here (he is son of Sir John Slade) and a Turkish Admiral, I met him somewhere at the table d'hôte in Pera. He tells me Europeans could not campaign in Asia for he has been there, and he says there are no roads, and only soldiers like Turks who can live on biscuits can march there.

I am anxious for the meeting of Parliament, Queen's Speech, etc. I wish you would send me that paper as there will be a rush for it here. I suppose we shall then hear when the next campaign will open. What tremendous exertions they seem making at home, building ships etc., the strength of the country is not yet half put forth. I am glad Campbell has got a battery, but I wish we were destined to be near each other, it is pleasant to be near someone who is tied by relationship in these times. I am glad you are suited with

---

* Kars, at the eastern end of the Black Sea had been besieged by the Russians since June 1855. It fell in November 1855. Teesdale was one of the British officers sent to help in its defence.

a horse, to have many of them tho' must be expensive keeping with these war prices.

Your affectionate Son

Hayda Pasha Barracks, Scutari   *January 14th 1856*
    My dear Mother — We have had beautifully warm weather til' the last few days, now suddenly we find ourselves in the middle of winter, changed all at once, and on getting up this morning found the ground covered with snow, and all day have experienced a heavy gale from the north, with snowstorms. These changes try people very much and cause a good deal of fever. I am most uncomfortable here, in fact since I have been in the army I never spent a more disagreeable, unprofitable, dreary time than I have here. I don't mind roughing it when necessary, but there is really no occasion for this. The snow beats in at all the five windows, covers the floors and all my things, and I cannot light a fire as the stove is useless, and I cannot get another. The water freezes in my basin, and I am forced to sit with all my thick coats on and my fur boots to keep warm. I have got the ham you sent me cooked, it is a very good one. . . .
    There was a ball at the Embassy on New Year's Day, to which I went — a very poor affair for such an important person as Lord Stratford de Redcliffe. They did not seem to think it worth while to make it pleasant, however, I saw all the swell Turks, and all the English at Pera.
    I hear the French are very badly off in the Crimea, a letter from an English officer to a cavalry colonel here says the French are suffering greatly,* all their roads have failed, and they come into our camps to buy, beg, and steal the rats our men kill in order to eat them. I found out yesterday that the *Imperidor* and *Thomas* are in, and I am going today to the head office to get my box and gun. I have been obliged to quit my room again, and come back to our house. It was so awfully cold, the water in my room froze and all that was spilt on the floor immediately turned to ice, so I told the colonel I could not live in barracks till proper quarters were provided, but the constant moving is nearly as bad as marching, and

---

* This was true, in sharp contrast to the first year of the war when the French fared better than the British.

I cannot settle down to anything. The weather has again been very fine and much warmer. We have not yet got out hounds. People here are much afraid that Kertele and all the Turkish contingent there will be taken. General Wrangle is before the town and they fear they will not be able to hold out. . . .

Your affectionate Son

Scutari   *January 24th 1856*

My dear Caroline — Some days since we heard here that peace was certain. The Czar having signed the agreement, Lord Stratford did not at first believe it, but afterwards he did, however the last few days have almost put the idea out of our heads, I don't exactly know why. The mail came in yesterday with papers up to the 13th and they seem to say there was no *chance* of peace, but the telegraph has given us later news. I thought it so certain I had actually thought of summer's leave to England. We are most anxious for the mail after next. For my part as far as I am concerned, I should like another campaign exceedingly, I should be pretty sure of leave next winter. . . .

Write and tell me all about the Maidstone ball, etc. I am surprised you did not think W. Scarlett gentlemanly-looking, he is a very good fellow. I suppose now he has cut his beard off. Did you not get introduced to him? I am still living up in Scutari; I hear Montgomery and Elliot are coming out again. I have no time to write more. Love to all.

Believe me your affectionate Brother

Scutari   *February 21st 1856*

My dear Father — It is some time since I wrote to you, but really there is so little to tell, that is the reason you don't hear oftener. I am off this afternoon with Richards to the plains of Troy, having leave to the end of the month, we take guns etc., but how we shall get on I can't say. We are to get out at the town of the Dardanelles, then we shall try to make our way by Rinkoy towards Mount Ida. I don't expect to get good shooting, but it is a great place to see, Kilburn comes too, and we go well armed, as I believe there are banditti about, when I get back I will tell you all about it.

Tell Joseph next time you write, that I write to him today at the 'Hotel d'Amerique', Rome, but have not heard from him. I fear I shall not be able to get you an Arab cob for the reasons I told you before. There was an Arab sold the other day in the 12th Lancers for £180, such a beauty. My chestnut horse is gone broken-winded, indeed few horses that have been out all the time are untouched in the wind. On Tuesday the hounds had a run of an hour and forty minutes and killed, all in the open country. I was out, but had to come home before they found as my horse was unwell, what bad luck! We always find every day, but have never killed before. There are jackals here, but the hounds won't hurt them, we dug out two large badgers the other day when digging for a fox.

I am thinking of getting leave to go to Jerusalem when the officers come back, but this is not certain yet. Peace seems pretty certain now. I wish we could have had another year at the war, I doubt if the peace will be a lasting one. Tell Mr Russell I will write to him on my return. Did you read about the new order, the Victoria Cross, it was much wanted and will I think give great satisfaction to the Army and Navy . . .

Believe me your affectionate Son

Scutari   *March 2nd 1856*

My dear Father — We returned yesterday from our shooting tour, having spent a very pleasant week indeed, though we had not much sport. We went to the plains of Troy and saw some of the tombs — Ajax, Hector, etc. — and a few of the remains which are now very small, so small indeed that the site of ancient Troy is not known for certain. There are pillars and marble slabs with Greek inscriptions left in different places, but it is now about 2,000 years since, and now woods and marshes inhabited by bears, wolves, etc., stand on the same ground which that great city once covered. For miles round there are ruins of different kinds, and if there were nothing left, it would still be an interesting spot.

We fell in with the consul's family, very nice people, we introduced ourselves and they were very kind to us; they were the first ladies I had spoken to for two years. We only brought home one wild boar, which was shot by one of the party out with us. I never got a shot at one, though I saw several, in fact the country is full of them, and in some places quite ploughed up by them. Coming home we got a passage in the *Medway*, a large English horse-transport steamer. I received a letter from Joseph by the last mail, he tells me he has written before, but the letters have never reached me. He talks of coming on here if he can make up his mind to the sea voyage. I intend to apply for leave again directly, as they are particularly liberal just now in this way. I shall try for six weeks, please tell Joseph this for I don't know where to write to him. I am thinking of going to Bucharest with an officer of the Carabineers, a very good fellow who speaks French and German well. We have not yet made up our minds. I want to go to Jerusalem, but he says that will not suit his purse, so I don't know where we shall go, perhaps to Greece and Mytilene, but we expect to settle and be off in a week or ten days.

Peace seems certain and I must say I am sorry for it, for I think England has rather lost prestige, though in truth she is strongest and best able to carry on the war. The French have been fortunate, and seem to think it best to leave well alone. Now we are so well prepared another year would gain us credit, impress our army, and not put us to much more expense, as the material is already paid for. People here seem to think Lord Stratford will get into a row, he had (*on dit*) £500,000 for the relief of Kars and never used it. Some here seem to think we shall not have peace yet. How about America? Our last news from home looks rather warlike, perhaps if we have peace with Russia, America will be more civil to us.

Halford and Hampton are come back, we expect the rest soon. Hampton was presented with a sword by his county, and made a great deal of, and so have several officers who went home. I hope nothing of the kind will happen to me, or it will have the effect of keeping me from home. I don't see any immediate chance of promotion, Fisher is come, but I have not yet seen him. I have not yet heard of the *Cleopatra*. You will hear again before long.

Believe me your affectionate Son

The Sultan is getting so Europeanized that he is giving the Turks great offence, and his last firman* concerning the privileges

* Official permit.

to Christians has crowned all; they even talk of a revolution, but I don't think they have energy enough to get one up. They are a degenerate lot, and stupid and ignorant to a degree and the whole population, women and all, smoke themselves perfectly idiotic.

Scutari   *March 17th 1856*
  My dear Mother — By the last mail I sent home a little box containing acorns from the plains of Troy, they are of the Velonia oak and they grow in great quantities there. The wild bears eat the acorns, and the husks are collected and sent to England for tanning leather, I hope they will grow but fear they are too dry. I have got a live tortoise here and am going to bring or send it home. Kilburn has one too, there are many here, and in Bulgaria you could find one in almost every bush. The parcels by Fisher came all right. I was rather in want of the handkerchiefs and socks. We have got a draft of a captain and four subs. (including Balders and eighty men as well as I can make out) coming out. The Government does not seem so very sure of peace.
  You ask me if I know Mrs Duberly, I do by sight very well, and should like to see her book, though I would not give a pin for her opinions. She is known in the camp by the name of the Vulture, from the pleasure she seemed to take in riding over fields of battle. I should think her feelings (if she has any) cannot be very fine, and she is certainly more fit to follow a camp than to live in an English drawing room.* . . .
  McMahon's father is on the court of inquiry, who for all the good that may come of it I think may as well be left alone. I am glad to see Lords Lucan and Cardigan are getting what credit they deserve, especially the former, whose injustice to the 5th at Varna will not soon be forgotten. The people at home seem determined to find someone to lay the blame of the miseries of the winter of '54 on, but I think it was more the fault of the system than the individuals. I have received the Russian grammar and other books you sent. It is very cold here and looks like more snow. The Turks

---

  * This is an illuminating view of the much-publicised Mrs Henry Duberly, wife of an officer in the 8th Hussars. Her book, *Journal Kept during the Russian War*, covers the period from the outbreak to the fall of Sebastopol and was published in 1855. She appears to have been brave and enduring but not popular, and her friendship with Cardigan caused some comment.

say we shall soon have more warm weather, but winter is never considered past (in Constantinople) till the end of April. I have not settled yet about a tour but I am still thinking of Jerusalem if we have peace.

Your affectionate Son

Scutari   *March 27th 1856*

My dear Father — The box per *Cleopatra* I got yesterday, the ship has only been in two or three days. I found everything in the box quite right, the ham was a good deal mildewed underneath, but I have had it scraped and wiped and hung up: nothing was broken. The writing desk is just what I wanted. Peace seems so certain and the time of our stay so uncertain, that I don't know if I shall have time to finish all the good things you have sent, so don't send any more. There are a good many things I now have that are no use here, and I dare say I shall send home a box of my warm clothes and all I don't want.

I wrote some time ago to Tredcroft to know if it were worth while to go to the Crimea during the Armistice; I only got his answer two days since. He strongly advises me to come, they see a great deal of the Russians and on the 24th there were to be races on the Tchernaya, and General Luders and his daughters were invited to see them by General Codrington. I am anxious to see a little of the Russians in a friendly way, having seen so much of them otherwise, and perhaps we may not have the chance again for some time. Yesterday I applied for leave to the Crimea for ten days, but was refused because there is a great review tomorrow of all the troops on the Bosphorus, and the Sultan is to be there, Lord Stratford and all the great people. After this is over I think most likely I shall start off for Balaklava, and stay with Tredcroft a few days, then come back, I don't want to be long away as I have another tour in my mind.

Halford, myself, and an officer of the 1st D.G. have arranged that as soon as we know for certain of peace, to apply for six weeks' or two months' leave and start for Jerusalem. There is a boat leaves for Jaffa and the coast of Syria on April 8th, they run every ten days or so, and we hope to get our leave and start by that day. I think we shall have no trouble when peace is signed to get leave.

We intend to see Damascus and all the places in this part, and then perhaps cross the desert to Alexandria and Cairo; we shall not be able to go further, as it will be too hot. If we could manage this tour it would be a great thing accomplished. Joseph says he would like to come too, if I were going anywhere, but I know from what I have seen of the interior here, he would not like the living and would not enjoy the life. I don't mind roughing it, and if you can put up with the discomfort there is something very delightful in Eastern life. There is something in the climate and way of living that makes one very indolent if you give way to it, and no wonder the Turks who are brought up here spend their lives in a sort of half-dreamy state, between smoking and sleeping. I hear the Armistice is prolonged, so it will not be too late to fraternize with the Russians on the Tchernaya. They are cleaning out the Russian embassy for the ambassador, who will I suppose soon be here. They say here the Turks are to give us the island of Candia.

Monday I was over at Pera, and was in time to see the Te Deum at the French embassy, Lord Stratford and the other ambassadors were there in full dress. Tuesday I was all day in Stamboul in the bazaars, talking and sitting with the old Turks, they like us much better than the French. Stamboul is a most curious place, I never get tired of going there, one sees something new every time. I go about into every hole and corner, and the Turks don't care so much about us as they used to, I mean they are not afraid of us. We walk through the mosques at pleasure, boots on, tho' they still look rather shy at us: but three years ago we could not get in without a firman, for which you had to pay about £15, and obliged to take your boots off. I hope we may be left here all the summer and come home in the autumn.

I hear Henley has exchanged with a man in the 95th another infantry officer, I am sorry for it. It throws over the subs. though it gives me a lift. The fellows have made a great mess about promotion. Burton wanted to go, but Montgomery hesitated about £200, and now we have peace he will not go for some time. Thompson is most anxious to go on half-pay. I hope he will be able to do so, he is kept at home by the commission now sitting; he is sure to make a mess of it, pretending to know more than he does, and he will contradict himself often enough. They will have some fun examining him, but for all the information they will get he might as well be here. We ought to have had two more steps if things had been well managed. I expect Burton will soon be major, and as major at home he has nothing to do, which will just suit him. If the war had lasted, I expect another year would have seen me at the head of the captains. I have been having some of the honey for breakfast, it is very good. If I go to the Crimea you won't hear of me for some days.

Believe me your affectionate Son

Scutari   *April 6th 1856*
My dear Father — I have got leave till the end of the month, and start with Hampton tomorrow for Mytilene, then perhaps we go to Cyprus, and if we can get there to Candia, we expect to get some shooting, but I fancy we shall have some roughish fare. I want to see the Greek islands etc., and I have now a good chance. If I have an opportunity I will write to you, but of course we shall be quite out of the world where we are going, so you must not expect to hear for some time. I could not get long enough leave to go to Jerusalem, and found it difficult to get four companions as they refused leave to Halford who had promised to go with me. There is a great talk about our going home; the general impression is that we shall be in England in a month or two, but even the General knows nothing about it. I suppose I shall know by the time we return. The Sultan is going to see a review of all the troops here, it has been put off very often, and I don't know now when it will be, I should much like to have seen it but if I wait it will make my time so short. The weather here has been very cold for some time, but the last two days have been beautiful and quite warm, so I am in hopes we may have nice weather for our expedition. It will be much warmer where we are going than it is here.

I have been having a Turkish bath, they are very pleasant when one gets used to them, but I should think they are too weakening to have them often; it is a long affair, to do it comfortably it takes quite two hours. This is to be quite a gay week here as we have a race-meeting which begins tomorrow, and which will I expect rather astonish the old Turks. Two days ago I saw the caravan of pilgrims start for Mecca; there is a party every year and they take

eight months to go and return; they had a great number of camels
for their tents and baggage, and their departure caused more ani-
mation than one could expect among the old Turks. In the evening
the whole of Constantinople was illuminated. We also had great
illuminations at the declaration of peace. . . .

Believe me your affectionate Son

Shepheard's Hotel, Cairo   *May 4th 1856*
My dear Father — I had a very pleasant week at Jerusalem after
a long ride of fourteen hours on a mule from Jaffa, and we fell in
with a very agreeable party of Americans, and also became
acquainted with the English residents, so we got plenty of information about the place. We saw the ceremonies of the Greek
Easter, and were there the day the Holy fire came out of the Holy
Sepulchre. In the Church, Greeks, Latins, Arminians have each a
part of the church, and as usual a tremendous fight ensued between
the former and latter people, such a disgraceful affair I never saw,
nor could I have believed. The battle lasted a good half-hour, the
weapons being sticks and stones (I was in a gallery out of the way)
and was at last settled by the Ottoman troops, before lamps,
pictures, incense vessels, statues, etc. were demolished. No wonder
the Turks don't think of Christians and Christianity when it is
shown them in this light. The Protestant bishop afterwards told
me four people were mortally hurt, and yet this happens every
year, sometimes worse, sometimes not so bad. There certainly requires more reform here than among the Turkish population.

The city is vastly interesting, and many places are pointed out
about which there is no doubt, such as Mount of Olives, the ancient
Temple, part of which is still to be seen, and many other places.
One day we went via Bethlehem to a convent near the Dead Sea,
where we slept, starting at daybreak for the sea, which we reached
at 8 a.m., had our breakfast on the shore, and then bathed in this
most curious sea or rather lake. We came out all smarting and en-
crusted with salt, promising ourselves to wash it off in the Jordan,
to which river an hour's gallop brought us (I say *us* for we had
picked up on the steamer an Irish barrister, Cowan). I must tell
you we had each paid the usual fee to the Arab chief or Sheik of
100 piastres or 17s for a guard and safe passage. Well we were con-

gratulating ourselves on our expected bath when an hostile Bedouin
tribe from the east of Jordan made a bolt from a hill opposite after
us. Of course we were soon taken prisoners, flight was useless as
we were badly mounted on tired horses. They marched us down to
the river and wanted us to cross, but we refused and pulled out
our pistols again. They, seeing there would be harm done if they
insisted, gave it up, so we filled our water tins, washed our faces
and then wanted to go, but the chief said no, we must pay for our
liberty, and wanted a great deal at first, but at last we got off for
£2 10s and he was near taking the Dragoman's clothes. We
immediately started off and did not pull rein till we got to Jericho
in about an hour, for they came after us and we feared a second
capture. I forgot to say our gallant guard bolted at the first alarm
and fled clean away. There were too many of them for us to fight
them, and our pistols were not all loaded, as we had been shooting
at partridges with them on the way. The Bedouins were fine-
looking men well armed, each with a lance full twenty feet long;
we were fortunate to be treated so well, for in general they are not
particular as to life.

The consul at Jerusalem made a great row about it, the Sheik
was put in prison and we got back all our money. We arrived at
Alexandria the 30th ultimo, saw Pompey's pillar and Cleopatra's
needle, and came on here on the 2nd passing through a flat but
fertile country. They are in the midst of their harvest, the corn is
all carried away on camels, much is already thrashed, and I
suppose will soon be exported. Alexandria and Cairo are much
before Constantinople. Here you see fine houses, squares and
European carriages. The Indian mail is just in, first came fifty from
Bombay, and yesterday the Calcutta mail brought 157 people. You
may fancy how large the hotel is, they cross the desert in vans and
come in, in batches of two dozen each. We expect the English
mail today.

Yesterday we went to the Pyramids of Giza and walked to the
top of the large one, from which is a magnificent view of the valley
of the Nile, and in another direction the great desert of Sahara
stretches away as far as the eye can reach. The pyramid is very steep
and you climb from stone to stone, very hard work under this sun.
The desert ends suddenly and you may put one foot on highly
cultivated land, and the other on the burning sand; this has a very

curious appearance. We went afterwards inside the Great Pyramid, you have to stoop and crouch for a long way, the fine dust and stifling heat make it very disagreeable. On reaching the sarcophagus chambers I nearly fainted from the suffocating feel, a thing I am not prone to, so did another Englishman there, I was very glad to get out again. There is a great deal to see in Cairo, but the sun is so fearful it is not safe to expose oneself much to its effects.

We leave by rail for Alexandria on the 7th or 8th, take the boat on the 9th direct for Constantinople, touching at Smyrna. I hope we shall arrive on the 14th when I will write to you again. We shall be a fortnight behind our time, I hope none of the regiments will be moving yet. We hope to hear some more news of what is to be done with the troops by this mail. Before I came away I was told by an officer just from England that the Cavalry were to be reduced two troops; General Yorke had told him so but perhaps the General was wrong, I hope so for it would put me on half-pay, which I do not wish. The French are preparing for the passage of 10,000 troops through Egypt to Madagascar to punish the natives for the murder of their countrymen. Love to all.

> Believe me your affectionate Son

Scutari   *May 15th 1856*

My dear Father — I arrived this morning from Alexandria, having had a beautiful voyage; it is quite cold here, I don't think there is any row about our absence. Burton's and Halford's troops sailed yesterday for England, we don't know when we shall embark. Fancy on my return I find that three weeks ago Hayda Pasha's Barracks were burnt to the ground and *everything I possess in the world is consumed,* but my horses, saddles, and swords; all my sketches, clothes, trunks, my journal which I have kept daily since leaving Queenstown, and which no money can replace, also a treasury bill for £60, which I hope to recover. The loss of my journal is worst of all, I had put down everything from the first day till now. The building was down in twenty-five minutes after the fire broke out, before Kilburn could get from the stable. I shall get compensation, but nothing will repay me for some things. My journal would have given lots of information to the Crimean commission, if I had liked. This leaves today, and I suppose we shall be off before I can write again; we don't know where we are to be quartered on our arrival in England.

Your affectionate Son

Scutari   *June 5th 1856*
My dear Father — We embark today at 2 p.m. on board the screwsteamer *Brenda* and most likely sail this evening. We leave about seventy horses, and 180 men of our own, and 190 men of the 10th. We shall I suppose land at Glasgow or Leith, and the 10th probably at Liverpool. I shall run down and see you as soon as ever I can, and as I have no kit I shall make it an excuse for leave as soon after I land as I possibly can. I will send you a line as soon as we land. Our ship is fitted here, and is not a good horse-transport; these Turks don't understand how to put up horse fittings. I am sorry I could not meet with a pony for you, but I have done my best to find one, there are no good ones to be had here. They have only given us three hours' notice of our embarkation which is not quite fair, as there is a good deal to arrange. I suppose you know we go to Edinburgh. The captain expects to make some English port in seventeen days. We coal at Malta and Gib. In haste.

Your affectionate Son

Steamship Brenda *off Malta*   *June 10th 1856 11 a.m.*
My dear Caroline — You see we have come some distance on our way home; we are now just going into Malta to coal and water, and hope to leave again tonight. I don't know if we shall arrive before the mail, which left Constantinople the same evening we did with my letter (they had to go by Smyrna) telling you of our embarkation; if we do it will take this to Marseille and you no doubt will get it before we arrive in England. In four days we expect to reach Gibraltar, and England about the 22nd. We are to run into Spithead for orders, but where we disembark I don't know; by our steamer's contract she is not bound to go farther than London. Horses and men are all well on board, though much overcrowded. We had had a strong head wind the last two days, since leaving Cape Matapan and rather a heavy sea, but a head

wind though it delays is good for the horses, as they get more air. I have been seedy only once, and am all right now, though the dinner table has been generally very thinly attended. I shall see you all soon I hope, so good-bye; the steamer is very shaky.

Believe me your very affectionate Brother

This day two years we were near the Dardanelles going out. We coal again at Gib.

George Hotel, Portsmouth   *June 25th 1856*

My dear Father — We disembarked at the dockyard today, having arrived at Spithead last night. We have had head winds the whole way, and sometimes very rough sea. We have lost four horses, two officers' horses, mine are all right except rather rubbed tails which will only disfigure for a short time. We leave this by rail tomorrow morning at 6 a.m. en route for Aldershot camp, where we rejoin the rest of the 5th and are to remain some time (I believe) before going to Edinburgh. I hope I shall be able to be with you in Lowndes Square on Friday, if only for a few hours, but I must soon get leave in order to find a new kit. I shall write a line tomorrow if I have time. Please get up my plain clothes ready to rig me out when I arrive. . . .

Believe me your affectionate Son

Index

Abdul Mejid, Sultan, 199–200, 201, 203
Aberdeen, George Gordon, 4th Earl of, 35
Airey, Richard, Baron, 166
Alexandria, 206
Allied armies, 21; physical sufferings, 4, 5, 6; Crimean landing, 4; last actions, 6–7; winter quarters, 91; before Sebastopol, 94, 149; and entrance to Baidar pass, 119–20; on the Tchernaya, 176
Anapa, 38
93rd Argyll and Sutherland Highlanders, 63; 1st Division, 16, 19; 'thin red line' episode, 75n, 78; praised by Raglan, 79
Austria, 19, 112, 185; peace negotiations, 7
Austrian troops, 25, 31, 33
Ayrshire, 161

Baidar valley and pass, 114, 119–20, 159, 185, 186
Balaklava, 126, 130, 131, 133; Allied position, 4–5, 81, 100; Bay landing, 59; TG at, 61 ff.; population, 63; hospital ship conditions, 72; physical conditions, 80, 100, 124; harbour horrors, 139–40; expected attacks, 146; electric telegraph, 147. *See also under* battles
Balders, Cornet, 161, 200
Balders, Maj. C. W. M., 31 and n, 51
Balders, Lady Katherine, 59
Baldjik Bay, embarkation, 54–5
Baltic, 4, 48, 176
battles: the Alma, 3, 58 and n, 100; Allied victory, 4, 59; TG wishes he had been there, 62; Light Cavalry, 62; failure to follow up, 84
   Balaklava, 125; cavalry battle, 5, 73; 'thin red line', 5, 75 and n;

TG on, 73–80, 122, 140; Russian defence, 75, 78; reports of, 99; anniversary Field-day, 188
   Inkerman, 106, 121, 181; military character, 3; 'soldiers' battle', 6, 113n; described by TG, 82, 87, 113, 115, 145–6; medals, 90, 91
   Tchernaya, 179
Belbeck, 185
Besussa, 170
Black Sea, 4, 46; fish, 177
Black Water valley, 114, 119
Blackwood's Magazine, on the campaign, 130
Bolton, Maj. Abraham, 168, 169, 179
Bosphorus, 15, 58, 138, 190–1; cavalry destination, 183, 185; troop review, 200
Bosquet, Gen. Pierre, 135
Bourgos, 89
Boxer, Admiral Edward, 156; death, 162
Bradshaw, Edward, 131
British army, 61, 68, 110; neglect since Waterloo, 4, 8; purchase of commissions, 7, 8, 93; promotion procedure, 8–9, 84, 129, 170–1, 172; flogging, 33, 38–9; winter needs, 85; officers' behaviour on sick-leave, 85; clothing, 110, 112, 121, 129; sufferings, 121, 122, 127, 128; mismanagement, 123; deserters, 127; numbers in the Crimea, 128; improved conditions, 134, 145, 147; new draft behaviour, 169, 177, 180, 187; embarkation orders, 185, 190
Brown, Gen. Sir George, commander Light Division, 18 and n, 20, 40, 155; at Devna, 32, 33; a fine soldier, 36; ill on board, 167
Bugukdin, 190
Bulgaria, 13n, 39, 42, 44, 140, 156, 170, 200
Burgoyne, Sir John Fox, 10, 47

Burnand, Capt. George, 52, 54, 63, 66, 83, 95, 101, 108, 117, 125, 137, 177–8, 188; promotion without purchase, 128; sends in his papers, 168, 169, 172, 177, 184; in Scutari, 102

Burton, Capt. (later Maj.) A. W. D., 50n, 62; desire to quit the service, 85, 101, 108, 202; and Lucan, 147; promotion, 203

Byron, George Gordon, Lord, 57–8, 58n

Cairo, T G and, 204–6

Cambridge, George William Frederick, Duke of, and Argyll and Sutherland Highlanders, 16 and n, 19–21, 33, 51; popularity with soldiers, 85; alleged madness, 90, 92

Campbell, Sir Colin, 37 and n; Highlanders' Brigadier, 70, 71; a good officer, 132; at the front, 149

Campbell, Brig. Gen. Sir John, death at the Redan, 164

Campbell, Capt. W. R. N., to leave the army, 93, 96, 101, 108; d. in 1854, 115–16, 117, 123

Campbell, Lt. of *Leander*, 142

Canrobert, Gen. François, 150, 155; replaces St Arnaud, 91 and n, 94; and Forey, 137

Cape Chersonese, 59

Cardigan, James Thomas, 7th Earl of, 2, 103; commander of the Light Brigade, 5, 23, 25, 26, 33, 36, 40; private yacht, 79n; TG on, 140, 142, 144, 151; to command the cavalry, 144

Carew, 79 and n, 97

casualties: Balaklava, 5, 75–6, 78; Inkerman, 6, 82; Traktir Bridge, 6; on the march, 25; Turks and Russians (wounded), 30; at the Redan, 180, 181; regimental, 116, 118, 134; inside Sebastopol, 183

Cathcart, Sir George, 84; death at Inkerman, 82

Cavalry, 116, 123; 'heavy' and 'light', 7–8, 106; transport ships, 14–15; marching conditions, 23, 24; disembarkation, 47; and the Alma, 60, 62; essential task, 89; living conditions, 94, 101, 102; TG on mounted police, 111; an improved force, 171; winter destination, 183, 185

Charge of the Heavy Brigade, 2; military importance, 5–6, 80n; TG on, 73–5 map, 74

Charge of the Light Brigade, 1, 103; cavalry battle, 5; military importance, 5; described by TG, 76–7, 79; disastrous instructions, 80n; Lucan and, 147–8

cholera, depredations, 4, 5, 32, 37–8, 43–6, 52–3, 59, 157, 160, 162, 168, 171, 192; in London, 37n; hospitals and, 39; abates, 59–60, 63, 71; among Russians, 60; worse than battle, 81–2; produced by cold, 85; belts, 104 and n; attacks newcomers, 169–70, 175

Christie, Capt., 139, 162

Chronicle, 109

City of London, 149

Cleopatra, 199, 201

Cluster, 138

Clyde, 135

Codrington, Gen. Sir William J., C.-in-C. Sebastopol, 189, 201

Comber, of the *Viper*, 170

Constantine, Grand Duke, 67, 82

Constantinople, 4, 161, 190; British quarters, 15–16; feast of Ramadan, 16; postal services, 22; officers on sick-leave, 85

Coy, John, Col. Shrewsbury's Horse, 7, 8

Crimea, 4, 7, 40, embarkation of troops, 54–6; climate, 107, 109, 110, 117, 121, 122, 124, 136, 147, 186, 188–9; graveyards, 139

Crimean War, reporting, 1, 37, 39 and n, 41, 68, 81, 99, 100; missed opportunities, 3, 6, 80n, 84; causes, 3–4; incompetence, 4, 6, 10, 123, 125; last events, 6–7; peace treaty, 7, 198; peace rumours, 35, 116, 128, 157, 195, 197; taxation of officers, 56; England and, 112, 123, 195; medals, 117, 121–2, 125, 177, 183–4; improved supplies, 131 and n; burial of the dead, 139, 147, 173, 174, 181, 183; fraternization, 144–5;

search for a scapegoat, 200; Armistice, 201, 202
Crispin, Capt., of *Fairy*, 12
Cubitt, Thomas, & Son, 55 and n, 59

D'Alouville, 194
Danube, 21, 27, 31, 33, 82
Dardanelles, 14, 197
Darrington, Charles, 103
Deverend (Devenish), 23
Devna, 24, 25–6; TG at, 26–39, 136
diseases, ague, 38; diarrhoea, 138; dysentery, 36, 87; fever, 32, 36, 38, 54, 72, 157; scurvy, 134; typhus, 37, 44, 139, 141
1st Dragoons, 40, 177
4th Dragoon Guards, 50; at Balaklava, 62, 64
5th Dragoon Guards, 9, 177; evolution, 7–8, 18n; equipment, 34; embarkation, 57; at Balaklava, 74, 75, 81; hard treatment, 81
13th Dragoons, 25
Duberly, Mrs Henry, *Journal Kept during the Russian War*, 200 and n
Duckworth, Capt., 44, 46, 96–7; death, 52
Dundas, Admiral Sir James, 21 and n, 88, 134
Dunkellin, Lord, taken prisoner, 71

Eastern Telegraph, 157
Egypt, 171, 183
Elliot, A. J. H., 76, 79, 103, 108, 125, 197; at Constantinople, 15; on Scarlett's staff, 97, 117, 148, 167; to exchange into the Guards, 169; promotion, 171
England, Sir George, 101
Esk, 134
Estcourt, Maj.-Gen. James, death, 166, 167
Eupatoria, 58, 96, 110, 111, 136, 137, 151, 185; British expedition, 154; Light Brigade and, 187, 188, 193
Europa, fire disaster, 31 and n, 192
Evans, Sir George de Lacy, commander 2nd Division, 21 and n, 36, 67, 101

Fenton, Roger, photographer, 148 and n, 157
Ferguson, Cornet, J. S., 11, 52

Ferrer, Gen., 174
Fielder, commissary, 106
Fisher, Lt. Edward, of 4th D. G., 47, 52, 53, 92, 97, 130, 157
Fitzgerald, Cornet H. E., 130
Forey (Forray), Gen. E. F., commander French 4th Division, 137 and n; alleged treachery, 136, 139
Fort Constantine, 176
Fort Paul, 184
France, 3, 4, 48
French army, 16, 19, 21, 25, 36, 84, 163, 185; transport ships, 13–14; and English troops, 22, 43, 48–9; dismounts the cavalry, 29; losses from cholera, 45; and Sebastopol, 47, 64, 66, 68, 69, 93, 94, 110, 111, 135, 136; soldiery 48, 63, 83, 86, 91, 116–17, 122–3; assault on the Malakoff, 164–5, 179; badly off in Crimea, 196 and n; Chasseurs, 48, 115, 118–19; naval forces, 57, 58; Zouaves, 22, 48, 93, 97, 119, 120, 137, 139, 142

Galeta, loss of *Avenger*, 13
Giffard, Capt., 150, 153
Godman, Caroline, m. of TG, 9
Godman, Eliza (*née* de Crespigny), w. of TG, 9
Godman, Frederick, b. of T G 155, 156; in the Crimea, 158 and n, 159–60, 161–2; *The Biology of Central America*, 10
Godman, Joseph, f. of TG, 9
Godman, Richard Temple (TG), arrival in Crimea, 2, 9, 60; character, 2, 10; his regiment, 7–8; promotion prospects, 8, 9, 52, 56, 95, 108–9, 130, 168, 176: marriage, 9–10; voyage out, 11–15; equipment and clothing, 16, 23, 27–8; rations, 20, 23, 26, 28, 32, 35–6 and *passim*; health, 23, 32, 41, 45, 51, 54, 65, 91, 98, 103; enjoys campaign, 31, 34, 45, 68, 108; leave possibilities, 38, 80, 186–7, 190, 192, 193, 199; and adjutancy, 51–2, 84, 113–14, 124, 127, 148; at Balaklava, 61–80; and siege of Sebastopol, 66 ff.; winter needs, 85, 92, 95, 98; (1855), 170, 175, 184; in action, 102; and women

Godman, Richard — *cont.*
  as nurses, 105–6; builds hut, 109–
  10, 112, 121, 126, 130–1, 133, 150,
  153, 160, 166, 170, 175, 177–8;
  skirmish with Cossacks, 114, 118–
  19; illness, 138–42, 143, 145; storm
  disaster, 165–6; gazetted to troop,
  169, 170–1, 171–2, 174; daily life,
  177; walks into Sebastopol, 180,
  182, 187; on the Redan, 181; re-
  ceives medals, 183–4; to remain in
  5th D. G., 185; at Scutari, 190,
  191–204, 206–7; brigade major,
  193; sorry for peace, 199; leave
  plans, 201–2, 203; embarks in
  Brenda, 207–8; at Plymouth, 208
Goldie, Brigadier, death at Inkerman,
  82
Gossip Hill (Balaklava), 73
Great Britain, 3, 4
Greer, Lt. R., 54n
Grey, Lord, to promote N.C.O.s, 128
Greys, 55, 59, 63, 162; at Balaklava,
  74, 75, 78, 99, 102; casualties, 77
Guards, 19, 45, 48, 91; at a loss, 53;
  deaths from cholera, 160
Gusleudgi, French expedition, 45

Halford, Capt. Charles A. D., 56, 62,
  85, 93, 98, 108, 117, 138, 192, 199,
  201
Hamilton, Richard, Col. Shrewsbury's
  Horse, 7
Hampton, Thomas L., 176, 199, 203
Harding, Lord, 108
Hay, Lt. Henry, 168
Hayda Pasha, 193, 206
Henley, Capt. James, 108, 146, 194,
  202
Highlanders, 48, 51, 59, 69, 194; at
  Balaklava, 62; at Eupatoria, 155
Himalaya, troopship, 11–15, 17, 19,
  83, 144, 146
Hodge, Lt.-Col., 4th D. G., 50n, 63, 83
Horse Artillery, siege of Sebastopol,
  70, 73
horses, 37, 63, 161, 177; transport of,
  11–12, 13–14, 18; at Varna, 21–2;
  at Devna, 33; lack of fodder, 44, 50;
  miserable conditions, 86–7, 90, 94;
  dying from cold and starvation, 98–
  9, 100–1, 113, 121, 123; stabling,

120–30; of TG, 19–34 *passim*, and
  throughout
12th Hussars, Russian regiment, 78
  and n
Hutchinson, Sir Edward, 124, 162,
  168

Illustrated London News, 38 and n,
  102, 112, 142, 178
Inglis, Maj. William, 29, 108, 130;
  wishes to quit army, 85, 101
5th Inniskilling Dragoon Guards, 8, 31
  and n
6th Inniskilling Dragoons, 120, 172;
  formation, 7; in Ireland, 7, 8;
  Crimean War, 8; amalgamation
  (1922), 8; in *Europa* fire, 31 and n,
  33; at Balaklava, 74, 75, 78, 99, 102;
  TG and vacant troop, 152, 162–3
Ireland, 11, 31, 43

Jason, screw-steamship, 161, 166; off
  Sebastopol, 57–60, 109, 110
Jasper, 172
Jerusalem, TG and, 204
Jones, Gen., 145

Kadikoi cavalry camp, 104–18; rail-
  way, 166
Kamara, 114, 118, 120
Kamiesele, *St. Hilda* off, 155
Kars, 199; Turks and, 194; Russian
  siege, 195 and n
Katcha river, 88–9
Kilburn, TG's regimental servant, 32,
  65, 72, 99, 103, 105, 113, 125, 137,
  176; illness, 96; a good cook, 145;
  photograph, 148; pack saddle, 160,
  saves horses, 166; at Scutari, 197
Killock, Capt., 83
King's Dragoon Guards, arrival, 171
Kirkpatrick, Edward, 56
Kotlubei, TG and, 40–4; cholera, 44
Kronstadt, 48

17th Lancers, 16, 25
Le Marchant, Lt.-Col. T., 93–4; and
  5th D. G., 8, 50n; unpopularity,
  50–1, 56, 94–5, 101; death, 64;
  possible successor, 93, 111 and n
Leander, 149
Leopard, 122, 153

2nd Life Guards, provides a surgeon, 95

13th Light Dragoons, 23

Livius, Capt., 26 and n

London, 155

Lowe, Major, 129

Lucan, George Charles Bingham, 3rd Earl of, Cavalry Division commander, 5, 99, 100; incompetence, 34 and n, 44, 105; his A.D.C., 45; and 5th Dragoons, 81, 83, 200; false reports, 83; at Balaklava, 88; and medals, 121–3; sent home, 135, 140; demands a court-martial, 142–3, 147–8, 151

Luders, Gen., 201

Lyndhurst, J. S. Copley, Baron, 35

Lyons, Admiral Lord, 88, 118, 134

Mackenzie Heights, 7

Mackenzie's Farm, 167 and n, 181–2

McKinnon, Edmund, 64, 177; medical board, 42, 43; on Thompson, 93

McMahon, (Sir) Thomas, 147, 184; commander 4th D. G., 50n; to replace Le Marchant, 111 and n, 158; at home ill, 113 and n, 129

McNeile, Lt. Henry, 29, 52, 54, 63, 66, 83; to sell out, 95, 101, 108, 117, 125, 139; to wait for his troop, 128; in England, 130

Malacca, 125, 131, 161, 167

Malakoff Fort, 145, 163, 164; French capture, 6, 169, 179–80, 182, 189; TG on, 181, 182

Malkins, 162

Malta, 13, 88, 149, 207

Mamelon Fort, storming of, 162 and n, 163; repulse of the Russians, 164

Marine Heights, 159

Marshall, Fred, 183

Maurice, Gen., 119

medical services, 23, 38, 45, 72, 177; Turkish, 30; hospitals, 39, 52; and cholera, 44; a disgraceful department, 72, 115–16; surgeons, 44, 52, 95; ambulances, 109, 116; London inquiry, 116; nursing staff, 139–40, 192

Medway, 199

Menschikoff, Prince, 82, 137; alleged death, 143, 147, 154

Militia, 107, 141, 151, 177

Montgomery, Lt. Robert, 103, 156, 160, 168, 197, 202

Moore, Mrs (w. of Col. Moore), 192

Mount Ida, 197

Nachimoff, Admiral, and Sinope massacre, 154

Naval forces, 6, 170; at Sebastopol, 67, 71, 110–11, 112; in Balaklava harbour, 89, 140; Russian, 182

Neville, Hon. Grey, 76, 79; death, 82, 91–2

Nicholas I, Emperor, 86; death, 140, 142, 144, 147, 154

Nicholls, artillery officer, 13, 32, 72

Nightingale, Florence, 1

Nolan, Capt., 76, 143

Odessa, 27, 31, 33, 82

O'Flaherty, Dr, at Scutari, 132

Omar Pasha, C.-in-C., 151–2; reviews troops, 30, 33, 40–1; at Sebastopol, 153, 154; and Kars, 195

Oneida, 168

Paget, Lord George, 6

Paget, Lady, 154

Park Hatch, Surrey, 9, 28 and n, 49, 93–4, 118

Parola, 12

Peel, Capt., of *Diamond*, 73

Pélissier, Gen. A. J. Jacques, 165, 188; reviews cavalry, 160

Pennefather, Sir John, 167

Pera, 15, 195, 196, 202

Perekop, 65, 92, 110, 127

Perry, Lt. J. E., court-martial, 54n

Pitcairn, surgeon, death from cholera, 44, 52

Polytechnic, sinking of, 89

postal services, 19, 22–3, 26 and n, 29, 32, 34–5; cancellation of Queen's head, 31 and n, 35; and dead, 45–6, 52

Prince, sinking of, 89

Punch, 34 and n, 133

Raglan, Fitzroy Somerset, 1st Baron, 10, 25, 41, 47, 65, 85; isolation from Alma, 4; and Light Brigade, 5, 6, 76, 79; lack of field experience, 21n;

Raglan — *cont.*
and 5th D. G., 50n; embarkation
for Crimea, 55; and Sebastopol, 67,
69, 70, 145, 150, 153, 156, 157,
160–1; and winter siege, 84; lives in
comfort, 89; TG on, 92–3, 142; not
seen about, 98, 100–1; promotion,
106–7, 130; incompetence, 116,
123, 125, 130, 166; and Lucan, 135;
superseded, 147; and Scarlett, 148;
and assault on Malakoff and Redan,
164, 165; illness and death, 166, 167
Redan Fort, Anglo–French assault, 7,
164–5, 179–81; blame for, 189
Retribution, off Sebastopol, 58
Richards, Lt. William, 168, 197
Rickets, George, 161
Rosley, Capt., death while dog-hunt-
ing, 186
Royal Albert, 112, 136
Royal Dragoons, 28, 57, 102; at
Balaklava, 74
Rud, Gen., plans of attack, 174
Russell, William H., 156; 'thin red
line', 1, 5, 75n; *The Times'* reports,
6, 39 and n; bets on peace, 128; and
Sebastopol, 187
Russia, 3–4, 112
Russian army, 101, 115; defeat at the
Alma, 4; and Balaklava, 4–5, 74–7,
78; cavalry morale, 5–6; at Inkerman, 6, 82; last actions, 6–7;
imperial guard, 27; and Sebastopol,
47, 61, 64–5, 77, 82–3, 99, 179–81;
arms, 89, 102, 157; soldiery, 83, 90;
treatment of wounded, 83, 87;
superiority in numbers and arms,
87; wounds inflicted by, 102–3;
plunder of their huts, 120, 153; in a
terrible state, 159, 172; spies, 164;
defence of the Malakoff, 164–5; at
Tchorgun, 170; Cossacks, 17, 25,
33, 41, 47, 60, 61, 65, 69, 78, 97,
111, 114–15, 118–19, 124, 157

St Arnaud, Marshal, French C.-in-C.,
41 and n, 47, 91n
St Hilda, TG and, 154–5, 158
St Jean d'Arc, 170
Sardinians, 158 and n, 172, 185
Scarlett, Hon. Sir James ('our Briga-
dier'), at Constantinople, 15, 18n,

19, 20, 23, 25; at Devna, 36; at
Kotlubei, 43; commander Heavy
Brigade, 50n, 55, 56, 96; at Balaklava, 75, 76, 79; and incorrect
reporting, 81; possible successor,
93; army service, 103, 108, 117, 130,
148, 149, 151, 178; at Sebastopol,
112–13; and Crimea, 149, 151, 165,
167, 188; in Scutari, 193
Scutari, 10, 15, 38, 54, 66, 72, 81, 92,
101; hospital conditions, 5, 72,
115–16, 134; possible winter quarters, 171, 182; stabling, 188, 191,
192; TG's quarters, 190–207;
embassy ball, 196
Sebastopol, 6–7, 31, 33, 111; strategic
position, 4; Russian troops, 40–1;
focus of attacks, 44–7; rumoured
fall, 55; viewed by TG, 58, 62, 182–
3, 184; Russian defences, 62–3, 64,
65, 104, 127, 134, 143–4, 149, 182;
siege of, 61 ff., 110, 116, 128, 130;
Allied position, 85, 87, 91, 106;
camp conditions, 86–7, 90n; arrival
of railway, 118 and n, 132, 133–4,
139, 141, 147; bombardment, 143,
145, 146, 148, 159–63 *passim,* 170,
179, 184; plunder of 181; on fire,
182; division of spoils, 186
Serpent Island, 58
Shrapnell, Henry, 10
Shrewsbury, Charles Talbot, Earl of, 7
Shumla, Turkey, 25, 27, 40; TG and,
29–30
Sidebottom, Capt. George, 96, 108,
117, 124, 146, 154; baggage, 161;
goes home sick, 168; death, 171
Silistria, 21, 25, 33, 41, 48; Russian
siege, 21 and n, 23, 25, 27, 33;
wounded in hospital, 30
Simferopol, 92, 154
Simla, embarkation ship, 57, 58, 190–1
Simpson, Gen. Sir James, 117, 178,
185–6; replaces Raglan, 147, 167,
168, 169
Sinope massacre, 154
Slade, Admiral, 195
Soyer, Alexis, visits Crimea, 163 and n
Stamboul, 191, 193, 202
Straits of Kertch (Kertele), 167, 197;
Allied expedition, 150 and n, 154,
155–6; Turkish atrocities, 159

Strangeways, Brig., death at Inkerman, 82
Stratford de Redcliffe, Lord, 154, 156, 196, 197, 201, 202
Swinfen, Capt. Frederick, 76, 79, 103, 108, 117, 121

Tannibazaar, 40
Tchernaya, 159, 172–4, 182; Armistice races, 201
Tchorgun, 135, 153, 159, 170, 173–4
Teesdale, Sir Christopher, 195 and n
Tenedos, 14
Thackwell, Gen. Sir Joseph, 36 and n
Thompson, Capt., 53, 89, 108, 129, 131; a great ass, 93; at Scutari, 195; at home, 202–3
Times, The, 124, 129, 147, 194; Russell's reports, 6, 39 and n, 41–2, 43; condemns Perry's court-martial, 54n; and Sebastopol, 69, 152; and gale of 14 November 1854, 117–18; letters from Crimea, 133; 'fund', 134; abuses Boxer, 162
Traktir Bridge, 6
Travers, Cornet Augustus W., an 'Irish savage', 168
Treaty of Paris 1856, 7
Tredcroft, Lt. Charles L., 191, 201
Trent, 58
Troy, TG and, 197, 198, 200
Turkey, Turkish Empire, 3–4, 30; climate, 32–3, 34, 36, 38, 41; fauna, 43
Turkish troops, 19, 20, 90, 151, 202; at Silistria, 21, 27; as soldiers, 22, 31, 83, 90, 194; and English troops, 26, 32–3; flogged for stealing, 39; Bashibazouks, 55; and Sebastopol, 70, 71, 73, 74, 86, 111, 152, 154; and

Balaklava, 75, 77; and Inkerman, 83; unpopularity, 90–1, 110–11; roadbuilding, 101; alleged atrocities, 160; and Christians, 192–3, 204; in Scutari, 192–3; at Kars, 194

uniform, abolition of stocks, 21 and n, 36; errors in reporting, 43; use of field glasses, 51 and n; flannel belts, 53; French suitability, 86

Valetta, 13
Valorous, 155
Varna, 18, 40, 57; Allied base, 4, 13, 161; TG and, 9, 15, 16, 18–33, 44–5, 53, 175; conditions in, 16, 18–19, 20; climate, 23; French occupation, 36; fired by Russian spies, 43; cholera, 43, 44; shipping, 46, 47
Victoria Cross, 198

Walmer Castle, TG and conditions in, 139–40
Watson, 49, 62, 72, 83, 88, 93, 106; in Constantinople, 15–16; in Scutari, 128, 132, 140
Wheatcroft, of the Inniskillings, 55
White, 5th D. G., 'a snob', 177; death in Scutari, 186
Widden, 33
Willett, Maj., death from cholera, 71
William Pitt, 83, 85
Wrangle, Gen., 197
Wyld, James, 55

Yalta, 92
Yorke, Gen., 184, 206
Yusuff, Gen., French commander, 22 and n